2-14-22

D0953099

BURNING
DOWN
THE HAUS

Police mugshots of East German punks

BURNING DOWN THE HAUS

**Punk Rock, Revolution,
and the Fall of the Berlin Wall**

BY TIM MOHR

ALGONQUIN BOOKS OF CHAPEL HILL 2018

Published by
ALGONQUIN BOOKS OF CHAPEL HILL
Post Office Box 2225
Chapel Hill, North Carolina 27515-2225

a division of
WORKMAN PUBLISHING
225 Varick Street
New York, New York 10014

Design by Steve Godwin.

A version of this book was originally published in Germany as
Stirb nicht im Warteraum der Zukunft: Die ostdeutschen Punks und der Fall der Mauer
by Heyne Hardcore in 2017.

Library of Congress Cataloging-in-Publication Data

Names: Mohr, Tim, author.
Title: Burning down the Haus : punk rock, revolution,
and the fall of the Berlin Wall / by Tim Mohr.
Description: First edition. | Chapel Hill, North Carolina : Algonquin Books
of Chapel Hill, 2018. | Includes bibliographical references.
Identifiers: LCCN 2018010846 | ISBN 9781616208431 (hardcover : alk. paper)
Subjects: LCSH: Punk rock music—Social aspects—Germany—Berlin—History—
20th century. | Punk culture—Germany—Berlin—History—20th century. |
Bergmann, Britta. | Berlin (Germany)—Social life and customs—20th century. |
Berlin (Germany)—Social conditions—20th century.
Classification: LCC ML3917.G3 M63 2018 | DDC 306.4/84260943155—dc23
LC record available at https://lccn.loc.gov/2018010846

10 9 8 7 6 5 4 3 2 1
First Edition

Contents

Preface

When I arrived in the eastern section of Berlin in 1992, I'd never seen any place like it. I'd never been to Germany or Eastern Europe before, and here I was in a high-rise student housing complex out near East Berlin's zoo, Tierpark. At first the city seemed to fit the East Bloc stereotypes I'd grown up with in suburban America: it was the grayest place I'd ever seen, cloudy and cold, shrouded in coal smoke. Add to that the eerie sound of zoo animals howling in the distance and the constant fear sown by rumors of roving gangs of skinheads, and my initial impression of East Berlin was grim.

But I quickly discovered a scene exploding with color and creativity behind the dilapidated, shrapnel-pocked façades of the central East Berlin boroughs of Mitte, Prenzlauer Berg, and Friedrichshain. Hidden behind unmarked doors, down ladders in empty lots, nestled among the crumbling bricks of a candlelit basement or a disused cistern, in the attics of half-destroyed buildings, even in abandoned bunkers and bank vaults, a kaleidoscopic new city was taking shape. The bars and clubs that made up this netherworld were dark and dirty, with extension cords meandering down from some distant outlet to power their sound system and a couple of buckets of water behind the bar providing the only means to wash glasses. They were radically egalitarian. They were open and welcoming to an outsider like me.

And they were so much fun I sometimes awoke the next day wondering if it had all been a dream. Once in a while I'd wake up and find I was still in a club, only on a different day. Some nights the bar staff would leave and tell us stragglers just to lock the door when we left. In warm months, sometimes we—it quickly became *we* in Berlin in those days—we, the people, together, the DJs and dancers and partyers, we would leave the club and go scale the wall of a municipal pool complex and swim naked together as the sun came up. Some of the venues existed for only a night or a few weeks. Others lurked around for decades. The people who congregated in them refused to sit passively aside while the city tried to find an identity and slowly determine where it was going. These people set their own agenda, created their own style, controlled their own environment. They came up with the blueprint not just for a new Berlin, but for a new way of life—a Berlin way of life.

I soon started DJing in some of those clubs and bars, and continued to spend long nights in many more. I moved away from the zoo, first to Friedrichshain, then to Mitte and Prenzlauer Berg, and a stay that was supposed to last six months stretched out for a year and then another and another and another. *That* Berlin—the shadow city being built largely out of sight and with utter disregard for the other one being thrown up in places like Potsdamer Platz and, later, along the banks of the river Spree—fundamentally changed my life and the way I think.

And it was in those clubs, during those years, that I first met East German punks and learned about the secret history of punk rock under the dictatorship. *Ostpunks*, or Eastern punks, ran or worked at most of the places I hung out; they had set up nearly all the first bars and clubs in the East and established in the process the ethos of the fledgling new society being built almost from scratch after the fall of the Berlin Wall. This kaleidoscopic world I had fallen in love with was *their* world, *their* creation.

At the time I had no idea I would eventually become a writer. But to an American reflexively skeptical toward the Reagan mythology surrounding the end of the Cold War, the story of East German punk seemed unbelievably important—perhaps more important than even the participants themselves realized. Here were the people who had actually fought and sacrificed to bring down the Berlin Wall.

My initial belief in the importance of this story was reinforced after I returned to the U.S. and recognized an ominous echo in developments in my own country: mass surveillance on a scale the Stasi could only have dreamed about, the widespread use of insidiously pliable charges like "failure to comply with a lawful order" to make arbitrary arrests, the struggle of protest movements such as Occupy, Black Lives Matter, and #NoDAPL in the face of a complacent or even hostile society.

In the West, we tend to harbor smug, simplistic views of the old Soviet Bloc and to dismiss out of hand comparisons of our system to authoritarian regimes like the one in East Germany. It's worth noting, however, that East German police—unlike our own—could not murder people in the street with impunity. Even today, we trot out images of foreign police brutalizing protesters in other countries to intimate the illegitimacy of governments in places like Egypt, Turkey, or Ukraine. But we rarely look in the mirror.

Our current inability to control state-sanctioned violence could not be more clear—even if white America goes to great pains not to acknowledge it. But perhaps even in an era when local American police departments deploy military equipment against protesters, use surveillance aircraft and lethal drones, and maintain CIA-style "black sites," there is still hope. Perhaps this story—about a bunch of unarmed, unruly teens and the cracks they managed to kick in the seemingly unbreakable system of repression in East Germany—is even more important now than when it first captured my attention. Back then I was fascinated to get to know people who had helped resist and eventually cast off the dictatorship. But I never imagined their stories might be of personal use to me and my fellow citizens in the "Land of the Free."

East German punks used to spray-paint the phrase *Stirb nicht im Warteraum der Zukunft*—Don't die in the waiting room of the future—on walls in Berlin. It wasn't about self-preservation. It was an indictment of complacency.

It was a battle cry: Create your own world, your own reality.

DIY.

Revolution.

BURNING
DOWN
THE HAUS

Official youth culture in East Germany: a Free German Youth rally

Introduction

By the late 1970s the Berlin Wall—actually two walls with a notorious death strip between them—had been up for little more than fifteen years, but it had already become a fact of life. A generation had grown up with it; its history and the details of its construction barely mattered anymore—it was a booby-trapped concrete reality, the physical embodiment of a division of the world that felt as if it could go on *forever*. The young on either side accepted the Berlin Wall as permanent—it had always been there and probably always would be.

Every aspect of life on the east side of the Wall was hyper-politicized, and nothing more so than popular culture. Already in 1945, several years before the official founding of East and West Germany as countries, American military observers were struck by the speed with which the Soviet Union fostered a renewed cultural life in the East after World War II. The Soviets did this not only because of its potential pacifying effects on the populace but, as American officials remarked, because they seemed to believe in the inherently edifying qualities of cultural institutions. A dozen theaters, two opera companies, five major orchestras, and countless cabarets and smaller music ensembles were established in the Soviet zone within two months of war's end. Of course, at the same time, Soviet secret police jailed 150,000 political enemies, a third of whom died from the harsh conditions in the prison camps. Between 1945 and 1947 the Soviets helped the German communist party found national organizations—like the Free German Youth, *Freie Deutsche Jugend* in German, or FDJ for short—meant to indoctrinate citizens and to monopolize social life and group activities from childhood on. On October 7, 1949, a few months after the founding of West Germany, East Germany—the *Deutsche Demokratische Republik*, or DDR—was officially founded. Four nights later, on October 11, 1949, 200,000 torch-bearing young members of the FDJ marched past a reviewing stand in front of the new nation's leaders. Erich Honecker, the thirty-seven-year-old head of the FDJ that night, would eventually rise to become the head of state in 1971. Clearly, integrating youth into the system was regarded as key to the continued success of the DDR. Which is one of the reasons youth culture in particular was so politically fraught in the East.

During Stalin's rule in the Soviet Union, East Germany witnessed similarly brutal policies, with a huge rise in the prison population in the early 1950s as well as the founding of organizations like the paramilitary *Kampfgruppen der Arbeiterklasse*—Combat Groups of the Working Class— as the infant DDR regime sought to consolidate power. One of the most momentous decisions in the history of the DDR was made in a matter of minutes on February 8, 1950, during a meeting of the as yet provisional People's Council: the founding of a Ministry of State Security, or *Ministerium für Staatssicherheit*. The first few letters of the two constituent parts of the final word—*Staat* and *Sicherheit*—lent the ministry the name the world would come to know and dread: the *Stasi*. By the mid-1950s the Stasi already had 16,000 employees, more than Hitler's Gestapo had employed in a unified Germany with five times as many inhabitants as East Germany; by 1952 the Stasi had also recruited 30,000 informants. Both of those numbers would continue to rise steeply.

As living conditions in the new DDR worsened during the early 1950s, hundreds of thousands of East Germans fled the country, and a heavily fortified border was erected between East Germany and West Germany—though not between East and West Berlin, leaving an island inside East Germany that was outside East German control. Continued economic woes led to the introduction of increased work quotas and longer hours at state-run enterprises.

Dissatisfaction peaked in 1953, as 120,000 people fled the DDR during the first four months of the year. Then, on June 17, workers in hundreds of cities and towns across the DDR went on strike to protest the new quotas, leading to wider demonstrations against government repression. At one point protestors across the country took over twelve prisons, thirteen police offices, and five Stasi command centers. The government was paralyzed, unwilling to take up arms against the populace. Soviet occupation forces had no such scruples: dozens of demonstrators were killed and perhaps 10,000 more sent off to prison camps after Russian troops retook the streets.

Throughout the late 1950s, hundreds of thousands of East Germans continued to flee, with the vast majority crossing from East to West Berlin. Some kind of barrier began to look inevitable. So inevitable, in fact, that in July 1961 alone—the month before the Berlin Wall finally went up—30,000 East Germans fled. Another 45,000 left during the first two weeks of August before the Wall appeared on the morning of August 13, 1961. It took just eleven days after the erection of the Wall for the first person to be killed trying to cross it. Over a hundred more would be killed in coming decades, most of them in their teens and twenties.

Still, even after the Wall was fortified in subsequent years—despite the broken glass shards and nails and razor wire, despite the mines and automated firing devices, despite the watchtowers and the border troops with orders to shoot—it was not entirely impermeable: Western radio wafted easily over it, allowing Western pop music to reach almost all parts of East Germany, with the exception of the low area around Dresden, an area known to East Germans as the *Tal der Ahnungslosen*, or Valley of the Clueless. East German officialdom had considered early rock "American cultural barbarism" and said Elvis's "so-called" singing "was just like his face: stupid, dull, and brutish." And yet, after the Wall went up, DDR authorities restated their stance on the politics of dance parties in a way that opened things up: a politburo statement dismissed the debate over whether certain types of dancing were influenced by Western "non-culture," adding that the politburo considered dancing "a legitimate expression of the joy of life" and did not intend to stipulate that kids were permitted to express this joy only in the form of a tango or waltz.

Bring on the twist.

Bring on the mashed potato.

But then, in 1964, Soviet hardliner Leonid Brezhnev deposed the more liberal-minded Nikita Khrushchev as the head of the USSR and declared an end to Khrushchev's de-Stalinization. Suddenly the East Germans needed to retreat from the more conciliatory approach they had taken after the construction of the Wall. The craze surrounding the Beatles—as well as demonstrations and a near-riot by hundreds of kids in Leipzig in October 1965 after authorities there banned almost all the local Beat bands—elicited commentary directly from head of state Walter Ulbricht during a meeting of the Central Committee of the Communist Party:

> I am of the opinion, comrades, that we should put an end to the monotony of the Yeah Yeah Yeah and whatever else it's called. Must we really copy every piece of garbage that comes from the West?

To lock things down on the youth culture front, the Party established new rules for licensing bands. It had always been the case that to work as a professional musician in the planned economy you needed credentials—you needed to study music and secure a license from cultural authorities. But from November 1965 on, even amateur bands needed to audition for and be certified by a licensing commission in order to play anywhere in public. And the certification process was not based on musicianship alone—political and aesthetic approval was just as important to securing an *Einstufung*. The days of teenage garage bands covering the latest British Invasion hits at school dances and FDJ youth clubs were over.

In 1971, the former head of the Free German Youth, Erich Honecker, now 59, took over the East German dictatorship—officially he replaced Ulbricht as General Secretary of the Socialist Unity Party, or SED. Honecker eased back the repression of things like Beatles haircuts and risqué clothing, yet during his rule the Stasi would also double in size to 91,000 employees, as well as nearly doubling the number of informants it ran, to 180,000—one for every eighty-three people in the nation of fifteen million. Honecker also believed in the overarching importance of homeland security, and in 1978, in a country that already had countless paramilitary organizations, he extended mandatory military training into primary schools.

A hardliner by nature, Honecker was nonetheless more open to rock music. But rather than import music by decadent capitalist puppets like the Doors or the Stones, he determined the DDR should foster its own rock culture. This led to a string of officially sanctioned East German rock bands dominating Free German Youth concerts and DDR youth radio during the 1970s. Bands with names like the Puhdys, Renft, Electra-Combo, Karussell, and Stern-Combo Meissen aped Deep Purple, Uriah Heep, King Crimson, Blood, Sweat & Tears, and Jethro Tull—and landed deals with the government record label, Amiga, the sole music manufacturer and distributor in the tightly-controlled East German media system.

It was against this backdrop that punk music drifted over the Wall . . .

East Berlin punks on Lenin Platz, in Friedrichshain, ca. 1982

I

Too Much Future

1

The very first punk in East Berlin went by the name "Major." She was fifteen years old and lived in a neighborhood called Köpenick, about a twenty-minute ride southeast from the center of town on one of the city's elevated S-Bahn trains.

It was September 1977.

Major's proper name was Britta Bergmann, and she had learned lessons about the Berlin Wall early. Britta had never known her own father, but she had an older sister whose father was a West Berliner who occasionally came to see the family in East Berlin. When Britta was five years old, her sister's father was over for a visit, and in the evening, when he said he had to be going, had to get back over to West Berlin, Britta had an idea.

"We'll come along," said little Britta enthusiastically.

She didn't understand why his face clouded.

"No," he said, confused. "You can't just come with me—you live in the East!"

That realization of what the Wall meant stuck with Britta.

Growing up, Britta was aware that her family had a history of opposition politics. Her maternal grandfather had been in the German communist party in the 1920s and spent time in prison after Hitler's rise; her maternal grandmother was officially branded an anti-fascist and placed on Heinrich Himmler's black list for, among other things, maintaining friendships with Jews and refusing to perform the Nazi salute. Despite their communist beliefs, life in Stalinist East Germany hadn't been easy for them, either, with her grandparents detained for weeks and accused of spying as a result of a friendship with a Swiss national. Britta grew up in her grandmother's apartment. Her grandmother was openly critical of the dictatorship and had a strong influence on her granddaughter's worldview—Britta learned not only to view government propaganda with a large dose of skepticism but to see the entire system as unjust and illegitimate.

All through school Britta suffered from the feeling that her choices were being usurped by the state, that—in more adult terms—she was being disenfranchised from casting a vote in the most crucial decisions in her own life and destiny, decisions about who she was and who she would or could be. She knew, she just *knew*, it was wrong that you weren't permitted to read whatever you wanted, that you couldn't openly express your opinions. Wrong that creativity, curiosity, and independent thinking were *verboten*.

I just want to be allowed to be an individual, to be who I am, to make my own choices.

In the summer of 1977, one of Britta's friends had a visit from a cousin from West Germany. The cousin told the girls about someone who had escaped to West Berlin by crossing one of the lakes that formed the border down in the southwest corner of the city, near Potsdam. Fifteen-year-old Britta felt inspired: she wanted to escape, too.

The future laid out for me in the DDR is NOT acceptable.

It's time for me to get out of here.

She and her friend secretly discussed the idea and soon both of them began to make plans—Britta even wanted to go scout out the lakeshore. In the end, though, the escape attempt did not go beyond teenage daydreams.

At the beginning of the school year in September 1977, Britta's sister gave her a stack of photos and pullout posters she'd amassed from the precious West German teen magazines her father brought her—images of ABBA, Boney M, Smokie, the cheesy chart toppers and heartthrobs of the day. As Britta leafed through the images, she suddenly stopped at one. It was a black-and-white shot of a band called the Sex Pistols.

What the fuck is this, she wondered, fascinated by their ripped clothes and sneering faces.

At school she asked around in class to try to figure out if anyone had heard of this mysterious band with the crazy name, the Sex Pistols. One kid in school knew everything about music, and sure enough he knew the Pistols: they were "punk," he told her. *Punk?* But wait, she thought, she'd heard that AC/DC was supposed to be punk, and she couldn't stand AC/DC. She hated hard rock. Not long afterward, though, Britta was listening to a Western radio station, Radio Luxembourg, and heard something that immediately caught her attention. The song started with a ragged, chiming guitar line and then the drums kicked in and then it got seriously loud, chugging along like some kind of overheated locomotive, a runaway train, and then the singer started—well, it wasn't exactly *singing*, the guy couldn't carry a tune, he was sort of howling in a tortured monotone, sneering and shrieking and growling . . . *There's no point in asking, you'll get no reply* . . . the song was like a punch in the gut and the singer sounded committed in a way she'd never heard before, almost possessed . . . *I don't pretend 'cause I DON'T CARE . . . stuff your cheap comment 'cause we know what we feel!*

It was as if the band was speaking directly to her. She felt like a switch had been thrown inside her, as if the song had activated something that had been buried inside her, something she hadn't known was there until this moment.

Holy shit!

She waited for the DJ to identify the band.

"That was the Sex Pistols, with 'Pretty Vacant,'" said the DJ.

The Sex Pistols!

Now *that* was what she had expected from the picture of the band, with their fucked-up hair and fucked-up skin and fucked-up clothing.

She hacked off her hair the next day, affecting the look she knew from the black-and-white photo of the Pistols. Then she started rummaging through her sister's stack of West German magazines for more shots of the band. Once she had a few, she began to modify her clothes to mimic the Pistols' look as best she could. She ripped holes in a shirt and then sewed the holes closed again with big, ugly stitches that were clearly visible. She cut out a swatch of white cloth and wrote DESTROY on it with a black pen, then sewed it onto the chest pocket of her jacket. Then she nicked the chain from a spare toilet plunger and attached it to the same jacket, stringing it from the chest pocket to one of the buttons. In one of the pictures Britta found, Johnny Rotten—the Sex Pistols' singer—had safety pins on the shoulders of his jacket. Britta could do that, too. She put a row of safety pins on the top of each shoulder of her own jacket—punk-rock epaulets.

You could hear the gasps at school when she showed up with short hair and her clothes ripped and stuck with pins.

One kid came up to her and greeted her based on her shiny metal epaulets: "Hello, Major!"

From that moment on, that was her name.

School authorities did not take her stunt so lightly. Any deviation from the officially ordained path was seen as threatening to the social cohesion the dictatorship nurtured with its system of youth organizations and propaganda, all designed to feed properly indoctrinated workers into the planned economy. The school quickly sprang into action, and the principal and Major's teachers—in consultation with the local youth services office—secretly deliberated on how to deal with her. As Major learned years later when she gained access to her Stasi file, the teachers felt they were incapable of molding an acceptable socialist identity out of Major, and they debated whether to have her committed to an institution where she could be treated for her "difficulties."

Major had problems in the classroom, too. Her grades fell as teachers began to look dimly on her work; they also gave her additional assignments, projects like preparing a poster about the good relations East Germany enjoyed with the Soviet army and writing a speech on the advantages of a planned economy. This was how the teachers hoped to reintegrate her into socialist society. Teachers also sent her home a lot, telling her she shouldn't return to class until she changed her clothes. She never changed her clothes. In fact, she continued to assemble more and more outfits, modifying more shirts and pants with paint and pins and pen markings, and adding homemade buttons with band names and phrases like I'M AN ENEMY OF THE STATE.

She had found the perfect vent. Punk sounded and looked and *felt* like liberation. Major had never doubted she lived in an illegitimate system, but she hadn't wanted to throw rocks or build bombs or murder anyone. She just wanted to be herself, and doing, saying, reading, and writing the things that would have made her feel like herself were all *verboten*. Becoming a punk imbued Major with a sense of power on two levels. First, the music seemed to give voice to the rage she felt inside and gave her the strength to survive in a system she hated. Second, the look provided an explicit way for her to show her opposition every time she stepped out in public.

Meanwhile Major's friend—the one she had talked about escaping with—had been corresponding with her cousin in West Berlin, and the two of them had naïvely mentioned the previous summer's teenage dream of swimming across the lake to the West; Major was mentioned by name. The girl's father came across one of the letters and he ratted out his own daughter, as well as Major, to the police.

On May 16, 1978, Major was ordered to report to a police station for questioning.

Led by a Lieutenant Müller of the *Volkspolizei*, the cops interrogated the sixteen-year-old all day and straight through the night. They also executed a search of her family's apartment while she was in police custody.

During the interrogation Major made a strategic error: she answered some of Lieutenant Müller's questions about punk, questions brought on by her outlandish look and then by things they'd found when they searched her apartment—song lyrics she'd jotted down while listening to the radio, poems she'd written that were deemed "politically negative." Major had discovered a bunch of bands she liked from Western radio: X-Ray Spex, Sham 69, Slaughter and the Dogs, Chelsea, the Clash, Cock Sparrer, the Buzzcocks, the Vibrators, the Stranglers, Stiff Little Fingers, Wire . . . She could rattle off a lot of names of bands she considered favorites by now. Unfortunately, most anything she knew about punk had to have come from Western media. This compounded the suspicions about Major stemming from her being mentioned in her friend's letter alongside chatter about something considered a very serious crime: *Republikflucht*. In essence, *defection*.

Major was finally released the next day, but the authorities anticipated more trouble from her. Anyone who self-identified with a youth culture that wasn't officially sanctioned was problematic enough. But in Major's case, not only was she a punk—or "pank," as the authorities sometimes wrote in reports—she had also written antisocial poems and broached the topic of defection with others. Any instance of attempted *Republikflucht* also triggered an automatic process: the Stasi had to be informed.

The Stasi started an official file on Major on August 27, 1978.

She was now on the radar of one of the world's most feared domestic spy agencies.

From that point on, Major was under constant surveillance. She was followed constantly and any mail she received was opened and read. The police never stopped tailing her, either. Lieutenant Müller was convinced he had ferreted out a dangerous enemy of the state in sixteen-year-old Major. And maybe he was right.

2

Tenth grade was the end of formal education for most East German students. At that point they began to be integrated into the planned economy through an apprenticeship in a specific field of work. Or rather, they were integrated more thoroughly—since even as students they worked several hours per week in factories as part of a school subject called *Produktionsarbeit*.

At the end of the school year in 1978, Major received the official assessment she would need to apply for any future apprenticeship or job. "She has great difficulty grasping the tenets of socialism," it stated, "but in *Produktionsarbeit* she was obedient." Major was convinced the assessment was meant to ensure she'd be steered into factory work rather than being allowed to enter a job field she might be more enthusiastic about. Once again her future was being preordained without her input.

Major applied for a number of apprenticeships and training school programs. She was shut out of them all. Doing nothing was not an option: working was not just a social obligation in East Germany; it was illegal not to work—and punishable by imprisonment.

The importance of work in the DDR was backed by law and enforced with the teeth of the state. People who didn't work weren't just lazy, they were criminally antisocial, guilty of *asoziales Verhalten*. As a policy, condemning lack of work as criminally antisocial was actually inherited from Nazi Germany. Work in an *Arbeitskollektiv*, or work collective, was also seen as a key means of integration, a way the individual formed a direct connection to socialist society.

The notion of *asozial* played a prominent role in developmental and pedagogic approaches in East Germany, too. The rehabilitation of wayward kids often involved shipping them off to work camps, where they could learn the value of honest work, social responsibility, and discipline. Unfortunately the work camps often translated to child factory labor—sometimes by kids still in single digits—in conditions that bordered on prisonlike.

In the end, Major's mother managed to secure her a spot in a program for typists. Officially, East Germany embraced gender equality, but the reality was often depressingly traditional; Major joined a training program that consisted exclusively of other girls. Not surprisingly, Major was the only punk. In fact, she had yet to see another punk *anywhere*, boy or girl. Her teachers and the director of the program constantly threatened her with expulsion because of her appearance.

Major quickly realized that as part of their surveillance efforts the Stasi had coopted people around her to work as informants. Of course, most of the people around Major were young like her—teenage typists. For a time in its history, the Stasi had debated internally about recruiting minors, but since 1968 the agency had actively sought to convert kids as young as seventh graders into informants, *Inoffizielle Mitarbeiter* in the Stasi's own terminology, or *IM*s for short, meaning something like "adjunct employees." The general population, not privy to the Stasi's internal jargon, called a Stasi informant a *Spitzel,* or "snitch." In a system where the state micromanaged the future, it was easy to get leverage over kids—*it would be a shame if you weren't able to get one of the few available spots in the job field you want . . . it would be a shame if your parents had to go to jail because you wouldn't cooperate and you ended up in an orphanage.* Of the hundreds of thousands of IMs the Stasi ran over the years, close to 10 percent were considered "youths," though not all of those were minors.

For the first year of her job training, Major lived as if she were on the run. She rarely slept in one place for more than a few nights in a row, switching between her grandmother's apartment—where she'd grown up—and friends' places, as well as the apartment of her ninety-year-old great-grandmother, who also lived in the Köpenick district. Moving around kept the informants and spies guessing; often she managed to ditch her tails by living so erratically. After about a year, the Stasi gave up chase— though Lieutenant Müller of the *Volkspolizei* did not give up his patriotic crusade to rid his district of her "negative-decadent" influence.

It was difficult to get an apartment at the time, so in 1979 Major registered herself at her great-grandmother's place, making it her official residence in the hope that she might be able to stay there when her great-grandmother eventually died.

Late that summer, while wandering through an annual local summer fair, Major saw something she had never seen before outside of her own mirror, a few Western magazines, and record covers: punks.

There are others!

Major had been a punk for nearly two years—totally alone, as far as she knew.

She made straight for them and they all chatted excitedly for a while. But there was no way to stay in touch—virtually nobody had a phone in the East, Major was moving from place to place all the time, making even mail difficult, and since she was still under surveillance, or so she suspected, letters would be intercepted anyway.

Major managed to hang in and finish the job training program, which landed her a minimum-wage job as a typist. She would have to work Monday to Friday from 6:30 a.m. to 4:00 p.m., using a typewriter from 1933.

In September of 1980, around the time she started her full-time job, Major ran into a few of the punks she'd met the summer before.

They told her about a meet-up planned for a few days later at a youth club in a nearby neighborhood. She went to the club—*of course* she went to the club! But only one other punk showed up, a guy she'd never seen before. They became friends. They arranged to meet again, and within a few weeks a handful of punks from the southern parts of the city—Köpenick, Schöneweide, Wendenschloss—began to congregate regularly at a youth club in a park called Plänterwald, which the punks called PW for short. In addition to the youth club, the adjacent amusement park, with its huge ferris wheel nestled in the woods, also became a punk landmark. At first there were just a few punks showing up at PW, then a dozen. As word of their Wednesday and Saturday gatherings got around during the autumn of 1980, the numbers began to rise.

One day a punk approached Major at PW, a guy she'd never seen before. He was tall and strikingly handsome, and dimples appeared on his cheeks when he smiled.

"What's your name?" he asked her.

"Major," she said.

"In that case I'm Colonel," he said, placing himself a rank above her.

His real name was Mario Schulz, but now he, too, had his nom-de-punk.

The gang of punks would sit at the side of the dance floor of the youth club waiting for something they could dance to, punk or ska, they didn't care. They took homemade cassettes of the Sex Pistols, the Stranglers, Sham 69, and all their other favorite UK bands—all taped off the radio—and offered them to the DJ. The DJs in official youth clubs were fully integrated into the system. They had to take a course and pass an exam in order to get a license to spin. But the use of homemade cassettes was common even among the officially-sanctioned DJs, since the cheapest and easiest way to get Western music was to tape it off West Berlin radio. And anyway, the DJs wanted to be hip and cool, too. So they'd usually play a punk song or two a night. The general crowd would run for the hills as the punks stormed onto the dance floor and threw themselves around wildly and pogoed. At first other kids thought the punks were cool, but it didn't take long before they started to take issue with them. Many nights ended in fistfights. For some of the punks, that became part of the thrill—waiting for the moment all hell broke loose.

Sometimes the punks would hit other youth clubs in the area—KWO in Schöneweide, FAS in Lichtenberg—but the pattern was always the same: wait all night for a Pistols song; hope to get out alive before the mainstream kids got up enough liquid courage to try to beat the shit out of the greatly outnumbered punks.

Major's great-grandmother had also died in the summer of 1980, leaving Major to occupy the apartment all by herself. Since Major had lived on the run, lived with the paranoia of being followed, she was happy to open her new place as a crash pad for other punks, whether they wanted to hang out and listen to music, sleep there to take a break from oppressive conditions in their family homes, or try to throw off police tails. Major's apartment soon became the hub of a burgeoning scene, a place where punks knew they could find each other even on nights when there wasn't a meet-up somewhere else.

It's a cliché to describe the East Bloc as gray, but there was truth behind the cliché. Many of the old buildings that had managed to survive Allied air raids during World War II were dilapidated or even derelict, with shrapnel damage on their facades from street fighting at the end of the war. The old buildings had a brownish-gray hue darkened by soot from the coal stoves still used to heat many apartments. Large sections of the city had been flattened by Allied bombing and never rebuilt; other sections had been rebuilt with cheerless sprayed-concrete facades and low-ceilinged apartments; on the outskirts of town the government had thrown up huge colonies of unadorned, monotonous high-rises. There were hardly any streetlights and virtually none of the posters, billboards, or signs splashed with advertisements that gave a lot of the color to Western streets—in a planned economy there was no need for advertising and branding. A leaden sky hung above the city for much of the year and the air was choked with the ruddy smoke belched out by all the stoves burning brown coal ripped from massive strip mines in central East Germany. In these surroundings, punks—splattered with paint and pins and homemade buttons and patches, wearing garish makeup, their hair dyed unnatural colors—might as well have dropped from outer space.

Thanks to their conspicuousness—as well as to nosy neighbors and informants—it didn't take long for the cops to take notice of the activity at PW and at Major's apartment. Major frequently received letters inviting her down to the police station: *zur Klärung eines Sachverhaltes,* which meant "to clear up some facts surrounding a case." What this usually entailed was being interrogated for up to forty-eight hours about the comings and goings at her apartment—after forty-eight hours the police needed a warrant to hold her any longer, so she would be released. During these sessions the police lectured her about the right and wrong ways to comport herself and made veiled threats about the consequences of doing it the wrong way—threats of arrest, beating, even threats of getting attacked in the dark, empty streets.

3

I n October 1980 a guy named Micha Horschig turned up at PW—alone. He was of medium height and build with spiky black hair and a downy mustache, not as imposing as the tougher-looking Köpenick kids. Micha had grown up first in Treptow and then in Johannisthal, a neighborhood sandwiched between the river Spree and the Wall, out beyond Schöneweide.

Micha had first heard the Sex Pistols in 1977 while laid up in the hospital—the guy in the next bed had furtively played him a few songs on a portable cassette player. As his school years drew to an end, Micha got deeper and deeper into punk, listening to Western radio shows, dressing in ripped clothes and giving himself purposefully weird haircuts, and eventually digging into anarchist literature. In an old set of pre-War encyclopedias he was able to find descriptions and excerpts of since-banned writings by Mikhail Bakunin, Pierre-Joseph Proudhon, and Max Stirner—the basis of an anarchist canon. Up to then, Micha had been a relatively happy member of communist youth organizations, despite elements of hypocrisy he found jarring—he'd been upset when a girl was barred from a Free German Youth event because she was a member of a church, for instance, and he could never understand why school teachers freaked out at the sight of a kid with a plastic bag with a West German brand name or logo on it. It was a *plastic bag*. Why would they care? Now, versed in anarchism and the history of anarchist movements, he began to have thoughts that were unthinkable in East Germany: Why had Karl Marx been willing to weaken the First International in order to seize power within the organization? Why had Marx been so intent on shutting out the anarchist factions that he stooped to using lies and intrigue? All of this ate at Micha. And it made him want to talk to other people as he tried to work things out.

Throughout 1978 and 1979, while working at an apprenticeship as a clock maker, Micha had spent all his free time discussing politics. He had found a willing partner in a fellow apprentice named Frank Masch. Frank identified himself as a social democrat, but Micha quickly realized that regardless of the label, most leftists—including a self-styled anarchist and a social democrat—could agree on basic philosophical principles like freedom, egalitarianism, solidarity, and the right of the people to participate in the political process.

Together with Frank, Micha began to go to bars and cafés and obsessively engage people in political debates. It wasn't hard to engage in some sense—people always wanted to know why he ran around looking so fucking strange. And what the hell was all this bullshit about anarchism he was spouting? Conversation started. The problem was that some people very quickly took issue with the sort of talk Micha wanted to have. The Stasi and their unofficial snitches were everywhere, and people squirmed. Sometimes a potential conversation partner would whisper to Micha, "Hey, keep it down, the guy back there is listening." Sometimes a kind bartender or fellow guest would whisper, "You better get out of here, that guy over there just *made a call*." Off he and Frank would run, getting out of sight before the police arrived.

But Micha did not want to whisper.

On paper, East German law enshrined free speech as a right. The right to freedom of expression was also trumpeted in state propaganda. Micha had decided to take it literally: *I will say what I want to say.*

Micha never started fights. There were just so many helpful defenders of the status quo, and when faced with Micha's maniacal drive to engage people on taboo subjects, they often answered with fists. After it happened a few times, something changed in Micha. He learned to go into beast-mode when attacked. If people wanted to fuck with him, they'd better be ready.

In 1979, Micha started a countdown to the end of the DDR: *ten years*, he thought, *that's how long it will take.*

He was sure of it.

Even though Micha had already considered himself a punk for two years by the time he turned up at PW that fall of 1980, none of the punks in Major's gang had seen him before, and they wondered whether he was a "real punk" or just dressed like one as a fashion statement. But when they started to talk to him, it quickly became clear that he was for real: Micha immediately took up the topic of politics, leading, of course, to anarchism.

This guy knows his shit.

The group immediately started to call him A-Micha—the "A" was for anarchy. Listening to A-Micha talk, Major realized he could articulate anarchist ideology with a clarity she had never heard before. Around his new friends, A-Micha was calm, level-headed, and responsible, and he came across like some kind of intellectual. He seemed more grown-up than Major's other buddies, even though he was the same age as the rest of them. Major was fascinated by A-Micha and the two of them started to hang out together, sometimes talking through entire nights. A-Micha began to crash at her place regularly.

A-Micha also dressed in a very creative way. He liked to sew zippers into the rips he made in his pants. And instead of painting buttons or bottle caps and then decorating them with band names or whatever, A-Micha just cut out scraps of paper, wrote on them with pen, and stuck them on his clothes with safety pins. The phrases he wore sometimes seemed crazy even to fellow punks—this was a police state after all and here was A-Micha plastered with the phrase *Haut die Bullen platt wie Stullen*, which was basically "Beat the pigs to a pulp." A-Micha was also among the first punks to wear the logo of Solidarity, the Polish trade union that came to international prominence in August of 1980 after staging a dramatic strike that spread from the port city of Gdansk to the whole country—among Solidarity's demands of the Polish dictatorship were the restoration of constitutionally-guaranteed freedoms of speech and of the press.

Some people dismissed Eastern punks as teenage rebels in thrall to the latest Western pop cultural trend, no-good kids who wanted to wind people up—this was their idea of fun, of *teenage kicks*. But Major had always seen it differently. She realized that her idea of fun—and the idea of fun she shared with her new friends—deviated from the path the government demanded everyone stay on together. Major and her friends were being political *by* having fun. It was that easy to be political in the DDR. To think differently, to speak out, or to stand out was to be political. And to stand out the way the punks did—in such an open, ostentatious way—was to be a political radical.

Keeping people on a preordained path, keeping them moving along together as one glacial entity—marching them through the Young Pioneers, the Thälmann Pioneers, the Free German Youth, and military service; steering them into apprenticeships, factory jobs, and creating productive members of society—wasn't as difficult as it might seem. In the DDR, as in most societies, conformity and complacency ruled the day. Everyone had a job and a roof over their head; everyone had refrigerators and 90 percent of households had TVs and washing machines; there was cheap booze and enough to eat. So people went about their daily lives and stayed within accepted sociopolitical boundaries without constant government coercion. Most people, anyway.

By the dawn of the 1980s, the physical brutality of the Stalin era was no longer necessary—or at least not *as* necessary—because once there was a "real existing socialism," that is, a *norm*, people tended to stick to the norm. Membership in communist youth organizations was not mandatory, and yet membership rates hovered around 85 percent. There was a lot of self-censorship, a kind of inherent sense of where the boundaries were and, *Hey, I don't want to go anywhere near them anyway, I'm happy just to fit in*.

As for those few souls who weren't inclined to fit in, people tended to *encourage* them to stick to the norm—nobody likes a person who makes things difficult for everyone else.

Still, it's important to realize that conformity and complacency didn't distinguish the DDR from other countries. For an entire century, most Americans went about their daily lives despite the gross injustice of Jim Crow laws: *Not my problem*. The total indifference with which most Americans reacted to Edward Snowden's revelations of mass warrantless surveillance is another example: *I've got nothing to hide*. Or white America's collective shrug at the militarization of its police forces and the ongoing flood of evidence of horrific police brutality: *They're not coming for me.* People look away. It's natural. People defend the norm without having to be prodded to do so. That's just the way people are. Until they really *do* come for you. Until you have to defend yourself. Until you bear the brunt of injustice. Or in the case of the DDR, until you were arrested and interrogated on a daily basis and your parents lost their jobs and your brother or sister was booted out of school and you were banned from your hometown or imprisoned and and and, and all because you spoke your mind, you objected, you failed to conform—you listened to the wrong music.

But that was still in the future as the leaves dropped from the trees in the woods around the PW club in the fall of 1980.

For Major and other punks, *encouragement* from ordinary citizens to stick to the norm, however, started immediately. It came in the form of insults—"you should be sent to the gas chambers"—and beatings at the hands of those defenders of the status quo who sure as shit weren't going to let a bunch of teenagers parade around like that, looking absolutely disgraceful, showing total disregard for society. No, those punks were going to learn a lesson.

Soon enough, groups of punks had to meet at the S-Bahn station at Plänterwald and walk to PW together—it was safer that way. Lone punks routinely got hunted down on the street by groups of law-abiding citizens out for blood. And often Nazi references flew along with the fists when people attacked the punks: "It wouldn't have taken Hitler long to get rid of the likes of you!"

Though A-Micha was calm, level-headed, and responsible, his new friends quickly found out that he really knew how to fight. Whenever the shit hit the fan, A-Micha defended his friends like the hero of an epic poem. Beast mode.

All the antagonism drew the little gang of punks closer together, all for one and one for all. Like the British band Sham 69 sang:

If the kids are united,
they will never be divided.

4

The first punk to show up at PW from the northern part of East Berlin was Michael Boehlke, who had grown up in Pankow, a neighborhood in the north of the city. Most of the southern punks were eighteen by now—like Major—but Boehlke was just sixteen. He was tall and willowy with somewhat sullen, deep-set eyes. He talked with a slight lisp. He had just finished tenth grade that summer of 1980 and had recently started his assigned apprenticeship as a machine fitter—*Facharbeiter für Anlagentechnik* in official terminology—at a cigarette factory in nearby Schöneweide. Someone at the factory had told him about the Wednesday night punk meet-up at PW.

None of the southern Berlin punks had ever been up to Pankow, and they looked at Boehlke as if he came from a completely different city, even a different planet.

"Hey, it's you," they would say when he showed up again, "the guy from Pankow!"

It didn't take long before they shortened the greeting to just "Pankow" and that became his name among the punks.

There were so few punks at that point that Pankow quickly got to know all of them by name. Not their real names, of course, as nearly everyone in the scene used an alias. Not just Major and Colonel and A-Micha, but also Erkner, Keule, Buzzcock, Fatzo, Special, and Spion. Taking on a new name was part of the ritual of becoming a punk. It was a rejection of a previous life and identity, a life and identity that had already been coopted by the regime—Michael Boehlke's life was already planned out, but Pankow's was just beginning, and he was the only one who was going to say where it was going. Using an alias was also extremely practical in a surveillance state bristling with informants, and in a scene where people would soon be subjected to constant police interrogation. "Give us a list of the people who were there!" *Um, let's see, there was Fatzo and Buzzcock and Pankow . . .*

One afternoon Pankow took a train to go see one of his new friends. He wanted to make cassette copies of the guy's records: *Never Mind the Bollocks* by the Sex Pistols and *No More Heroes* by the Stranglers. On the way there, three guys attacked Pankow on the train—*god damn punk!*—and broke his nose. Pankow went and made the tapes anyway, black eye, bloody nose, and all.

Getting beaten up was nothing new for him. Pankow had been an outsider his entire life. He'd grown up in a violent home, where his father frequently beat him and his mother—he had shown up for the first day of first grade with a broken nose, compliments of dad.

The household was always on edge.

The contrast between the outward show his family put on versus the violent reality meant that Pankow developed a deeply ingrained sense of skepticism from an early age—things were not as they seemed.

Pankow was naturally left-handed, but when he started to learn to write in school they forced him to switch hands. He already had been made fun of for being so scrawny, and now he started to develop speech impediments, mumbling and stuttering. By the third grade everyone else could write properly but Pankow still couldn't. Somehow he was never held back. He just sat there year after year thinking, *I'm an idiot, there's something wrong with me. Why am I unable to do the things everyone else has no problem doing?*

Pankow felt more and more isolated.

He didn't think of himself as political, but he definitely thought East Germany was a fucked-up place. Sometimes he sat out in front of his housing block and stared disdainfully at the neighborhood. Many party leaders and other prominent figures lived in the area, it was neat and leafy, with folks washing their cars on the weekend or taking strolls in a nearby park built around a Baroque chateau, and Pankow hated it all, hated the people and especially the other kids, and resolved not to be like them.

I feel different.

But what could he do?

By his early teens, his aggression began to boil over.

One night near the end of tenth grade he and a friend snuck out and smashed all the ground-floor windows of their school. When he showed up the next day, his name was called while the students were all assembled for a flag ceremony. Pankow was admonished in front of the entire school for wearing his denim vest with AC/DC scrawled on the back. On the way home that day he spotted a Mercedes parked on a side street—some well-connected party member's car. He eyed the star on the hood. Then he went over and broke it off. That star would fetch a good price, he knew.

He started negotiating at school the next day—what could he get for a genuine Mercedes hood ornament? In the end he traded it for a West German music magazine—and it would change his life.

Inside the magazine: a photo of the Sex Pistols.

This was what he had been searching for.

I feel different.

I want to look different, too.

As his school career came to an end, Pankow began to change. He spray-painted an anarchist A on the back of an old suit jacket he'd found. He went into the woods in a local park and tore holes in some of his T-shirts.

Then one day Pankow grabbed the family scissors and bounded down to the cellar of his building. He gave himself a punk haircut, spiky and purposefully fucked up. When he went upstairs he impulsively decided to ring the doorbell rather than going straight in. His father answered the door, took one look at Pankow's hair, and punched him in the face.

Pankow's mother didn't really mind his new look—she even seemed to take a certain glee in the way he attracted attention, the way heads craned out of windows when her son walked down the street. But Pankow's father could not stand it. He forbade Pankow to eat at the family table. He screamed at Pankow and smacked and punched him.

It didn't matter. Pankow was committed to punk. Even though he had yet to hear much of the music and hadn't met any other punks—he thought for a while he might be the only one in Berlin—he knew he had found what he had been looking for. After getting constantly hassled and beaten up by other kids in the neighborhood for his outlandish look, Pankow bought a spiky dog collar, thinking it would make him look more intimidating. Instead of shrinking from the attention and hoping not to get beat up, he went on the offensive: whenever someone started to mess with him, he would glare at them and shout, "You want to get your face smashed in?"

Things at home kept deteriorating. Shortly after he started his job training at the cigarette factory, Pankow decided he could no longer take it. He threw a few things in a bag, slammed the door shut behind him, and never went home again.

5

The first place Pankow fled to was a friend's apartment on Göhrener Strasse, just down the road in Prenzlauer Berg. The friend lived in the rectory of Elias Church, which was run by an opposition-friendly minister named Georg Katzorke.

Things quickly got complicated there when Pankow fell for the minister's daughter. The next place he landed was an apartment on Wörther Strasse, near the water tower in central Prenzlauer Berg. A friend of Pankow's had just fled the country, so Pankow squatted the guy's now-empty place. There were two versions of squatting in East Germany. In one version, people took up residence illegally—that is, without the mandatory permission of the state housing authorities—in an officially recognized apartment; this is what Pankow did on Wörther Strasse. But the more commonly understood version of squatting also took place. An official East German report put the number of empty properties in the country at 235,000; they were concentrated in the central parts of cities like Berlin, Leipzig, Dresden, and Halle. By the early 1980s the government estimated that 800 people were squatting in East Berlin's Prenzlauer Berg neighborhood alone; that number would double by the end of the decade. It was one way opposition-minded youths started to carve out physical space for themselves, living inside East Germany but outside the state.

The problem for Pankow with that first apartment was that the Stasi turned up, thinking Pankow was an accomplice to his friend's escape. Pankow had to find another place, and fast. This time Pankow squatted a derelict building—the more common idea of squatting.

It was around this time that Pankow first met the punks in PW. And it was also around this time the PW punks decided to make a foray to Alexanderplatz, the central square of East Berlin surrounding the Fernsehturm—the signature building on the skyline that soared above the city, its bulbous disco-ball-like lounge skewered on the needle-like TV tower. The PW punks had heard that West Berlin punks occasionally hung around Alexanderplatz, and they wanted to see for themselves.

As Major and the gang wandered around the square, they stumbled on a self-serve café at the foot of the Fernsehturm. Outside the café were a punk and two long-haired girls. The punk took one look at Major and the PW punks and said, "Are you guys from West Berlin?"

"No, we thought you were!"

Everyone started laughing.

For the rest of the day, and the next day, the PW punks hung out there and met all sorts of punks from other parts of Berlin as well as from villages on the outskirts of town. Now they all knew about the meet-ups in Plänterwald. Soon the Wednesday and Sunday gatherings at PW began to attract a hundred people. And smaller groups of punks now met daily at Alexanderplatz or nearby Rosa-Luxemburg-Platz.

Word about Major's apartment also spread, and at times she would have more than twenty people crammed into her place, hanging out, drinking, listening to music, sleeping over. Her neighbors began to track the comings and goings and work with the police. Often as soon as people showed up, so did the cops—hammering on the door and forcing their way in, asking everyone for ID and clearing the place, often by force. Sometimes the kids then had to spend the night at the police station being interrogated.

Punk kids were used to being asked for ID. Authorities could stop anyone, anytime, and demand to see papers. Because punks stood out, they could hardly leave home without being hassled by the police. If you didn't show your papers or didn't have them with you or, as happened to punks a lot, you no longer looked like the photo on your ID, it was off to the police station for up to forty-eight hours. Sometimes it was straight off to the police station anyway.

Major and her gang hated the cops and the cops hated Major and her gang. And even though she was afraid—getting arrested or physically roughed up was scary—she never showed it. As a point of pride.

I will not be intimidated!

She was determined to remain an ugly pimple on the face of real existing socialism. She wanted people to notice her and wonder if maybe there was something wrong, something false about the glorious image of society perpetuated by the dictatorship.

Scared, yes, Major was scared. But her rage was stronger than her fear.

One time the cops showed up at Major's place and kicked in her door so violently that they splintered the bottom half of it. It was hard to find a carpenter in the DDR and for weeks her apartment was just open for anyone to crawl in, including the cops. Another time the pigs gathered Major's visitors, took them one by one into her kitchen, and beat them so savagely that when she finally got home after her own detainment and interrogation, the walls and cabinets and floor and even the ceiling were splattered with blood.

It just made Major more determined.

I will not quit.

A-Micha's parents kicked him out of their home in late 1980. He started to crash at Major's full-time. It was A-Micha who cleaned up the blood in her kitchen after the savage police beating.

Pankow meanwhile started spending more time at Alexanderplatz, getting to know the punks there. They got detained a lot, but their philosophy was similar to Major's: *we're here, motherfuckers.* They wanted to be right there in the center of town for everyone to see. Which was exactly what the cops didn't want—they didn't want those eyesores mucking up Alexanderplatz, they didn't want tourists gawking at those disgraceful negative-decadent teens, those no-good kids trying to piss everyone off and embarrass the government.

One afternoon Pankow walked into a café everyone referred to as "the Tute" and spied a baby-faced punk, one he'd never met before. Pankow had just shaved part of his head—he was always trying new styles, aiming to rattle people as much as possible—and was wearing a homemade Cockney Rejects T-shirt. Pankow walked up to the round-faced guy and said, "Hey, babyface!"

"What do you want, skinhead?"

The two of them struck up a conversation and immediately hit it off. The baby-faced punk was named Kaiser and he lived with his parents in one of the hulking apartment blocks right across from Alexanderplatz, facing the Fernsehturm. Kaiser's father was a journalist; his mother, an academic researcher.

Kaiser had gotten into punk music a few years earlier because of the sheer speed of it. He loved hard, fast music; he loved the fact that Ramones albums didn't have any slow songs on them. He loved the Dickies and the Sex Pistols, fast, fast, fast. After he discovered punk he spent hours with his finger on the record button of his tape recorder, waiting to catch something worth taping on one of the West Berlin stations he could pick up on his radio. He'd been emboldened to start to dress punk by a girl in his school named Jeanny—she was the first person he knew to give herself a punk haircut and wear ripped-up sweaters like Johnny Rotten of the Pistols. Jeanny's extreme look had shocked everyone at school, but she said she felt a sense of confidence when she walked down the street and people swore at her and spat at her feet and said she should be gassed. Lade, a boy Kaiser had been friends with since kindergarten, was the next classmate to go full-on punk. He hacked his hair off and then stood it up with a mixture of shaving cream and water, and he wore a ratty trenchcoat he decorated with punk symbols and hand-painted slogans. Together, Lade and Kaiser began to delve into punk philosophy, getting their hands on illicit copies of books by Bakunin, the nineteenth-century father of collectivist-anarchism. What started out as simple teenage rebellion quickly became pointedly political for Lade and Kaiser. For them, punk and anarchy were inherently fused, and in this musical-political *Weltanschauung* the two boys felt they had found the means of self-expression they'd been looking for. They were also convinced that they were pretty damn smart.

Now, over cups of coffee on Alexanderplatz, Kaiser impressed Pankow with his political knowledge. He and Pankow laughingly began to dream up a terrorist organization.

"We'll blow up the People's Congress!"

They named their imaginary teen terrorist cell SA 80.

Kaiser also told Pankow he played in a band. The band was called Antifaschistischer Schutzwall, or AFS for short. *Antifaschistischer Schutzwall* was the East German government's official name for the Berlin wall: the anti-fascist protection barrier.

Whoa, thought Pankow, *that is cool! An actual band!*

Pankow could hardly believe it, it seemed so far from the world he knew in his sleepy neighborhood. *An actual punk band—in East Berlin!*

Kaiser could tell Pankow was impressed, so he dashed off the address of the band's practice space on Metzer Strasse and invited Pankow to drop by and check it out if he wanted to.

To call AFS a band was a bit of an exaggeration on Kaiser's part—not that Pankow cared. But so far AFS had mostly stood around looking cool in a moldy basement space they'd squatted and lined with egg cartons and rotting rags to muffle the sound they generated—when they played at all.

A number of garage bands had sprouted up in the East Berlin punk scene, but none of them amounted to much. Typically a group of kids would agree to form a band and then spend the next few weeks or even months celebrating the fact that they had formed a band before even picking up their instruments together. AFS was a little further along than that, but only because AFS had formed out of the ashes of a couple other garage bands. One was called BetonRomantik, or Concrete Romantic, a send-up of the government's love of poured-concrete construction. That band was formed around a guitar player named Micha Kobs, one of the few people in the scene who could actually play an instrument properly. Kobs had grown frustrated with his bandmates. None of them had learned to play well enough to get beyond the first three bars of "Anarchy in the UK" by the Pistols. Kaiser's experience up to then had consisted of playing the bass line of Public Image Ltd's "Public Image" for a few hours together with a drummer he knew named Alexander Kriening. But as a result Kaiser figured he had all the skills he needed. Kaiser had then joined forces with his school buddy Lade, whose own brief-lived band had imploded when his guitar player and bassist decided they only wanted to play songs by the Police, who released their third album in the fall of 1980. "You can do that punk shit by yourself," they'd shouted angrily at Lade when they quit. At that point Kobs joined Kaiser and Lade to form AFS. The original plan was to have Lade sing while playing the drums, but it was all somewhat less than ideal—Lade could barely play the drums anyway, and then to have him sing as well, though he had only started singing because he couldn't really play an instrument . . . . The band needed something else. A different drummer or perhaps a different singer. *Something*.

Kaiser wasn't there when Pankow went around to Metzer Strasse a few days later, and neither were the other band members. But another punk named Lobethal was there. Lobethal and Pankow hung out in the dingy basement for a while. Lobethal played drums and would eventually get a band together with some PW punks including Special, Jerry, and Fatzo. He started playing and had Pankow pick up the mic and sing along. Pankow didn't realize it, but Lobethal was running a crappy tape recorder, as he often did when he played.

"*Donnerwetter, Donnerwetter*," shouted Pankow—it was an exclamation used like "holy crap"—"*Alle Leute werden fetter!*"—everybody's getting fatter. "*Jeder ein Versager ist, der nicht seine Scheisse frisst!*"—Everyone's a loser who doesn't eat his own shit!

The next time Lobethal saw the members of AFS, he played the tape of Pankow.

Whoa.

This guy!

Suddenly, all the wrangling over who should play which instrument and what the band needed seemed unnecessary. They had found a frontman. His lisp, his aggression, the way he screamed—Pankow was the shit.

AFS had a real singer now, and maybe, just maybe, they could become a real band. The name AFS, however, was too dangerous.

Soon they had a new name to go with their new singer: *Planlos*—No Plan.

Fuck the rules, fuck the youth organizations, fuck the factory jobs.

Fuck the system.

We'll do what we like—or nothing at all.

We have no plan, and we like it that way.

6

By the beginning of 1981, as punks became more visible, the authorities concluded they needed to get more aggressive. The *Kriminalpolizei*'s political division, K1, and then the Stasi's *Abteilung XX*—Department XX, the division responsible for subverting underground political activity— stepped in to institute a cohesive policy of repression.·

Groups of punks started to attract attention from security forces everywhere they went. When caught in public they were subjected to threats, physical intimidation, and arbitrary detainment. Many were expelled from schools, training programs, and jobs, all of which led to strife at home. More and more of them sought out living space between the cracks, occupying legal apartments illegally or squatting in Prenzlauer Berg or Friedrichshain. In order to live outside society, as they were being forced to do, they had to create space beyond the dictatorship's web of do-gooders and their snooping ears and eyes. Many of the punks started to receive regular summonses to police stations, where they were questioned about their political beliefs, the slogans written on their buttons and clothes, and their circle of friends. Over and over again.

One fourteen-year-old girl was kicked out of school and told she could return the following school year only if she wore "normal" clothes. Her parents told her she would alter her look or they would have her committed to a juvenile detention home. When she would leave the house, they would insist on first seeing the ID papers of whatever friends she was going to be with—presumably to pass the details on to the cops. After all, they told her, "We're not going to end up in court because of you!"

She told her parents she'd rather *die* than be "standardized."

About 250 punks were forced to sign documents identifying themselves as potential criminal elements, which automatically added them to a registry of such elements. They were ordered to stay away from other punks and warned about consequences if they didn't. Most chose to ignore these warnings.

A-Micha had finished his training program and started working as a janitor. He had been forced to sign one of these documents stating that he was a potential criminal element and told he could not fraternize with a long list of people—basically every punk the security forces knew about. He thought about the ultimatum for two days and then decided: *Fuck it, I'd rather go to jail than stick to it.* He kicked himself for being so naïve as to report to the police station in the first place. From then on he knew better; he just ignored the summonses. If they wanted him, they could come get him.

And then one day the *Kriminalpolizei* did pick A-Micha up at work—he had ignored a summons—and took him in for an interrogation. When they dropped him back at work a few hours later, his boss fired him.

A-Micha knew he needed to work or else they could send him to jail as *asozial*—for not working. He was becoming increasingly reconciled to the idea that he would probably go to jail at some point, but he wanted to go for the right reason, for something he valued—for voicing his political opinions—not for some stupid bullshit. He started to go to the central post office at the main train station. The postal service hired day labor. A-Micha went each day at seven, and when he was lucky he was able to get a day's work. This kept him legally employed and put money in his pocket.

It wasn't long before the police did indeed try to pick him up as *asozial*. But A-Micha told them he had been working at the post office, go check it out. And sure enough, he had signed in on many occasions and a post office administrator told the investigators that A-Micha had worked hard. The police found a solution: the next time A-Micha went to the post office, the personnel director said he had been barred from hiring A-Micha ever again.

Now A-Micha was really in a vulnerable spot. He had only a few weeks to find something again or he would almost certainly get thrown in jail. Desperate, he finally landed a job as a gravedigger in a cemetery in Baumschulenweg, not far from where he had grown up. Crisis averted. But not for long: the boss at the cemetery was an old Nazi who rhapsodized about the German Forest and the German Oak and told anti-Semitic jokes. And as a manager he was so spiteful and petty that one person on A-Micha's shift eventually tried to kill the guy with a shovel, chasing him all over the cemetery.

Pankow sometimes got hauled in multiple times over the course of a single day. He'd be detained, and then once he was released, the first cops to drive by would take one look at him and stop. "Papers, please." Off to another police station. He soon realized that in a place like Alexanderplatz he had some leverage. The police mostly wanted the punks—who with their ripped clothes and safety pins and outlandish haircuts stood out so provocatively against the conformist masses—out of sight. Especially out of sight of tourists, and Alexanderplatz was full of tourists. Typically a couple of plainclothes officers would walk up and clamp a person's elbows and then walk them away. Most people went quietly, allowing arrests to happen without much of a commotion. But as Aleksandr Solzhenitsyn wrote in *The Gulag Archipelago*, his famous 1973 exposé of the Soviet Union's institutionalized system of repression, "You really can and you really ought to *cry out*—to *cry out* that you are being arrested!" Pankow did just that. He would cry out when the police grabbed his arms. He would go limp or flop to the ground. He would do everything to draw attention to what was happening. They would have to drag him, screaming, across the wide open space. And Pankow found that when he created a scene, sometimes the arrest would be aborted.

Ordinary citizens also continued to attack punks. One night Pankow, Colonel, Fatzo, and another punk found themselves alone in FAS, the club in the Lichtenberg district. The place was packed with soccer hooligans. At one point the DJ came over to Pankow and whispered to him.

"Something's up," he said. "You guys better get out of here."

Pankow and the other three left the club. But just behind them the door slammed open again and a horde of hooligans came racing out, looking to chase down the punks and beat them to a pulp. Pankow and the others ran for their lives, eventually hiding in a dark courtyard to evade the fifty or so would-be keepers of the socialist order. The following week Pankow returned. He and about fifty punks strutted down Frankfurter Allee, went into the FAS club, and trashed the place. A-Micha arrived at FAS later that same night, after his friends had left. When he walked in, the crowd parted—nobody wanted a piece of a punk after the show of force Pankow had mustered.

Shit was getting out of hand.

Meanwhile Pankow's band, Planlos, started to rehearse and write songs. You might say they were disciplined—they practiced every day. But then again it was fulfilling a need. This was the music they wanted to listen to when they hung out, and they couldn't make that music without each other. This was their gang, these were their best friends. They hung out together constantly, whether it was at PW, the fountains at Alexanderplatz, or their rehearsal space. It was all about camaraderie and solidarity.

The band had a melodic quality that distinguished them from the chugging discord of a lot of the other garage bands. In part this was because Kobs, their guitarist, turned out to be a gifted musician and had an ear for a catchy tune; in part it was because the entire band seemed to have set themselves a high standard. There were bumps along the road. Lade couldn't keep time very well, and still seemed to want to sing. At some point he came out from behind the drum kit and Pankow played the drums. Kaiser and Kobs liked the original lineup better. Lade had a good voice, but he wasn't the frontman that Pankow was. Lade went back behind the drums.

The first song they put together was called *"Überall wohin's dich führt,"* or "Wherever You Go." Lade wrote it.

Überall wohin's dich führt
wird dein Ausweis kontrolliert,
und sagst du einen falschen Ton,
was dann geschieht, du weisst es schonn . . .

Wherever you go
You're asked for ID
If you say a false word
You know what happens next
It doesn't matter where you look
Cameras are everywhere
Accompanying you step for step
"Security" always follows you
You speak your mind openly
And what will happen?
You can only hope

Something has to happen
Who wants to stand around passively?
Were you really born
To be subordinate to it all?

Observations like that were the sort of thing that got people sent to jail. The members of the band knew that. But as far as Pankow was concerned, this was the logical next step. He knew the country was fucked up and wanted to do something about it. Being a punk was cool, but being in a band like this, with lyrics like this, was exactly the outlet he had been looking for, a forum where he could speak his mind and vent his rage. But he wasn't crazy. After he'd memorized the words of a song he always burned the handwritten lyric sheets. He didn't want to leave any physical evidence around.

Kobs wrote a lot of songs, too, and he stored his notes beneath a false bottom in his lowest dresser drawer. One song Kobs wrote was *"Ich stehe in der Schlange am Currystand,"* or "Waiting in Line at the Currywurst Stand," about being followed by agents of the state. The lyrics translated:

Waiting in line at the currywurst stand
I don't turn around—I've already seen you
You are my shadow wherever I go
A dark spot on the sun

If I think too loud, you are there
Where's the monitor? Behind the camera
In the bathroom you piss next to me
I may not see you, but you're there
You're breathing down my neck
In the U-Bahn you strafe me with your gaze

Another Kobs song translated as "Modern Times" and inveighed against complacency: "Modern man keeps his mouth shut and is silent" despite a list of problems Kobs touched on in the song, including environmental degradation and the looming threat of nuclear war. In another song Kobs mentioned the dead pigeons that fell from the sky—the East sometimes undertook aerial pesticide campaigns and it would literally rain dead birds.

As soon as bands started to write lyrics like *that*, punk in the DDR transformed into something uniquely Eastern, even stridently Eastern. The social conditions for punk in Britain didn't exist in East Germany anyway—there was no unemployment or homelessness, no anxiety about basic needs. The problem in the DDR wasn't No Future, the rallying cry of British punk. As Planlos guitarist Kobs liked to say, the problem in East Germany was Too Much Future. Your whole life was planned out for you almost from birth and it felt unbelievably stifling; there was no space, literal or philosophical, to live outside the system or even to express criticism of it.

Planlos—No Plan—was the exact opposite of Too Much Future.

7

At 7 a.m. on February 17, 1981, Major, now eighteen, heard banging at the door, violent banging. Three friends had stayed the night: Major's boyfriend and another couple. Now the four of them found themselves being taken down to the police station—police, not Stasi. Lieutenant Müller had never relinquished his feeling that Major was a dangerous enemy of the state. The other three were asked about Major, about her habits, even her sexual habits, while Major herself was interrogated for forty-four of the next forty-eight hours. She lost five pounds during that time, fed only a cup of mint tea and two hardtack biscuits—the emergency rations given to soldiers. They took all the buttons and safety pins out of her clothes and removed her shoelaces. When she had to use the bathroom she was accompanied by a male officer who never let her out of his sight.

While she was in custody, they searched her apartment. They brought all the punk stuff they found to the police station—posters, articles, song lyrics, her own poetry and notes and sketches—and made her watch as they burned it all. Nobody told her what she was being charged with, but burning all the punk materials seemed designed to ensure she *wasn't* charged with a political crime of some sort. If the police had evidence of political motivation for her crimes, they would have to turn the case over to the Stasi. Lieutenant Müller wasn't going to let that happen. He wanted her in jail on his terms.

The cops began to grill her about workdays she had missed—twenty-one in the space of three months. They said the unexcused absences were enough to charge her with *asoziales Verhalten*, the crime of failure to work.

In addition to *asoziales Verhalten*, the cops piled on other charges. Initially they wanted to try to charge her with prostitution. A guy who had crashed at Major's place had tested positive for a venereal disease and the cops knew it. They took Major to a place people jokingly called Gonorrhea Castle—the central registration office for sexually transmitted diseases, in Christburger Strasse—and forced her to have a gynecological exam. They wanted evidence to make the bogus prostitution charge stick. No dice. Major didn't have any sexually transmitted diseases. Next they decided to charge Major with "incitement to antisocial lifestyle." The woman who had stayed over the night before the arrest had run away from home and stopped going to school; she was a minor. Major could take the fall for her truancy.

The forty-eight-hour time limit came and went, and Major realized she was really being charged this time. They led her out to a windowless van and shoved her into one of several cramped, pitch-black cells in the back of it. They drove her around for a while and then dropped her at a pretrial detention center, *somewhere*, who knew where, never telling her what day or what time it was; she was totally disoriented and still didn't know what exactly they had charged her with.

In pretrial detention she was treated roughly, always addressed as "prisoner" and had to go to the bathroom in the presence of male guards. The cell was poorly heated in the cold early months, and she found herself spending entire days pacing back in forth in the tiny room. She was lucky to get fifteen minutes outside every second day, when she and other prisoners were forced to silently goosestep up to a pen on the roof of the prison called the *Schweinebucht*, or the Bay of Pigs. Sometimes the guards forced her and other prisoners to stand for hours on a line painted in a hallway—if she lost her balance and stepped off the line, she was pummeled with a baton.

She would end up spending three months in this place before her case went to trial. In court her lawyer wouldn't call any witnesses who might offer statements in her defense. Despite being paid well by Major's mother, the lawyer showed no interest in trying to mount a real defense. The trial ended quickly.

The verdict: one year in prison followed by five years of *Berlin-Verbot*, meaning Major would be strictly barred from entering her home town when she got out of jail; she would not be able to see her family and friends; the nightmare would continue.

At the close of the process, the judge asked the obligatory question, "Does the defendant have anything to say?"

Not to be cowed into silence, Major stood up and began to state, "I wish before witnesses to . . . "

The judge interrupted her, trying to cut Major off.

A punk girl named China, who had managed to get a seat in the courtroom, gasped.

Major continued. "Before witnesses to state—"

"Silence!" shouted the judge.

Now Major was shouting, too, not to be drowned out: "—to state: I hereby renounce my DDR citizenship!"

The judge did not answer.

Major was shipped off to a women's prison in Dessau. The complex was ringed by a double wall topped with barbed wire, with menacing dogs roving the strip between the two walls. There were half a dozen barracks. Major shared a room with thirty other women, all of them stacked tightly into ten triple bunks. Elsewhere on the grounds was a set of buildings where the prisoners had to work. The prison laborers worked around the clock, with the prison population divided into three shifts, waking and sleeping according to their work schedule. A normal shift was eight hours, but sometimes Major had to work ten or twelve hours—with just a five-minute cigarette break and a twenty-minute meal break. On top of all the other humiliations, the women frequently had their underwear stolen from the prison laundry line.

Major and other inmates were forced to get injections. Medical staff told her the shots were vaccines, but Major always suspected they were something else. It was certainly possible—it emerged after the fall of the Wall that doctors were complicit in the systems of control, administering phenobarbital and antipsychotic drugs, among other things, to inmates with no medical need for them, as well as attesting at times that a person's unwillingness to comply with authorities indicated a mental disorder.

The prison authorities also coopted the inmates into a military-style self-policing hierarchy—one top prisoner oversaw six others, each of whom oversaw one of the barracks; those women in turn oversaw a series of lieutenants who served as foremen in the work camp and marshals in the barracks; there were also lieutenants in charge of specialized things, like dragooning fellow inmates into sticking to the official hygiene regimen. Basically, the authorities had recreated *inside* something like the system the government used *outside*—with its army of informants—to enforce conformity: a third of the inmates voluntarily conspired to keep the other two-thirds in line.

Sometimes it's difficult in retrospect to understand the government's paranoia about teenage punks, but then again Major's arrest came just months after Alina Pienkowska, a young nurse at the Gdansk shipyards where Poland's Solidarity strikes began, took on a leading role in the ongoing drama, first by alerting union groups further afield to the strike and then with an impassioned speech that kept the strike going at a critical juncture. The threat represented by Solidarity was deemed so dire that later that year, in December 1981, Poland would declare martial law, rolling out tanks in scenes reminiscent of crushed uprisings in Hungary in 1956 and Czechoslovakia in 1968.

In any event, the constant hassles and violence, the attacks and beatings and arbitrary detainments—and now the harsh jail sentence against Major—further politicized the East Berlin punk scene and made what had been something of a nebulous cause into an all-out crusade against the dictatorship.

In the wake of Major's arrest, a newly urgent rage started to burn inside A-Micha, a rage against the state and its henchmen, a rage that burned in a way it hadn't before, a hot rage. A-Micha had already been a radical, but now, perhaps, he was a revolutionary.

8

While Major was shut away being interrogated day after day, the first public punk show in East Berlin took place, in March 1981. Or rather, the first ever *semi*-public punk show: it was staged in the Yugoslavian embassy by a diplomat's son who had started a band called Koks, slang for "cocaine."

The diplomat's son was named Ilja, and Kobs knew him from school. Planlos went to the Koks show together as a band—Pankow, Kobs, Lade, and Kaiser. They were still working on songs at that point and had yet to play a gig. Where would they play? They didn't have an amateur license and they sure as hell wouldn't get one singing about being tailed by Stasi agents at the currywurst stand.

That night the room in the Yugoslavian embassy was packed with dozens of East Berlin punks.

This is going to be legendary, the Planlos gang agreed, *a real punk show!*

One of the kids at the show was Ronald Lippok, the drummer in a school band called Vitamin P. Ronald considered himself "anti-political" rather than "apolitical." For him punk was primarily about having fun, and he didn't think of himself as a dissident. He was just sick of the expected regurgitation of political incantations at every turn, sick of professing love of state and party, sick of all the bullshit.

He had been particularly repulsed by his mandatory military training in school. During weapons training his teacher had shouted at him while they were shooting at human-shaped targets: "Shoot him in the nuts! In the nuts!"

No fucking way.

I'm not shooting anyone in the nuts.

And especially not for you assholes.

He had gotten into the Sex Pistols and Ramones while listening to British military radio—he taped DJ John Peel's show every week. At first Ronald thought punk was just a new version of the hard rock he loved, stuff like Black Sabbath. Then, however, he ran into real live punks in East Berlin, people like Colonel, and it hit him: *Okay, something is happening here, this is interesting.*

He realized punk was much more than a twist on hard rock. It was something completely different. Punks all seemed to know each other, they automatically talked to one another on the street or the subway when they ran into each other, whether or not they'd ever met. Punks were rejecting all the bullshit Ronald hated and creating some kind of parallel world.

Soon both Ronald and his brother Robert cut their hair, the talismanic ritual that marked a rejection of hippie culture and blues-rock and entry into the punk subculture. Almost as soon as he changed his look, Ronald began to get arrested and hauled off to police stations for questioning. This new world was the most exciting thing he'd ever experienced. In those early days of punk, all sorts of people came together under the punk banner—blue-collar kids and kids with educated parents, soccer hooligans and would-be intellectuals. The scene was a total social mashup: some of the kids just wanted to get drunk and go looking for fights, others were into dada and surrealist art, others were into politics—whether that meant joining church-based peace groups or becoming self-styled anarchists like Lade and Kaiser and A-Micha.

Ronald's father worked as a blasting engineer with the state road-building *Kombinat*. He tolerated his sons' new enthusiasm, even if it did affect him at work. One day, in fact, Ronald's father was called into the office of the *Kombinat*'s Stasi agent and asked to sit down. The agent threw photos down on the table. They were surveillance shots of Ronald and Robert with their punk haircuts.

"Your sons seem to be under a bad influence," the Stasi man said.

"Hmmm," said the Lippok boys' father noncommittally. He didn't like the pictures, but he wasn't going to condemn his boys or ask them to change. In fact, he was about to help them. His *Kombinat* had an official band, like a regimental band in the military, and when the state-road-building *Kombinat* had some surplus instruments, he managed to snag Ronald a drum kit.

Ronald started a school band, which covered the Pistols and Ramones and even wrote a few elementary songs of their own. The other thing Ronald got hold of from the *Kombinat* band was an East German rhythm box, and soon he was getting into synth-punk pioneers like Suicide and Throbbing Gristle. Later in the year he would join forces with a band called Rosa Extra—named for a brand of East German tampons. Their first gig together was at a school cafeteria; the school administrator who allowed the gig was subsequently relieved of duty. Rosa Extra played just three more gigs before Ronald was called up for army duty, and the cops broke up every one of them before the band could finish their set. Still, kids were finally getting their first tastes of live punk rock.

As pockets of punks elsewhere in East Germany caught wind of developments in the capital—usually by making their way to Plänterwald, based on rumors of weekend punk meet-ups—bands began mushrooming all over the country: Schleim-Keim in Erfurt, Müllstation in Eisleben, Restbestand in Magdeburg, Virus X in Rostock, Rotzjungen in Dresden. The singer in Rotzjungen was the first person in the city of Dresden to wear his hair in a Mohawk.

An informal national network was starting to take shape.

Nowhere was there more happening than in Leipzig, the country's second city, home to more than half a million people. A small punk scene had been smoldering there and punks in Leipzig—still barely more than a dozen brave souls in early 1981—had experienced much the same response as punks in East Berlin: they were constantly shouted at and insulted by the citizenry, punched around whenever those people were drunk enough to get belligerent, and regularly harassed by the *Polizei*. But then in the summer of 1981, graffiti went up on the walls of crumbling buildings in the decrepit parts of town announcing the arrival of a band: Wutanfall. The name meant

Rage Attack and it was spelled with a big fat anarchist A. Sometimes it was shortened into a sort of logo—a big W with the anarchist A formed out of the peak in the middle of that W.

The members of the band had met only recently, at a concert by an officially-licensed group, Keks, that played a few Sex Pistols covers as part of their live set. Once they started hanging out together, Chaos, who would end up being the singer in Wutanfall, quickly started pushing the idea of a band.

Chaos had never been one to sit around.

He had always hated the drabness and boredom of his surroundings and was looking for an outlet for his frustrations. In his early teens he'd gotten into boxing and had plenty of scrapes in and out of the ring, but he'd always been interested in music, too. He caught a glimpse of the Pistols on a West German TV show in eighth grade and it was as if a match had been struck inside him. He wasn't sure what punk was, really, but it was obvious that this was the music he'd been looking for, quick and powerful, *bam*, like a punch. Not long afterward he'd been barred from a school trip when he showed up with safety pins stuck in his clothes and his eyes smeared with black makeup like Dave Vanian, the singer of the British band the Damned. He'd been sent home that day, but he also knew for sure he'd found his thing. Punk.

Chaos's parents weren't happy with his look or the troubles he started to encounter as a result of it. They screamed at him and beat him. His home life became unbearable. Chaos took to leaving home in relatively normal outfits and changing into his punk gear at a new friend's house, another punk named Ratte, who was politically tuned in and conversant in anarchist philosophy. Chaos perused the Weimar-era writings of prominent anarchist, military critic, and Nazi opponent Erich Mühsam, but he didn't see himself as political—for Chaos, punk was about teenage kicks, about doing what he wanted to do. He eventually left home at seventeen and squatted in a run-down hole of an apartment in eastern Leipzig that had been vacated when a friend of a friend left for West Germany. Chaos's new place was in a particularly grim section of the city, a neighborhood distinguished by its high quotient of misery, destroyed buildings, and drunks. As in the centers of all of the cities of East Germany, the streets in central Leipzig were lined with empty storefronts, vacant lots, and buildings with their guts spilling out the doors and windows in the form of bricks and rubble; some of the roads were in such a state of disrepair that they could barely be called paved. On the rare occasions Chaos ran into another soul on the street, as likely as not he'd hear, "You should have been gassed!"

The aggressiveness of ordinary people toward him and other punks surprised Chaos at first. But at the end of the day he wanted to provoke a reaction. He'd taken a trip up to Berlin earlier in 1981 after he heard rumors about the meet-ups at Plänterwald. The rumors, he'd found, were true. In fact, the scale of the scene in Berlin had blown him away. He befriended a few of the Berliner punks and started to feel as if he was part of a snow-balling scene, as people from all over the country met at PW or the ferris wheel in Plänterwald and then started to visit each other in towns across East Germany. The number of punks visiting Liepzig was about to spike, too, because Wutanfall soon took the scene by storm with their fast, aggressive sound—basically DDR hardcore.

Together with Imad and Typhus on guitar, Zappa on bass, and Rotz on drums, Chaos went at the band the way he went at everything, attacking it full on. The band assembled a couple of homemade guitars and an assort-ment of pots and pans and pickle barrels as drums, and set up shop first at Imad's apartment and then in a half-exposed attic on Sternwartestrasse—Zappa and some other punks lived there, in the building below.

Working with a friend named Ray Schneider, Chaos co-wrote the lyr-ics for the first song Wutanfall cranked out, a sonic gut-punch that would remain an East German punk anthem for the rest of the decade: *"Leipzig in Trümmern,"* or "Leipzig in Ruins."

> When the Combat Groups of the Working Class
> march before your house,
> and the children in school
> are trained for war,
> the father of the nation speaks by torch light
> of freedom to the German youth,
> the police won't leave you alone . . .

Leipzig in ruins, Leipzig in ruins

Open pit mines scrape away villages
and government officials toast it with champagne,
nobody cares about nature and forests
everything flattened and covered with concrete . . .

By the time Wutanfall had a couple of rudimentary songs, they decided to play a show. It was the opposite impulse of Planlos, who spent all of 1981 writing and rehearsing their songs—though sometimes there were as many people hanging out in Planlos's basement rehearsal space as would attend the first Wutanfall show.

Near drummer Rotz's apartment, in an area on the northern edge of town packed with typical East Bloc high-rises, there was a garage-like structure that functioned during the week as a communal laundry-hanging center. On weekends, people could rent the building for parties for next to nothing. Wutanfall rented it for their first ever gig, falsely registering the event as a birthday party.

On the day of the show, Chaos went over to a friend of a friend's apartment and cajoled him into rejiggering a radio into an amp for his vocals. The friend, Reudnitz, was new to the punk scene but handy with electronics, and he came through. The band dragged their scrappy instruments to the laundry building and set up. The band also strung bread rolls from the rafters with twine.

By show time, the place was packed. They had invited a couple dozen friends, and everyone came. Just to be safe, they locked the doors before they started playing. And then all hell broke loose.

As the band attacked their instruments, Chaos started singing—or rather, screaming like he was being flayed alive. Like he was possessed.

This is the most liberating feeling I've ever had, thought Chaos as he howled and the crowd throbbed and pogoed.

He hadn't expected the listeners to go so crazy, and he hadn't expected the band to sound so good. They were rough and raw and noisy, but it worked. It really worked. It was magical.

We have to keep this going.

What had started out as a lark suddenly felt important to Chaos.

During a song called "Hunger," Chaos jumped up, teeth bared, and ripped chunks out of the dangling bread rolls like a starved animal. When the jerry-rigged radio he was using as his vocal amp quit near the end of the show, Chaos grabbed an axe and violently hacked it to bits.

All of Chaos's frustration and anger—his white hot RAGE—roared out of him when he sang.

We have to keep this going.

It was an insane gig. Nobody had ever seen or heard anything like it. This was something new, something different, something none of them—Chaos, the rest of the band, the people in the audience—had ever experienced.

Kids ran out of the building chanting, *"überall, überall Wutanfall."*

And almost immediately, the band logo turned up in graffiti all over Leipzig, with its lurid, dripping anarchist A.

Wutanfall was a bona fide sensation—after one gig.

Before Wutanfall, Chaos had a better idea of what he *didn't* want to do than about the things he *did* want to do. He wasn't thrilled that he would be starting his apprenticeship as a carpenter that fall of 1981—he had always hated the way his whole life was predetermined by the state. Too much future. *No matter what happens*, he thought now, *I will not end up like that, in that pack of lemmings, pissing my life away in this gray hellhole, everyone informing on each other, everyone working for nothing, and then keeling over at seventy, no way, no fucking way.*

Now everything was different. Now he had the band. This was something Chaos wanted to do, something he had to do. He had always felt hemmed in when he got angry, unable to run, unable to escape the rage and creeping dread. Now he could burn all of that out of his system. Give him a mic and he could channel that incandescent rage into a laser, leaving scorched earth around him, and at least a brief calm inside him.

We have to keep this going.

Wutanfall continued to meet up in their rehearsal space and write songs. They slowly accumulated better equipment. First some real guitars, later a small kit of proper drums, at some stage even real amps. Chaos continued to write with Ray, describing the ills they saw around them and scrawling lyrics in a notebook. But Chaos was careful. Nothing he wrote ever said straight out "fuck the DDR" or "fuck the Stasi." Still, at times he worried that what was in his notebook could come back to haunt him. But it took time to write and then memorize the songs.

The next time the band booked the laundry building and started to play, the police immediately descended on the place and busted up the gig. It didn't matter. For Leipzig's punks, the flame had been lit. And as for the police, well, Chaos had always wanted to push against the boundaries of the system. He knew there could be consequences. But Chaos hadn't reckoned with the force of the blows that would eventually rain down on him and his friends.

The police would be back.

9

The K1—the political division of the criminal police—had expected to be able to dismantle the punk scene by April 1981. It hadn't worked out that way. April had come and gone and if anything, from a police perspective, things seemed to be getting worse. Despite the examples they'd made of Major and others, despite the expulsions from schools and apprenticeships, and despite the constant detainments, hassles, and beatings, the punk movement was not only hanging on but growing, all over the country. In fact, the harsh treatment had hardened the punks' convictions and further convinced them of the injustice and hypocrisy of the system.

Working in conjunction with the Stasi, the K1 now sought to solve the punk problem by eliminating punks from public view. They instituted a blanket ban of punks in bars, cafés, restaurants, and youth clubs. And they made it clear that any establishment caught ignoring the ban stood to lose its license.

Suddenly East Berlin's punks had no place to meet, and any group spotted on a street or in a subway station, no matter how small, had to reckon with a speedy police response.

Then in July 1981 a deacon named Uwe Kulisch, from Pfingst Church in the central East Berlin district of Friedrichshain, bumped into a few punks—led by Colonel—on the street. After hearing about their struggle to find places to meet up without being dragooned by the police, deacon Kulisch suggested the group drop by his church during what he called an *open evening*. The deacon explained that as part of a program called *Offene Arbeit*, or

Open Work, the church opened space for use by young people who were not part of the congregation.

Pfingst Church had been built at the turn of the previous century, situated mid-block on Petersburger Platz, flush with the apartment buildings on either side. The brick building had once been handsome, with flame-shaped High Gothic flourishes, but it was now blackened by a thick layer of soot.

At the next open evening, about ten punks, including A-Micha and Colonel, showed up and drank tea uneventfully with a few other freaks—regulars at the Open Work evenings.

"Could we bring some friends with us next time?" they asked at the end of the night.

"Sure."

It was a fateful decision.

More than twenty punks turned up at the next open evening. And a church out in Friedrichsfelde—close to where Major and the original pocket of punks had cropped up—told a group of punks who showed up on its doorstep that they should try the Pfingst Church, too. That doubled the number of punks again at the next Open Work evening.

By the dawn of the 1980s, the country's Lutheran churches had come to host a lot of youth activity—much of it oppositional in nature, at least as far as the government was concerned. It wasn't that East Germany had experienced a renaissance of religiosity. On the contrary, most of the church-based activity had little or no direct connection to god or theology. And it wasn't that the Lutheran church as an institution stood in opposition to the government—a full 5 percent of church officials would turn out to have been working as Stasi snitches; others just wanted to avoid conflict with the state; still others saw the church's proper role as strictly limited to spiritual matters. What was true, though, was that the church was so decentralized that individual congregations or ministers or even lay deacons could pretty much get up to whatever they wanted, regardless of what regional or national church leaders might have liked.

The East German Church had recently achieved a unique and unprecedented level of autonomy: in March 1978, dictator Erich Honecker had met for the first time with a national church delegation and settled on a new status for the Lutheran church, described as *Kirche im Sozialismus,* or church within socialism. As a practical matter, the agreement granted the church formal independence and acknowledged it as beyond the reach of uniformed security forces—and thus, even if it wasn't the intent of the new understanding, any rogue oppositional activity within church walls was largely off-limits to police. From 1978 on, churches could in theory operate as free spaces where people were able to discuss politically taboo topics and speak their minds. The question was, how far would the government let churches go before they ignored or even revoked this autonomous status? It wasn't necessarily a question most church leaders wanted answered, but when Pfingst Church opened its doors to the punks, the risk of confrontation spiked.

Prior to 1978, the church's role in society—particularly its role in the lives of young people—had a fraught history in East Germany. Quite aside from the communists' distaste for religion as an ideological tool of capitalism and imperialism, the Party didn't want the church to undermine the government's monopoly on youth activities. During the Stalinist era, DDR authorities had hounded the church relentlessly. In 1952, the Communist Party tasked Honecker—then still a rising star and head of the Free German Youth—with cracking down on the church, and in particular on church youth groups. Chaplains at schools and universities were barred from carrying out their work, and some of them were among the first arrested in a wave that saw more than seventy theologians detained and thousands of students expelled from school. An array of sanctions against church youth groups were announced, and a propaganda campaign insinuated that the church was being steered by sinister Western forces. The government eventually reversed course, but the damage was done. People worried—correctly, as it turned out—that there would be subsequent crackdowns, and church youth groups never regained much membership.

By the beginning of the 1970s, however, the political climate had changed. Honecker was now the head of state. Despite his hardline mentality, Stalinist tactics were out and the desire for international legitimacy was in. Also, the population was far less religious by then—just 7 percent of East Berliners were churchgoers—and many religious traditions and rites of passage, like confirmation and first communion, had been successfully displaced by politically palatable alternatives. More than 90 percent of East German fourteen-year-olds, for instance, had a *Jugendweihe*, a secular initiation party that effectively replaced religious coming-of-age rituals.

The church, too, had changed. Or at least a handful of innovative pastors had. Under their leadership, some churches began clawing their way back into the youth-culture scene. Beginning in the early 1970s, a new kind of youth outreach had taken root, particularly in the southern state of Thüringen. To liven up their moribund youth ministries, pastors there began to bring in young outsiders of various stripes—hippies, freaks, objectors to mandatory military service, even alcoholics. The newcomers were not members of the congregation, and often not religious at all; in fact they were almost all atheists. Rather than try to integrate these new groups into traditional youth ministries, the pastors invented a new category of service: Open Work. Eventually Open Work evolved into something more formally oppositional: rather than simply opening church space to a broad range of troubled kids and trying to help them with their problems, the new vision held that it was perverse to try to reintegrate troubled youth into the society that was breaking them down in the first place. That is, it was *society* that needed to change. The church hierarchy was not receptive to this series of innovations and constantly tried to force more overtly religious content on these increasingly independent entities and schemed to find ways to bar Open Work groups from access to church facilities. Even so, by 1976 an East Berlin church institute had started training deacons specifically to work with marginalized youths—Kulisch, who brought Colonel and the others into Pfingst Church, was one of them—and by the late 1970s Open Work had taken hold in parishes all around the country.

Friedrichshain was a hotbed of youth outreach in East Berlin, with programs in several churches, including Galiläa, Samariter, Auferstehung, Advent, Andreas-Markus, and Lazarus. Eventually Pfingst Church became the focus of Open Work in Berlin. But it was a slog. Through 1978, Pfingst was led by pastor Hans Reder, a vehement opponent of Open Work—and a Stasi snitch under the code name "Beier." He later became the superintendent of churches in Weimar, where in 1985 he had the Open Work group in that city thrown out of its church quarters and criminalized; in

1988 he violated the 1978 agreement shielding the church by calling in police to forcibly remove a small group of protestors who had barricaded themselves in Weimar's Herder Church. Subsequent pastors at Pfingst were not much more enthusiastic about Open Work, though an activist congregant successfully steered a group of marginalized youth into the church.

After much haggling with wary church leadership, Open Work took up residence in a three-room apartment in the bell tower of Pfingst in May 1979. Complaints began immediately, both from within the church and from neighbors and local authorities.

Despite the 1978 arrangement with Honecker, the Kriminal Polizei had opened a file in 1980 called *Kreuz*, or Cross, to monitor and undermine youth activities in several local churches. They had snitches and even plainclothes officers with recording equipment at many events, all in an effort to stifle the "political-ideological influence" of the church that was, as they saw it, "defaming and misrepresenting socialist conditions in the DDR."

The K1 and Stasi kept particularly close tabs on church officials they disliked. Lorenz Postler, another deacon who began to work with the punks, was eventually surrounded by more than a dozen Stasi snitches. Stasi meddling in state housing authorities also ensured that Postler would have constant trouble getting and retaining living space for his family, which included three young children.

For now, though, thanks to Uwe Kulisch, the punks had a new meeting spot, a seeming safe haven. Pfingst Church had replaced PW.

The punks started to meet at the church twice a week that July, and by the fall of 1981 more than a hundred punks would turn up every Monday and Friday night. They were allowed to make themselves at home in the bell tower rooms. What they did to the second-floor space wasn't exactly in keeping with normal church style; it wasn't in keeping with the bohemian coffeehouse style of a lot of other Open Work spaces, either, dominated as they had been by hippie-era aesthetics. The punks started by spraying graffiti all over the walls—using the same kind of slogans they sprayed on the walls of their squatted apartments. One was: DON'T DIE IN THE WAITING ROOM OF THE FUTURE.

10

East German punks had already perfected the art of confrontation. A few had even started to play with Nazi imagery—the ultimate taboo in a country explicitly founded on anti-Nazi ideology. Faced with ever more brutal treatment by the police, some punks wore yellow star patches, making reference to the patches the Nazis forced Jews to wear. Others wore red armbands with white crosses on them and the word CHAOS written in black on the cross, meant to make people look twice because of its similarity to the armbands worn by Hitler's SA and SS.

Then the authorities spotted some public graffiti they found particularly disturbing: *DDR=KZ*, meaning *East Germany = a concentration camp*. A punk named Spion had spray-painted the slogan. He was the singer in a garage band called Ahnungslos, or Clueless. In the course of investigating the graffiti, the police also found drafts of Spion's song lyrics, and he was thrown into prison for a year.

Despite the K1 crackdown, the East Berlin punk scene was exploding. It wasn't just the number of punks turning up at Pfingst church each week that was growing, it was the overall scale of the scene. Everyone could feel it—people like A-Micha no longer knew every single punk in the city. There was a whole new generation. And it was huge.

Out in Grünau, beyond Plänterwald, a group led by a newly strident punk named Speiche also began to spray—using cans of rust primer. Speiche had recently been dragged out of a tram by police on his way to his job at a bakery; they had taken him to the station house, beaten him, and forcibly cut off his Mohawk.

Speiche was slightly older than most of the other first-generation punks—he'd come to it a little later in life, when he was already seventeen, though he was reading anarchist literature before that. One advantage of being a baker was that Speiche worked overnight, with very few people around. He listened to the radio all night, and some of the coolest music came on during those hours. Speiche was into hard rock—KISS, AC/DC—but also liked a lot of the more obscure stuff. He had started taking his cassette recorder and stacks of tapes with him each night and recording hour after hour off the radio. Soon he was known among his friends as the guy with the huge stash of music. Then one day, armed with his trusty handheld cassette recorder, he and two friends had been riding on a tram on the outskirts of East Berlin when four guys wearing leather jackets and chains all over their clothes got on—*real live punks!* They were huge—not just larger than life, but physically imposing. At the time, at seventeen, Speiche was the opposite. He was slender in the extreme: he weighed under eighty pounds. Speiche and his friends were listening to music from his stash of radio recordings. As some generic 1970s rock played through the tinny speaker, the punks growled at him to turn it down.

But a Sex Pistols song came on next.

"Hey, turn that up!" said the punks.

The next two songs on Speiche's tape were by the Clash and the Damned.

"Where'd you get all that?" the punks asked Speiche.

"Recorded it myself," he said.

The four punks invited Speiche and his two friends to join them at a nearby biergarten. Speiche let his cassettes play. And the punks kept hearing songs they didn't have.

"Is there a jack in that recorder?" the punks asked Speiche.

There was. It was possible to run a line from his handheld cassette recorder to another one.

They asked for Speiche's address. They wanted to come by and copy some of his music. This wasn't ordinary rock and roll, they told him, it was punk.

"This is protest music," they said.

Three weeks later the punks were at his door. Three days after that Speiche hacked and dyed his hair into a punk 'do. He fell in with other punks from the area and started to attract the attention of the police and his fellow citizens. The attacks—always by people who were far bigger than him—just hardened his beliefs; he also took up martial arts. Soon he was a force to be reckoned with in street fights, and within a few years he began to train others in the scene to defend themselves, too.

Speiche's shift to punk was in keeping with the personality profile the government already had on him: he'd been judged a hopeless case at age ten, impossible to mold into a good socialist citizen. This despite the fact that he had always been quite politically aware: at age eight he had written a letter to American communist and civil rights activist Angela Davis, who was then awaiting trial on conspiracy charges related to an armed takeover of a California courtroom. Speiche wrote that if he could, he would free her and together they would free the world. This sense of mission never left him. He also became hyper-attuned to a sort of shakiness he began to sense in the East German system—a shakiness he first detected when he saw the fear he and his punk friends elicited from the police.

By 1981 he had an anarchist star tattoo to go with his Mohawk.

The graffiti campaign that Speiche and his friends undertook in Grünau that same year culminated in spraying a phrase on a wall directly across the street from the local police station:

REVOLUTION GEGEN DIE BULLEN GESELLSCHAFT

In essence:

OVERTHROW THE POLICE STATE

Graffiti had become a major problem.

11

On August 12, 1981, a group of teens stumbled out of a basement bowling alley in East Berlin at closing time. Midnight. It was the night before the twentieth anniversary of the building of the Berlin Wall. The streets were quiet and dark; the teens were loud and drunk.

One of these teens was Esther Friedemann. She had grown up in the northern neighborhood of Pankow. Her parents were both doctors; her mother worked at the Health Ministry and was a representative to the UN's World Health Organization.

Though Esther had started dressing oddly at the end of school, she had encountered more trouble as a result of her mouth than her punk look. Esther wasn't what you'd call diplomatic. Or quiet. Finished with school after tenth grade, Esther started an apprenticeship as a cabinetmaker. She'd started hanging around with other punks as she met them—at parties, at Alexanderplatz, and less frequently at the occasional concert in a rehearsal space. She loved the concerts.

An entire room of cool people!

Among her friends were Pankow—who had grown up in her neighborhood—Colonel, and Kaiser. She'd seen those guys get hauled off by the cops at Alexanderplatz, but she herself hadn't had much trouble with the police.

On that summer night of August 12, Esther, now seventeen, and a boy named Robert Paris peeled off from the others and headed home. Robert's place, on Stargarder Strasse in Prenzlauer Berg, was on Esther's way home.

Esther had recently seen a West German calendar at a friend's place—it was one of those word-a-day type calendars, but in this case a funny political phrase accompanied each new day. She had flipped through a few pages. For August 13, the day the Berlin Wall had gone up back in 1961, it said, *Zwanzig Jahre Mauer, wir werden langsam sauer*, which was a rhyming phrase that meant: "Twenty years of the Wall, we're starting to get pissed off."

Ha.

Hey, now that it's past midnight, that's today!

Robert had a can of spray paint in his bag, bought at an auto parts store.

Wouldn't it be funny if I sprayed that on a wall?

They knew it was technically illegal to vandalize, but on the other hand they didn't think it was a big deal.

Come on.

On Greifenhagener Strasse, a quiet street one parallel over from Schönhauser Allee, a major avenue, Esther took the spray can and started to paint the phrase on the side of a building.

Zwanzig Jahre Mauer, wir werden langsam sauer.

Twenty years of the Wall, we're starting to get pissed off.

Somebody walked by and looked at them. Esther and Robert realized they'd better scram. They took off running, first up Greifenhagener and then down onto the platform in the sunken S-Bahn train station. They ran to the other end of the platform and re-emerged up on Schönhauser Allee and then headed down that road, with the raised U-Bahn tracks looming above them.

A car screeched to a halt next to them.

Police jumped out.

Esther and Robert froze.

Busted.

The cops took them to a police station at Senefelder Platz, a big red brick building. But soon they were transferred in a police van to a facility in Pankow—a courthouse with a prison behind it. A prison for political prisoners and people who'd tried to flee the country.

Still, Esther wasn't too worried. She wouldn't turn eighteen for a few months. And all she had done was some minor vandalism.

Then they started to interrogate her.

Who was behind this? Who else was involved? Where did you hear that phrase?

She told them about the calendar. Why lie? What was the big deal?

They put Esther in a cell with a West German woman who'd been caught trying to smuggle silver out of the East, and an Eastern woman who'd tried to escape the country.

Esther was denied any visitors for the first month of her detention.

Why am I being treated like a dangerous criminal?

After a month her mother received a visitor's permit. But when she came to see Esther all she did was scold her.

I don't need this.

But she knew that was how her mother was. And though Esther didn't find out until later, her mother had lost her position as a rep to the World Health Organization as a result of Esther's political indiscretion.

Her trial started three months after her arrest—on the day of her eighteenth birthday. That way, they told her, she could be sent to a real prison instead of a juvenile detention center.

Esther was sentenced to eight months and Robert to six. But Robert's mother, a prominent photographer, and father, a painter, both had plenty of connections; Esther's mother also asked a famous writer she knew for a favor. In the end, the sentences were suspended and both Esther and Robert were released in late November, only a week after the end of the trial.

Prior to her release, Esther had to sign a bunch of paperwork. As she sat and signed various documents, an officer sitting across the desk from her said, "Don't even bother to try to file a petition for an exit visa when you get out. For one thing, you're not getting out of the country anytime soon. And for another, you'd better take your whole family."

Esther thought she knew what he meant. Her sister had a coveted spot at a university and her parents had good jobs. Or at least they did when she had last been home.

When she got home she learned that her father, like her mother, had suffered professionally. He had actually lost his job. But unlike her mother, he never voiced a word of complaint to Esther. Even when she went back to hanging out with the punks and refused to join the straight world.

If anything, she thought, his eyes had been opened by the experience.

He seemed to understand.

Esther needed a new job, too. Even if she finished her apprenticeship as a cabinetmaker, she knew a job would be impossible to come by now. So she convinced her aunt—a tailor—to take her in as an apprentice. Soon enough she would be making pieces on the side out of things like mattress liners and fabric salvaged from decades-old dresses and selling them to artists and officially-licensed musicians who had plenty of money but no place to get cool clothes. She would become able to sustain herself almost entirely outside the system.

12

Attendance at Pfingst Church's Open Work nights spiked during the second half of 1981. The members of Planlos, the PW gang, punks from all over Berlin and even from Leipzig, Dresden, and Magdeburg began turning up. Hundreds of punks. Even those who supported their presence in the church realized the punk nights created quite a spectacle, with beer bottles rolling down the stairs of the bell tower, puddles of liquid here and there, couples practically having sex in the open, loud music, wild dancing, and the occasional makeshift musical performance by a nascent band—*those lyrics!* But there were also at least somewhat structured discussions of everything from dealing with strict parents to a wide array of political topics.

And then there was the graffiti.

Outsiders had a particularly rough time when confronted with anti-Nazi graffiti, like crossed-out swastikas. Even negated like that, it caused chills down the spine—and, for the uninitiated, creeping doubts about the punks' politics. Almost all of the graffiti in the church would have been regarded as criminal if painted anywhere outside. It was a ticking time bomb. There was a sign outside the punk rooms stating NO PHOTOS, but if the Stasi could secretly secure photos of the space it could cause all kinds of trouble.

A report from an informant detailed one of the evenings on December 7, 1981: an estimated three hundred punks came, "predominantly 15-20 years old, and of them about 100 girls." The rooms were filled beyond capacity, with, according to the informant, people packed in like sardines, lying on top of each another on old mattresses and broken pieces of salvaged furniture. "There were few meaningful comments and for the most part insubstantial conversations, punctuated by burps and vulgarity . . . the vast majority of these people come here because they can behave the way they want to. They can enjoy total 'freedom' here," the report sneered. "Defamation of the government was no rarity." Still, even while the informant denigrated the goings-on, the report went on to detail discussion groups that addressed such themes as freedom, anarchy, the desire to be able to speak one's mind openly and without fear of arrest, and police brutality. "Overall, the so-called demands were mostly attacks on the People's Police and other state and security organs."

That same December night, about ninety punks got candles at the church and then, at the end of the evening, sat on the steps of the nearby Frankfurter Tor U-Bahn station with them—regardless of the intent or lack thereof, it was the sort of non-sanctioned mass public act that set off hysterical warning bells among DDR security services. Ten days later the church superintendent was summoned to a meeting with representatives from the Interior Ministry and from the government office in charge of liaising with churches. They reminded the superintendent that the church was responsible for everything that happened inside it, and insisted she do everything in her power to hinder the propagation of anti-state sentiments. Then the Ministry demanded that "youth dressed as 'punkers' be barred from entering the church" in the future.

"The church," an Interior Ministry representative insisted, "cannot become a catchment basin for this element!"

The superintendent, however, had no intention of ending Pfingst Church's relationship with the punks or altering its approach to Open Work.

The deacons who worked directly with the punks took their real-life concerns seriously, and helped them deal with trouble at work and in school and even with the police. Deacons like Uwe Kulisch and Lorenz Postler would accompany punks to meetings with employers and bureaucratic offices, and help deal with irate parents who sometimes showed up looking for their kids, who had left home and taken up residence in illegal apartments and squats. The deacons helped get lawyers for punks who continued to have constant run-ins with the police.

Still, many other church workers, not to mention congregants, found the presence of this horde of belching, boozed-up, foul-mouthed, outlandish-looking teens utterly shocking, even scandalous. Perhaps a bigger problem was that the punks also cleaned out the beer and schnapps at nearby markets before every meeting, causing outrage in the neighborhood around Pfingst—well, that and the fact that the punks used surrounding buildings as urinals as they staggered homeward from the church at night. The solution to the first source of neighborhood ire was to make beer available at the church itself. That put off more of the Pfingst staff and congregation.

The punks, however, were in heaven.

They finally had their own space. Their own *world*. They could play their music, dance, drink, talk shit. All of this and no cops busting down the doors to detain them.

As the punks began to be exposed in greater number to the other oppositional groups and ideas being sheltered by the church—disarmament and peace groups, and, later, environmental and human rights groups—they began to see how different they were. It wasn't that punks didn't sympathize with the goals of those groups; they did. But they didn't share the same attitude. Those groups wanted reform. Punks wanted more fundamental change: to cast off the system, to destroy it.

Trying to convince the government brass to change this or that was pointless.

You want to engage the Party in dialogue?

Count us out.

Top-down change?

Fuck that shit.

It was all about bottom-up politics.

The punk approach was also contradictory: they wanted to change the system, yes, but for the most part they also tried to operate outside of it, almost as if it didn't exist. And the free space in the Pfingst bell tower, while allowing them to find common cause with other groups, also made it easier for them to operate outside the system.

They planned to live the life they wanted, not ask the Party to provide it.

Create your own world, your own reality. DIY.

Punk.

Revolution from below.

13

Throughout 1981 Planlos had regularly performed in front of people in their dank cellar rehearsal space—inviting friends over from the Pfingst Church, hosting out-of-town punks, and staging parties that were little short of public gigs. But they had yet to play out. After rehearsing obsessively for an entire year, Planlos were satisfied with their sound and ready to make their live debut—at a blowout on the final night of 1981 in an artist's atelier on Lychener Strasse, in the bohemian Prenzlauer Berg district.

As the punk scene had exploded over the course of 1981, artists and alternative literary figures all over the country had quickly taken an interest in adorning themselves with punks. Avant-garde poets like Sascha Anderson and Bert Papenfuss turned up at the bell tower of the Pfingst Church on occasion, reading their works over distorted electric guitar. Anderson, who was originally from Dresden, started performing with an art-punk band from Dresden called Zwitschermaschine, and Papenfuss eventually collaborated on song lyrics with Berlin's Rosa Extra.

The problem was that punk was all about simplicity and confrontation. Punk bands did not mince words. The poets, on the other hand, crafted opaque neo-dada verses that nobody could understand. Their work was considered decadent and subversive by the dictatorship because it didn't conform to officially sanctioned standards, but what did it fucking mean? *Every satellite has a killer satellite*—that was Sascha Anderson. *Go across the border / on the other side / stands a man and says / go across the border.* Huh?

The dictatorship might not have loved that kind of stuff, but, some punks wondered, did it really hurt the authorities?

Of course, the punks didn't object to being invited to the parties these artists hosted. After all, free booze was free booze. And free *space* was pure gold. Many people in the alternative arts and literature scene seemed to have an almost inconceivable level of autonomy, able to publish or exhibit in the West—and as a result, were much less economically tethered to the state than most people. And they apparently didn't get knocked around all the time by the police. There were other differences, too: Most punks lived either with their parents—often in intensely hostile conditions—or in transient situations: crashing with friends, illegally occupying vacated apartments, or squatting in ramshackle buildings. Artist ateliers seemed swank by comparison.

For Pankow, the upcoming New Year's Eve gig represented the fulfillment of everything he'd been trying to do. But he also knew it was dangerous. He'd been arrested almost daily during some stretches in 1981, and that was just for walking around near Alexanderplatz. Who knew what would happen when he started screaming the band's anti-state lyrics in a semi-public setting.

He was extremely nervous in the lead-up to New Year's Eve. On the day of the show, Pankow told friends, "I might be going to jail after tonight."

But he was still looking forward to the gig. And if he was going to get locked up tomorrow, he planned to make the most of tonight.

This is it.

This is THE night.

And it was. It was epic.

The artist who threw the shindig on Lychener Strasse had wanted one band—Rosa Extra—and expected about fifty guests. Rosa Extra had invited Planlos; Planlos had invited Unerwünscht—Unwanted—a band Planlos shared their basement rehearsal space with; then the brother of Rosa Extra drummer Ronald Lippok insisted on playing a set with a noise act he had put together on the fly.

More than three hundred people turned up.

The party was *insane*.

The atelier soon looked like a war zone. Glass got smashed. Wild dancing dislodged the chimney pipe several times, filling the atelier with coal smoke.

Planlos had a batch of eight or nine fully formed songs, and their playing was tight. It paid to have practiced the songs to death. Because now they absolutely killed it. Another advantage: many in the audience that night already knew the songs. They'd been to Planlos's rehearsal space or seen the band rough their way through a song or two in the bell tower of the Pfingst Church. So now, as the band launched into their songs, the audience not only went crazy, bouncing off each other and pogoing and creating a seething, swarming mass of bodies all united in sweat and smoke and solidarity, they also *sang along* with almost every word.

In fact, throughout the show, audience members grabbed the mic from Pankow and sang verses themselves. He found himself constantly running after the mic. The crowd shouted along as the band ripped through *"Überall wohin's dich führt"*:

> Wherever you go
> You're asked for ID
> If you say a false word
> You know what happens next . . .

> Were you really born
> To be subordinate to it all?

The crowd shouted along as the band cranked out *"Ich stehe in der Schlange am Currystand"*:

> Waiting in line at the currywurst stand
> I don't turn around—I've already seen you
> You are my shadow wherever I go
> A dark spot on the sun

In Kobs's "Modern Times," the band sang about how people just kept their mouths shut. But the kids at the party—hundreds of them—were not keeping their mouths shut. They were singing and screaming against the system along with Pankow.

As the band left the premises, they looked with amazement at the state of the place. Inside the atelier, in the staircase, out in the courtyard, everything was a mess.

Holy shit.

The band members had been punks for about two years when at midnight the calendar switched to 1982. They'd all had their troubles, at home and at large, and they'd all been harassed by the police for nearly all that time, slugged by fellow citizens and cops alike, interrogated by the Stasi. Their suspicions about the rotten nature of the DDR had long since been confirmed, and now, they felt, they had done something concrete about it. They had raged against the system, out loud, publicly.

Were you really born
To be subordinate to it all?

Not tonight.

14

On January 27, 1982, China, a punk who had been at Major's trial back in 1981, was arrested, subjected to multiple strip searches and body cavity searches, and placed in pretrial detention for five weeks. The charge, according to the arrest warrant: she had distributed a total of twenty hand-typed statements saying, among other things, that she lived in a "mousetrap" where "no freedom of opinion existed."

The statements, it turned out, were from her diary.

She was sixteen.

On February 16, 1982, Major was released from prison. Upon release, the terms of her *Berlin-Verbot* were explained: for the next five years she was forbidden to visit Berlin or any towns bordering the capital. Her compliance would be monitored by the authorities. She would be "rehabilitated" in Turnow—an isolated village about fifty miles southeast of Berlin—where she would be expected to work at an industrial textile cleaning facility. She had to report to the local council every week, and could not leave the town of Turnow without permission. She was barred from trying to change her job or her place of residence without written permission of the authorities.

She was taken directly from prison to Turnow. She was not just the stranger in town, but the criminal. The place she was supposed to live was a decrepit cabin with an outhouse instead of a toilet.

Major didn't wait a single day before hopping a train back to Berlin. She stayed until the following day, February 17, before returning to Turnow. She did not, however, report to work.

On March 3, 1982, the local mayor of Turnow sent officers to Major's residence to find her and demand she report to work. As soon as they had left, she again joined her friends in Berlin for three days.

Four weeks after her initial release from prison, Major was arrested again. This time she was quickly sentenced to eighteen months. When this second prison term ended the following year, she would be taken directly to the border and sent to West Berlin.

The vise was tightening.

The punks' haven in the Pfingst Church was imperiled as well.

Imperiled from within, it turned out.

In a series of reports from late March, 1982, the security organs boasted of twenty-five visits by informants to various Pfingst events just since January. The state basically succeeded in creating a split within the Pfingst Church that eventually had to be arbitrated in a church court. In the simplest terms, the local parish council tried to unilaterally kick out the punks by simply padlocking the tower rooms in early April, and other factions within the church sued the local parish council to reopen it.

For several weeks in April, it was unclear what would happen. Punks gathered in front of Pfingst each Monday and Thursday, unable to get in.

After a few weeks, good news came: the local parish had lost its case and Pfingst would reopen to the punks. There was a downside, however. The church court had decided to let the parish undertake some renovations for a few months, meaning for the immediate future the punks remained on the street.

The closure affected all participants in Open Work programs, not just the punks. But by then most people associated with other subsets of Open Work had come to develop respect for the way the punks dealt with the authorities. The long-haired peaceniks, for instance, were in the midst of a struggle of their own with the government. Beginning in November 1981, church-based peace groups had started to wear circular white patches embroidered with the Biblical citation *Schwerter zu Pflugscharen*, or swords into plowshares, and a depiction of a statue called "Let Us Beat Swords into Plowshares," by

Yevgeny Vuchetich, which the Soviet Union had presented to the United Nations in 1959. Despite the image of the officially sanctioned Russian statue, the patch had drawn the immediate ire of East German authorities—the government had its own peace initiatives and did not accept the legitimacy of this nonsanctioned activism. The government crackdown on the patches reached its peak in March 1982, with police forcibly removing them from people's clothing. For the peaceniks, this was a new and shocking level of harassment. But by then they had witnessed firsthand the more severe treatment the punks experienced—and were *still* experiencing. So rather than creating a wedge between the different groups, the closure of Pfingst Church contributed to a growing feeling of common cause between them—a feeling that would have great consequences in the future.

In the fall of 1982, six months after it was closed for "renovations," the Pfingst bell tower reopened. When the punks came streaming back, now on Mondays and Fridays, a church official who had supported the continuation of Open Work and of taking in the punks came to survey the scene. She was struck: the ranks of punks seemed to have actually grown during the lockout.

The Stasi apparently agreed. In a report from August 1982 detailing connections between the church and punks in the southern city of Erfurt, the secret police estimated the nationwide number of punk "adherents" at one thousand. Punk "sympathizers," however, who were likewise "recognizable by their appearance," ran to *ten* thousand.

In a country of just fifteen million, ten thousand was a hell of a lot of troublemakers.

Jana Schlosser performing with Namenlos at Christus Church in Halle, 1983

II

Oh Bondage Up Yours!

15

J ana Schlosser left home in 1982. She was seventeen.

She had just finished the tenth grade and was about to start a job-training program to become a nurse in the psych ward of a local children's hospital in Halle, where she had grown up, a hilly, crumbling, soot-choked city about a hundred miles south of Berlin. Halle was in the most toxic region of East Germany, surrounded by massive open-pit coal-mining operations and petrochemical plants; the mounds of smelly yellow-white foam that floated along and lined the banks of the slow, dark river that ran through town made it that much harder to ignore the stench of the poisonous water.

Home had not been a happy place for Jana. Her parents were very strict, obsessed with tidiness and order. Her father chauffeured apparatchiks around as a professional driver, and her mother took inventory for the official trade organization for hospitality enterprises—bars, hotels, restaurants. Her parents weren't party members but they didn't oppose the state, either. They were ordinary workers; politics was not important to them. When Jana started to experiment with her look, they didn't view it as a political act, they just didn't think it was proper.

Towards the end of school, Jana—who had straw-colored hair, a razor-sharp nose, and a willful chin—had started to cultivate a sloppy sort of hippie look, wearing long batik skirts in bright colors, and had sampled the alternative scene in Halle. Because of the local arts college, there was a vibrant community of artists—though Jana thought a lot of them were a bit aloof. The city had also been a hotbed of environmentalism and peace activism for several years, with a lot of the action centered around a young, impulsive deacon named Lothar Rochau, who worked at a church in a high-rise section of town. Rochau had arrived in Halle in 1977, just twenty-six years old, and built up a youth group that began to attract attention both from less tolerant church leaders and from the Stasi. As a lay employee, Rochau's position was somewhat more perilous than it would have been as a minister, and local church authorities disagreed about whether his activities should be permitted and protected. Rochau's critical misstep—for which, in 1983, he would actually be cut loose by the church, arrested, jailed, and then expatriated—was to take his activities beyond the church walls. He organized public demonstrations, candlelight vigils, and bicycle rallies, among other things.

Jana found herself drawn to the freaks, the dropouts, the long-haired activists. Some of them had squatted apartments among the derelict buildings in the bombed-out old town center. In Halle, as in other cities in East Germany, the government had opted to throw up new high-rise blocs around the edge of town rather than rebuild the war-damaged old center. Jana sometimes wandered around the hollowed-out downtown and looked into empty buildings and squats.

Whoa, look at this place!

Some still had pieces of furniture in them.

It would be cool to move into a place like this!

To live my own way!

She was trying to figure out where she fit might in, seeking a way to express her strong sense of individuality. She was curious, and she wasn't the type of person to quash that curiosity.

Then one day near the end of school her mother gathered up Jana's bohemian clothing and burned it all.

If you didn't like that look, Mom, I can definitely be more extreme.

Jana had read an article about punk in a West German magazine she'd found. It was a piece was about Nina Hagen—the East German émigré who'd become a West German star—and included a sidebar about punks in East

Berlin. It said they hung out at an amusement park called Plänterwald along the banks of the river Spree.

Punks.

A whole community of them.

In East Berlin.

One night, secretly listening to a West German station she could pick up on the radio she had in her bedroom, huddling under the covers so her parents wouldn't hear, Jana's ears perked up. It was a show about punks in England, and Jana found herself riveted even before the music came on. Punks got their clothes out of garbage dumps, they reported, and decorated them with safety pins. The report talked about punk ideology. Jana had only the vaguest idea of what anarchism was, but some of the slogans sounded cool.

And then came a song by the Sex Pistols.

Even playing softly under her covers, the song gripped her. It felt like something from *inside* her, something that had always been there.

This sounds exactly the way I feel.

That is when it all started.

16

Jana roped a friend of hers into becoming a punk. Together they made things she thought they needed to be punk. Using clay and safety pins they shaped homemade buttons and baked them in the oven so they could paint slogans on them. Jana found a discarded old striped jacket. She took a white pair of pants and splashed paint all over them.

This is what a punk looks like . . . I guess.

Her friend's parents freaked out immediately. It was too much for the other girl, who promptly gave up.

Jana was now the only punk girl in Halle.

She soon learned there were about a half dozen punk boys. One of them was Moritz Götze, who had started a band.

They briefly became a couple.

Moritz's band had come together under the auspices of a local church youth group.

"We're starting a band," Moritz told Siegfried Neher of Christus Church in the industrial eastern section of Halle, not far from the main train station but very much on the wrong side of the tracks. The minister was a rock music fan and himself a guitar player.

"But you don't know how to play instruments or read music," Neher had replied.

"That's exactly why we're starting a band! We're going to play worse than anybody in the entire country!"

On Saturday, June 19, 1982, the band played a youth workshop at a church on the outskirts of town. Neher, who was in attendance, had to tune the instruments for them. It was pure chaos, screaming and noise, and Moritz called the group Grössenwahn—Delusions of Grandeur. Wutanfall followed Moritz and Grössenwahn that night and the Leipzig band blew the crowd away with their speed and intensity and their no-holds-barred lyrics. At that point even the Berlin bands would admit that Chaos was the best frontman in the DDR. And everywhere Wutanfall played, new kids were inspired to challenge the boundaries in their own lives. Punk ranks were swelling.

Jana kept pushing her look further and further. She took to wearing lots of earrings and chains. She started to experiment with her hair and began to inch toward the full-on Mohawk she would eventually wear.

One day she decided to try to dye her hair with the ink from some felt-tip markers. She combed it into her hair and left the brush in the bathroom. Apparently the ink clung to the bristles: her mother went to brush her own hair and suddenly Jana heard her screaming in the bathroom.

Her parents had reached the breaking point. They had been hammering her about her looks, repeating the same phrase over and over: "Either you dress like a normal person or you get out."

Now it was just *Get out*.

"Get out!"

Leaving wasn't difficult for Jana.

She thought back to the article she'd seen about punks hanging around at the Plänterwald amusement park in Berlin. She wanted to see that. Maybe she could find a community there, a group where she'd fit in. At the very least she wanted to explore the possibility. Through his family, Moritz Götze knew some artists and artisans in East Berlin and gave Jana an address in Prenzlauer Berg. He said she could just knock on their door and they'd let her sleep there.

She packed a few things and headed to the train station.

17

In Berlin, Jana went straight to Plänterwald, walking the fifteen minutes from the S-Bahn station toward the Ferris wheel in the woods.

She sat down on a bench in the amusement park and waited. No punks. People kept walking by and insulting her.

"Hey, the haunted house ride is over there—get back to work!"

Eventually somebody told her that the punks met there only two days a week. Two *other* days. The West German magazine hadn't mentioned that.

Shit.

She got back on the S-Bahn and went to Alexanderplatz.

As she wandered around the bleak, concrete plaza she spotted two punks. The two Berlin punks obviously had the same thought that she did.

Aha, a fellow punk!

The pair of punks took her around that evening and introduced her to others. Jana had made her first links to the Berlin scene.

Back in Halle but unwilling to go home, Jana squatted an apartment downtown. She found a three-story building, completely empty. There was no electricity or water, but she moved in anyway—alone.

She also continued to go to work for a time, though she had to carefully hide her hair now that it was shaved on both sides and dyed bright colors. She wore a scarf on her head and didn't put on any of the outlandish eye makeup she'd started wearing.

One day a child tugged playfully at her scarf and it came off.

Oh!

The children all shrunk back, some gasping, some snickering.

"What happened to your hair?" they asked.

She told them she had a scalp condition.

She didn't last much longer at the children's hospital.

One weekend afternoon, strolling through a street fair, she encountered her parents and the family dog. The dog pulled at the leash and tried to come over to Jana; her parents pretended she wasn't there and walked past without a word.

Another day she ran into two punks on the street. She knew the handful of Halle punks and these guys were unfamiliar, so of course she started talking to them. It turned out they were from Berlin and had just escaped from a juvenile detention center. They were on the run.

"I have three floors in a house I squatted," she told them. "You can stay with me."

All three of them were excited. The punks started exploring the grounds of the house and discovered an apple tree in the overgrown yard. They built a campfire and roasted apples. They painted an anarchist slogan on a wall:

MACHT KAPUTT, WAS EUCH KAPUTT MACHT

Translation:

DESTROY WHAT'S DESTROYING YOU

But the authorities were looking for the two Berliners, and now Jana was involved. One day the three punks spied the cops snooping nearby and decided they better split. They climbed over a garden wall behind the house. In the adjacent yard was a theology student. He hid the three of them.

The house was now burned for Jana—she couldn't go back to living there.

And she knew that the authorities would eventually come for her, too.

Going back to her parents' house was out of the question. She wanted to do the things she wanted to do, the things she thought were fun, as often as she wanted and for as long as she wanted.

I don't want to have to listen to the radio under the covers.

She snuck into her parents' place to collect a few things and hopped a train back to Berlin. She locked herself in the bathroom when the ticket-taker came along. She didn't care if she got caught—her identification papers still listed her parents' address, so any fines she got would be sent home to mom and dad. In Berlin she returned to the place where Moritz's family friends lived.

She knocked.

A girl about Jana's age answered. She was small and skinny, almost boyish, with wavy dark hair. She had on black overalls covered with patches and strange high-top boxing sneakers that were falling apart.

She said her name was Mita. She said she was new there. Come on in, she said, absentmindedly tapping out a beat on her hip.

18

Mita Schamal grew up in a village just outside Berlin. Her mother was an artist who had been trained in structural ceramics and her stepfather was a potter. In fact, she was from a family of potters—all her aunts and uncles were potters, too.

Mita finished school in the spring of 1982 at the end of tenth grade, with no desire to continue. She was sixteen. She didn't know what she wanted to do next.

The most sensible solution was to stay in what was essentially the family business and become a potter.

Artisans and artists had a level of freedom that came with not being part of one of the large state enterprises. For instance, as head of her own workshop, Mita's mother was permitted to take on apprentices. She was also able to arrange an apprenticeship for Mita that would pass muster with authorities. But Mita insisted on one condition: she didn't want to have to stay in her little village on the outskirts of the city. So her mother agreed to have her spend three weeks of every month in Prenzlauer Berg and work as a guest apprentice at her aunt's ceramics atelier; for the fourth week of every month Mita would be at home under the tutelage of her mother.

In September 1982, Mita moved to her aunt's on Schönfliesser Strasse, which became her official place of residence. Mita had a tiny room, more like a closet. She slept in a loft bed, which took up almost the entire footprint of the room. She stowed her things beneath the bed. Her room was actually part of the apartment where her aunt's husband lived; they had recently split up. Mita's aunt's husband lived at one end of the atelier and her aunt now lived at the other end with her new boyfriend, Sascha Anderson, the dissident poet who worked with the art-punk band Zwitschermaschine.

Not long after her move, Mita was standing on the platform at the Schönhauser Allee U-Bahn station when a mob of punks came streaming up the stairs and along the platform. One of them walked over to Mita. He struck her as a friendly, funny guy.

"Hey, sweetie," he said, "do you want to tag along with us?"

"Sure!" said Mita.

The guy's name: Colonel.

She hopped onto the subway with Colonel and his gang. They headed to Alexanderplatz. Mita was thrilled. She'd only just arrived from the boonies and here she was exploring the city with a gang of punks.

Mita was already friends with some other teens involved in the alternative scene. Though she considered herself basically apolitical, together with her family she had gone to church-sponsored events, traveling as far afield as Dresden to protest the deployment of intermediate-range nuclear missiles in East Germany. If, like Mita, you were raised in a family with any sort of outsider leanings, you ended up spending time in churches and getting to know other kids from similar backgrounds.

In the ninth grade Mita had attended an arts camp to learn gravure printing, where she befriended a kid named Moritz, who had a school band in Halle. It had turned out Mita and Moritz's families also knew each other through the informal network of East German artists and artisans: Moritz's father, a painter, knew Mita's mother as well as her grandparents.

Mita had started traveling to Halle once in a while by train to hang out with Moritz and his friends. For Mita's parents it was natural—Moritz was practically family anyway, and nobody worried about kids traveling on their own in the DDR.

Moritz had been in the process of transforming his school band into something more serious. Mita got to know the other guys in the band and took a shine to the drummer, Mike. The drums fascinated her, and Mike taught her some basic rhythms. Back home in her village outside Berlin she took to practicing the patterns anywhere she could—on pots and pans or an old suitcase, on her knees while riding on the school bus. She became obsessed with learning the drums, picking up fills she could add to the basic rhythms Mike had taught her.

At Christmastime in 1981, Mita spotted a kiddie drum kit for 100 East German marks and begged her parents for it. They bought it for her: a cute little kick-drum, a snare, and a cheap clattering high-hat. She played it incessantly. Fortunately, living out on the fringes of Berlin, the closest neighbor was hundreds of yards away. When Mita moved to her aunt's in Berlin in September 1982, she took the kit with her and stashed it under the loft bed.

When Jana knocked on the door at Schönfliesser Strasse in the fall of 1982, she and Mita quickly realized that Mita's friend in Halle was the same guy Jana had ended up getting together with just before fleeing Halle— Moritz Götze. East Germany was often a small world.

Jana and Mita instantly hit it off.

19

ita told Jana she could crash with her in her tiny closet-like room. Together they started to go to the punk hangouts and work their way into the scene. Jana found the punk scene in Berlin so much bigger and cooler than she had ever imagined, hundreds of people, hundreds of people *like her*.

Jana decided she wanted to meet Pankow, whom she'd heard so much about. Tall and willowy with a distinctive way of walking, a big puff of dyed blonde hair, the singer in a band called Planlos. She found out he worked the early shift at a cigarette factory, and one afternoon she waited outside the factory for Pankow's shift to end.

Pankow walked out and saw a woman with a massive Mohawk and a totally destroyed trench coat that was splashed with paint. He'd never seen anybody like her before. Suddenly he didn't feel like such a badass after all.

What the hell is she doing here, of all places?

She made a beeline for Pankow.

Huh?

"You must be Pankow," said Jana.

"Yeah," said Pankow.

"You look cool," said Jana.

They became a couple.

They became inseparable.

Sure, once in a while it bugged Pankow that everyone stared at Jana when they were out together; he was used to getting the biggest reaction wherever he went. But there was no way to top Jana. Forget it. When it came to winding people up based solely on looking extreme, Jana was in a league of her own.

By her own description, Mita followed along behind the new couple like a puppy. Jana, Pankow, and Mita began to spend all their time together, day after day, night after night. Mita was quite innocent and naïve, and wasn't self-conscious about being a third wheel. Even in the bed all three of them sometimes had to share in Mita's tiny room. Sometimes Jana and Pankow would be having sex and they would realize Mita was staring at them with wide eyes.

"Hey Mita," Pankow would say, "we're trying to fuck here."

"I want to try!"

"No, Mita, for god's sake!"

The three of them spent several weekends just bumming around, scouring the country for other punks. They went back to Halle and found the punk scene blossoming, with parties being held in squatted buildings on Wolfstrasse, Spiegelstrasse, and Wallstrasse. They took trains to Leipzig, Magdeburg, and towns along the Baltic Sea. They went to Erfurt, where they wandered around town and met one punk and then another and finally met a big guy named Otze, who had a band called Schleim-Keim that had played church concerts. The local punks treated Otze like god—a god prone to heavy drinking and random violence, but a god all the same. There were pockets of punks all over the country, it seemed.

Jana, Pankow, and Mita were unknowingly creating something like a national network.

For a few weeks the three of them lived as if there were no rules. They traveled without tickets, they stole food off people's tables in restaurants, they hid in dumpsters in dipshit towns and jumped out to scare passersby. They hung out with people like Chaos in Leipzig and formed friendships that would last their entire lives. The circle of friends who made up the original core of the Leipzig scene included members of another fledgling band, HAU, formed by Wutanfall guitarist Imad—the initials stood for a made-up German phrase, Half-baked Anarchist Underground-movement. The two bands actually had intertwining, almost interchangeable members for a time. The singer in HAU, Stracke, had been at the first Wutanfall rehearsals and even sang with the band on occasions when Chaos couldn't make practice. HAU also included Chaos's friend Ratte on bass, who became very tight with Jana, Mita, and Pankow during their visits.

Jana was determined to stay in Berlin now, which she saw as the center of the punk universe. She wanted to stay more than anything. But there was a problem: you couldn't just move where you wanted in East Germany. That was illegal. She was in essence a fugitive in the eyes of the law.

To live in Berlin, Jana needed an officially recognized job and she needed to register with the local police precinct to establish legal residency. She found a job as a cleaner at a church. It was really the only place she could work looking the way she did at that point. To register with the police you needed a rental contract, and Mita was happy to provide a bogus sublet contract stating that Jana was living at her place.

One morning Jana took the bogus rental contract and headed to the local police station.

To the local cops, Jana looked as if she had dropped in from outer space— Mohawk, chains, earrings, fucked-up clothes smeared with paint and stuck with pins.

"You are not recognizable in the photo on your ID," they said. "Come with us."

They threw her in a car and drove her to another police station. At the next station they photographed her from multiple angles and then interrogated her until nighttime. To be released, she had to promise to return to Halle.

She was released and returned to Mita's place. She sat there trembling.

I want to stay here.

I will not let them stop me.

Then she began to think.

Okay, they are looking for me now. But they are looking for a punk.

There was an easy solution.

She knew how to disguise herself. She'd done it at the children's hospital back home. So Jana started to wear a scarf over her head. She wore long dresses. She wore a pair of serious-looking metal-rim glasses.

Then she tested it out by walking past a police station. No reaction from the cops out front.

One day, in her new disguise, she and Mita ran into a punk Mita vaguely knew. The guy had already attracted a lot of attention from the police and one of his closest friends was serving her second stint in prison. The guy came across as cerebral—and *hyper*-political. Jana had never heard anyone talk the way he did.

It was A-Micha.

A-Micha's gravedigging days were over. He and some of his coworkers had tried to get their boss—the one who spouted Nazi rhetoric—ousted from the cemetery. It had not gone well. Instead, several of the workers, including A-Micha, lost their jobs. Fortunately, by then he had gotten to know deacons Uwe Kulisch and Lorenz Postler, and they realized A-Micha would probably be thrown in jail very quickly if he didn't find a job. They helped him land one as a handyman at a church facility on Göhrener Strasse in Prenzlauer Berg—the rectory and meeting halls of the nearby Elias Church, the same place where Pankow had crashed when he first fled his parents' home. Postler, whose father had also worked for the Lutheran church, had grown up in Elias Church.

A-Micha had a band, too. Or used to. Sort of. He played guitar with a few other guys in a combo they called Alternative 13. The drummer lived in Rostock, several hours away, up on the Baltic Sea coast. That made it difficult to function as a proper band.

Mita had always been impressed with A-Micha—in addition to his various musical interests he was into archeology, which she thought was cool. And he was funny. The day she and Jana ran into him, A-Micha totally ignored Jana in her glasses and dress and scarf. But Jana, too, was impressed with him.

Still, Jana's new look served its purpose. She went to the local police station again and presented her rental contract. Luckily they had failed to jot down her name the last time she'd come—they'd been in too much of a hurry to whisk her off to the other station for interrogation.

This time, it went like clockwork. She got the necessary stamp on her ID papers and she was officially a resident of East Berlin.

She didn't waste any time digging into her new home in the way she knew best—by causing chaos. One night she and Mita ran out of matches while walking around in Prenzlauer Berg and went into a bar to buy a pack.

"Let's see your papers first," said the proprietor.

"Are you crazy?" said Jana, "We just want to buy matches!"

"You're not getting anything here," said the proprietor.

These assholes, they just want to fuck with us because they feel like they get fucked with all the time. People just want to pass the pain on to anyone they have a chance to lord it over.

This kind of shit happened to them all the time.

People hissed at them on the street or on the S-Bahn, people said Adolf must have forgotten to have taken care of them, people got in their faces and threatened them.

Jana and Mita went back out of the bar again, angry, with no matches.

It's so fucked up.

Jana and Mita smashed in the front window of the bar.

Then they ran.

20

Jana had always written down the feelings and thoughts going through her head. Sometimes these notes took the form of poetry.

Now when she listened to Mita drumming, whether it was on her little kit at home or tapping out a rhythm when she and Jana were out and about, she started to mouth her poems to the beat.

An idea was starting to take hold in Jana and Mita's heads: they should start a band.

Jana and Mita had also gotten to know Lade, the drummer in Pankow's band, Planlos. Mita now traded her only punk record—a compilation LP from West Germany—to Lade for two tom-toms to flesh out her own little kit.

Jana and Mita ran into A-Micha again, and this time, with Jana back in her normal look—that is, looking like the most badass motherfucker in the DDR—A-Micha took an instant interest in her. He struck up a conversation and told her about his band, about practicing in a garage near a high-rise apartment block in Rostock, about how impractical it was having a drummer in another city. Then he went on to talk about the lyrics he wrote, which led to his anarchist politics. Jana shared at least some of the same explicitly political feelings as A-Micha, even if she expressed them differently. Jana constantly got stopped, asked for ID, taken to police stations for questioning, interrogated, quizzed about her "associates," asked to identify people in photos, insulted, threatened, all for not sticking to the preordained path, for daring to look different, for doing her own thing. And while the attention from the authorities was frightening, she would never admit it, maybe not even to herself, no fear, and anyway, who knew whether there was really anything to be afraid of, anything serious, though she sure as hell tried to avoid being alone in public. *Papers, please . . . come with us.* Once when the Berlin transport police had ordered her to come along, she had just sat down and refused. *I wonder what they'll do, I wonder whether anyone else will say anything?* They called for backup. Only one bystander had told them to leave her alone. That man was shoved aside by the cops and all Jana got out of her refusal to cooperate was an extra hour of interrogation, well, that and they'd confiscated her spiked bracelet. And it all fucking pissed her off.

"I write, too," Jana told A-Micha.

They began discussing lyrics, trading phrases and ideas.

When A-Micha wrote, he tried to flay the system—to peel everything back and expose what was festering below. He was blunt and politically focused. Jana touched on political themes but tended to couch them in human terms. She focused on the impact of the system on individuals. Of course, either way, what they both said and wrote would have made most people gulp and look over their shoulder in case someone nearby might be straining to listen; what they both said and wrote would cause panic in an average East German citizen—the mere act of hearing it uttered would make you suspect. But for Jana and A-Micha, what they said and wrote was both a protest against the system and a reaction to the system's attempts to crush them—every hiss and insult and arrest and interrogation just made them and their statements harsher and more resolute. And every hiss and insult and arrest and inter-rogation made it more fun and daring and rewarding to keep going. Despite the creeping fear instilled in everyone, the feeling that you really had better censor yourself to ward off unseen and unknowable consequences, Jana and A-Micha both loved to speak out, to break the rules, to speak and write as if there were no consequences at all, or at least none that mattered, or none that scared them. Silence was not an option. They had to speak and write and sing and scream. They had to direct their rage outward, like the spikes on their bracelets.

Jana and A-Micha clicked. And, Jana was quick to remind him, Mita was a drummer. With A-Micha on guitar and his buddy Frank Masch on bass—they'd been friends since they'd spent so much time bar-hopping together talking politics, and Frank had also played with A-Micha in Alternative 13—they had the makings of a band.

Beneath Mita's aunt's workshop was an empty basement.

The new band set about soundproofing part of the basement to use it as a rehearsal space, lining it with egg cartons, old clothing they found in dumpsters, cardboard, and whatever else they could scrounge up. They wrapped a few pipes that ran through the space with old rags; twine and more rags soundproofed the old wooden lattice-work door to the space. The problem was that Mita's aunt and uncle and Sascha Anderson weren't the only residents in the building. There were normal people living there, too, and they didn't want to hear drums banging, regardless of what sort of band they were accompanying. Despite the soundproofing, the band usually practiced only for an hour or two in the early evening so as to avoid attracting attention.

It was a rush to start to put together songs. They worked well as a team, everyone could understand the goal of finishing a song, of getting all the parts to fit together, *hey let's try this*, coming up with a chorus, *man this is cool*. What a feeling, creating their own music, screaming their protests at the brick walls of the basement. One chorus went:

Aufgepasst, du wirst bewacht vom MfS

Translation: Watch out, you're being surveilled by the Ministry of State Security—the Stasi. But that wasn't enough for the band. They altered the final chorus:

Aufgepasst, du wirst bewacht vom MfMfSSS

That final repetition, *SS*, drew an implicit comparison between the DDR's Stasi and Hitler's Schutzstaffel, the notorious SS with its logo of two lightning bolts. To a regime that styled itself as the political opposite of Nazism, this was the ultimate insult.

Another song was called "*Nazis wieder in Ostberlin,*" that is, "Nazis back in East Berlin."

After the minister of Elias Church, where A-Micha worked, told him he feared there would be a crackdown on the punks, the band wrote a song called *"Der Exzess."* The lyrics sounded like a manifesto and translated, in part:

Is it worth it to march for a man who doesn't love you
Is it worth it to march for a man who just kicks you
Is it worth it to march for a man who hates you
Is it worth it to march for a man who jails you

Say it, speak it, shout it out loud, the truth is so distant
Say it, speak it, shout it out loud, and let the informant listen

If we go to prison for [saying it, speaking it, shouting it out loud] you can all be sure,
We'll be out again eventually and then we'll be terrorists

Working together, Jana and A-Micha made two-minute Molotov cocktails that the band took glee in lobbing into the world. Fuck reform. This wasn't about tinkering with the system, it wasn't about wheedling the dictatorship into taking military education out of middle school or stemming the tide of unacknowledged pollution. This was about rage. Fuck the system, fuck every last one of them.

They called their band Namenlos—Nameless.

They were careful about hiding any lyrics they wrote down. In Mita's aunt's atelier was a shelf with lots of pots and vases, and they stashed any scraps of paper with lyrics in one of the pots with a top.

Still, people close to Mita's family quickly caught wind of the kind of music and lyrics the new band was making. A lot of artists harbored dissenting opinions; a lot liked to have punk bands perform at their parties. But artists and literary types didn't risk public anger and police harassment just by walking down the street. Being a punk was completely different. Every fiber of your being was a dissenting opinion, an open affront to the system, a break from the future planned for you and everyone else, you were protest incarnate, twenty-four seven.

One day a friend of Mita's aunt, a woman from the art scene, pulled her aside and said, "Mita, do you understand how dangerous what you're doing is? You'd better think long and hard about it."

"I don't have any choice," Mita told her. "I *have* to do it."

And in her head she said, *If your generation isn't going to do anything, then we'll have to.*

For Mita, playing a song like *"Der Exzess"* was the best form of protest she could imagine. She felt *compelled* to do it.

Say it, speak it, shout it out loud.

Let the informant listen.

Mita and Jana and A-Micha and Frank knew it could be dangerous to say the things they said in their songs, but they didn't yet understand just how dangerous it could be.

21

Berlin was the undisputed capital of East German punk rock and Leipzig its second city. But in this mostly communal scene, the only true star was a hard-drinking farm boy named Otze, whose music took shape in a pig stall miles away from those urban centers. The spring of 1983 would mark a turning point for him, too.

Otze was born Dieter Ehrlich in 1963 in the hick town of Stotternheim, a hundred and fifty miles south of Berlin, in the state of Thüringen. He had three brothers and a younger sister, all of whom lived within the walled yard of an old farm complex, where his parents and grandparents also lived. His father was a butcher. Dieter Ehrlich had his first run-in with the law at age eleven, when he was nabbed for stealing a bottle of cheap liquor. He wasn't particularly successful as a student, and at the end of the sixth grade, having already been held back twice, he was pushed toward an apprenticeship in a metal shop that built equipment for strip-mining operations.

"Ehrlich is barely able to write his own name," wrote his supervisor in a report for the criminal division of the police, who were keeping tabs on him. "He is very unstable, and shuns work . . . he tried to craft wire into safety pins of approximately 50 cm in length, about which his work colleagues could only shake their heads. They think Ehrlich is not normal for making such things."

Dieter Ehrlich started to become Otze one day in 1978, when he heard

Sham 69's "If the Kids Are United," taped from a West German radio station by his brother Klaus. Dieter and Klaus listened to the song nonstop for weeks.

Soon Otze started to dress punk. He stuck a safety pin through his earlobe and another through his cheek. Using a needle, he crudely tattooed the word *punk* on his arm. At the metal workshop he made himself a big skull-and-crossbones medallion and started wearing it, dangling from a thick chain. He and a couple friends scavenged the local dump for leather jackets. It took a few days for the half-rotted things they found to soften up, and even then the boys looked and smelled like swine. But that was the idea—the *ideal* even.

Over the next few years Otze started hanging out with other punks he found in Erfurt, the nearest town and, with about 200,000 residents, a major metropolis by the standards of the state of Thüringen. The gang of area punks hung out at the biggest café in central Erfurt, and other highly visible locations—as well as at church events, and, eventually, in derelict buildings some of them began to squat. They were always putting themselves on public display.

Otze was big and stocky and became a one-man wrecking crew whenever he or other punks were challenged or attacked. Otze would physically remove bartenders from their own bars—pluck them out from behind the bar and launch them bodily out the door—if they refused to serve him for being too ostentatiously punk. And his metallurgical skills never abandoned him, whether that meant arming himself with handmade brass knuckles or equipping his buddies with metal rods he had swiped.

The punks from greater Erfurt quickly developed a reputation for brutality and were in constant rumbles. It was always about confrontation for these backwater punks, about revealing the open sores on the body politic. They constantly forced the cops to hide these sores—meaning to detain, chase off, or beat down Otze and his mates.

Otze gained local notoriety long before his legend spread throughout the workers' republic. Neighbors in his tiny village were scandalized by his appearance and behavior. One night he and his brother Klaus came home in the middle of the night, kicking a beer can in the middle of the street. Beer came in bottles in East Germany, and to get a can of the stuff you had to go to a special shop where they sold Western goods for Western currency. So the sound alone piqued the interest of village residents as the pair stumbled along the street, waking everyone up.

As one of the Ehrlich boys tried to kick the can, he missed and put a boot through the basement window of one of the houses on the street. They continued home.

The next morning, the occupant of the house with the broken window—a middle-aged man named Bernhard—knocked on the door of the Ehrlichs' family compound. Otze and his brother were hungover, still in bed, but Klaus answered the door.

"Are you guys crazy, kicking in my window?" shouted Bernhard. "The basement is going to be full of mice by the time I'm able to get a replacement window."

Klaus waved his hand dismissively and stumbled back into the family house. Then Otze appeared at the still-open door. He pushed the angry neighbor aside and walked out into the street.

Bernhard followed.

Next door to Otze's house, a cat was dozing on another neighbor's postbox. Otze grabbed the cat, walked down the street to the broken window in Bernhard's house, and flung the creature into the basement.

"There you go," growled Otze to Bernhard. "No more mice."

By late 1980, Otze had travelled up to Berlin to find kindred spirits there, too. He and a friend took a train to the capital and went out to Plänterwald, where rumor had it the punks hung out. There they ran into two punks who took them to a squatted apartment. The door opened and Otze could not believe his eyes: there must have been fifteen punks lying around the filthy, graffiti-covered apartment.

Back home, with no access to albums and no local punk bands to go see, Otze decided to make his own music. He began to teach himself to play various instruments, beginning with drums—they were the easiest thing to come by, since he could make himself a primitive set using buckets, pails, and tubs from around the farmyard. His first bass drum was fashioned from an old desk drawer. Otze's brother Klaus took up guitar. They ripped the headphones out of a tank driver's helmet to create microphones, retooled a radio into a rudimentary amp, and started playing together, eventually bringing in buddies to play bass. Inspired by a famous West German punk band called Slime, they called themselves Schleim-Keim—basically, Slimy Germs.

Soon people from Weimar were stopping by, members of a couple of bands called the Creepers and the Madmans. Otze's parents and other siblings had never seen so many freaks before.

As Schleim-Keim began creating songs, Otze wrote all the lyrics and sang, but he remained seated at the drums. By 1981 Otze had financed some Czechoslovakian-made drums by becoming a two-bit version of an arms dealer: on the rare occasions he showed up for work, he surreptitiously crafted brass knuckles, which he then sold to soccer hooligans.

In December 1981, Schleim-Keim played Thüringen's first major punk show, in the Johannes-Lang-Haus, a church facility in Erfurt. Otze wore a homemade T-shirt for the occasion that read FRESST SCHEISSE, or EAT SHIT. The show drew every punk in the region, but nobody had seen anything like Otze before.

Despite the huge impact of Schleim-Keim's first public performance, shows were hard to come by. At first the local church leadership hadn't known what to make of Otze—or of the punks who had started to make up more and more of the crowd at their youth outreach programs. They'd never seen pogo dancing, for one thing. But as Otze started coming to outreach nights to meet up with friends and drink—there was no hard stuff, but beer was always available—he and Wolfgang Musigmann, the clergyman who set up the concerts at Johannes-Lang-Haus, got on fairly well, despite the rumors floating around that Otze had punched some other minister in the face.

In the summer of 1982, Musigmann staged another punk concert at Johannes-Lang-Haus, lining up Schleim-Keim as the local act alongside Wutanfall from Leipzig and Paranoia from Dresden. Otze took an instant dislike to the guys in Paranoia. They had on nice leather jackets and pants. They didn't smell like real punks to him.

They must have rich relatives in the West.

Wutanfall played first. As singer Chaos writhed and spat the lyrics and the band careened through its songs, the crowd went *off*, bouncing wildly around the church hall.

Paranoia played next, and during their set they somehow broke one of Otze's homemade amps—before Schleim-Keim had a chance to play. Just as bad, the guys in Paranoia didn't even apologize. Otze was furious. He started throwing punches. Show over.

Later that night—one of those warm June evenings when the dying light lingered—a bunch of Erfurt artists and literary types threw a party in the courtyard of their building. Zwitschermaschine, another Dresden band, a bit older and artier, were playing the party, and a lot of people from the Erfurt and Weimar punk scenes showed up, along with people from the church show earlier in the day. Otze and his band went, too. After Zwitschermaschine finished, Wutanfall played a few songs. But their set began to fall apart, and Otze and Schleim-Keim would not be denied a chance to play. They pushed Wutanfall aside and ripped into their songs on what was a much better PA than at the church facility.

Schleim-Keim's performance that night, with nothing to contain them but a few decaying walls and the night sky, was no less staggering than their first show six months prior.

It sounds like they're slaughtering a fucking pig, thought Conny Schleime, the singer of Zwitschermaschine. *It's like Otze is trying to use his drumsticks to pummel the entire shit pile that is this country.*

The mastermind of Zwitschermaschine was Sascha Anderson, the dissident intellectual who was living in the same Berlin atelier where Mita of Namenlos would soon move in—Mita's aunt's place. Anderson had been impressed with Schleim-Keim, too. Six months later he contacted Otze and asked him and his band to participate in a secret project he was working on—getting an album of East German punk music released in West Berlin. The album, Anderson said, would be called *DDR von unten*—East Germany from below—and the West Berlin label Aggressive Rock Productions was going to put it out. Otze was intrigued, not least because according to Anderson it would mean getting paid in hard currency: *West* German marks. And West German marks meant the chance to buy better music equipment.

The idea to make an album and release it in West Berlin had a long backstory. In early 1982 a West Berliner named Dimitri Hegemann had gotten to know the members of the band Rosa Extra at a party he attended in the East. A musician himself, Hegemann almost immediately became obsessed with making an album of DDR punk. The problem was making the recordings—any proper music studios in the East were part of the state's media monopoly, and the equipment for an illegal home-studio was hard to come by. Hegemann checked in with Rosa Extra every once in a while, but from the other side of the Wall he couldn't really do anything practical to help them. Rosa Extra finally approached Sascha Anderson, who was a major figure in the underground, connected to artists, poets, and musicians in Dresden, Weimar, and in Berlin. Anderson loved the idea and, in exchange for having his own band get in on the project, he connected Rosa Extra to a guy in Dresden who was known for throwing great parties. The guy worked as a roadie and driver for officially sanctioned bands. He also had access to an isolated house a few miles outside Dresden, where he was able to set up a drum kit, microphones, and an antiquated Eastern mixing board and tape recorder and record music without any nosy neighbors complaining or snooping around.

The one thing missing from the project, in Anderson's eyes, was a wildly aggressive, abrasive punk band, something people in the West wouldn't believe was possible on the other side of the Iron Curtain. Both Rosa Extra and his own band, Zwitschermaschine, were more arty than, say . . . *that band he'd seen in Erfurt!* The one that sounded like a pig being slaughtered! Schleim-Keim!

That was when he called Otze.

On a weekend in early January, 1983, Otze and Schleim-Keim traveled to Dresden to record in the makeshift studio. Anderson assured Schleim-Keim that he would take the heat if anything went wrong, but the trio was skeptical what that would mean in practical terms. They decided to use a pseudonym, Saukerle—in essence, "Pig-dudes." But it didn't matter, because unbeknownst to them, there was a Stasi informant in their midst. The recordings wouldn't remain so secret after all.

Soon after that weekend in Dresden, the Stasi visited Rosa Extra singer Günther Spalda and told him a story they'd heard about a Western record label, some Eastern punks, and an album. "That sort of thing could land a man in jail for five years," they said, "maybe ten." *Just saying.*

Rosa Extra backed out of the project.

Sascha Anderson arranged for a West German diplomat to smuggle the remaining tapes of his band and Schleim-Keim across the Berlin Wall for him—Anderson had contacts everywhere, it seemed—and the albums were quickly pressed. Only 1,500 copies of the album *DDR von unten* were manufactured and very few made it back into the East—though cassette copies circulated widely. Its existence, however, hit Eastern authorities like a nuclear bomb.

The money Sascha Anderson had promised Otze never appeared, but the Stasi quickly did—even before the release of the *DDR von unten* LP. Anderson, it turned out, was an IM, a Stasi snitch. Thanks to Anderson, the Stasi had been following Otze closely since December. Otze's parents had been felt out about becoming informants but had declined; Otze's mother wasn't much more friendly to the dictatorship than he himself was, and she was famous among punks for having once yelled at them out the window, "If the goddamn Stasi wants to treat us like antisocial elements, we might as well act that way!" His neighbors, fellow musicians, and punk peers had likewise been approached. Surveillance sites had been set up to keep tabs on the family home.

When the Stasi's Department XX confirmed Otze was away from home for a few days in March 1983, a group of non-uniformed government employees arrived at his family's compound. They presented themselves as agents from the employment office. Otze hardly ever went to work, which was illegal. The agents said they needed to search the grounds. There were armed sentries posted outside the house, and Otze's mother realized what was really happening. As soon as she realized it was a Stasi raid, she took care of the most damning piece of evidence she knew about. She called to Otze's little sister, Heidi. The little sister was handed a shopping basket and sent shopping—with Otze's lone promo copy of the *DDR von unten* album stashed beneath a cloth in the bottom of the basket.

"Don't come home until all the cars out front are gone," Otze's mother whispered to Heidi.

Department XX agents rifled through Otze's room and belongings, the band's shed rehearsal space, everything. They took photos of all his posters, buttons, stickers, sketches, notes, and homemade T-shirts—including the one that said FRESST SCHEISSE, the shirt he'd worn at the band's first concert.

But they never found his lyric sheets, which he kept carefully hidden in a chimney flue.

The Stasi did not relent. At the end of March, 1983, Otze was arrested. If nothing else, they could hold him because he hadn't turned up to work since October. Otze landed in pretrial detention, subject to the usual routine of humiliation and control: stripped, a body-cavity search. During the interrogations that followed, the Stasi agents made clear they knew the words to at least some of his negative, hostile songs, and accused him of seeking to cause international damage to the country by conspiring to get recordings to West Berlin.

"You'll get ten years," they told him: Unauthorized recording for a foreign power.

After the initial interrogation, they threw him in an isolation cell. He spent two weeks in solitary confinement.

Ten years.

Ten fucking years.

Otze stared at the walls. During the day, he was not allowed to lie down on the hard wooden cot. Not allowed to do calisthenics. He was not allowed to do shit. He just stared at the walls. For many people, that was enough to change them.

After two weeks, he began to be interrogated by a team of four men.

He was just happy to be talking again.

That changed as the first interrogation dragged on for thirteen hours.

Otze never equivocated about the band itself.

Stasi officer: "Are you aware of a punk rock music group by the name of Schleim-Keim?"

Otze: "*Ja*. Such a group was founded in 1981 by me and my brother . . . We founded the group because we had fun making music and we thought that there were far too few punk bands in the DDR. In my opinion, young people want to hear something different from the usual disco music and old blues."

Stasi officer: "Is the punk rock group you founded by the name of Schleim-Keim registered or licensed?"

Otze: "No, that is not the case. We have never sought government recognition as a music group." He explained that they didn't believe they needed a license because they had never played in a public space; he told them about a couple of church gigs.

But when they asked whether the band ever used any other aliases—fishing for Saukerle, their pseudonym from the *DDR von unten* LP—Otze denied it. And when they asked whether he and his band mates had ever tried to publicize their music—with recordings, for instance—he said never.

Finally, they played some of the home recordings of the band they'd confiscated during the raid of his home, harping on the lyrics, that expressed a "pessimistic outlook on life, with anarchistic traits, general discontent, and a fundamental opposition vis à vis the governmental order."

Ten years.

Otze refused to admit the anti-government lyrics were about the DDR.

"It's about South Africa," he said.

"Then say that in the song!" screamed the interrogator, pounding his fist on the desk.

Still, without sufficient hard evidence or a confession, Otze was released again after four weeks in detention—despite the offensive lyrical content of his songs, despite the obvious illegal Western contact necessary to get the recordings out, despite playing concerts without a performance license, despite it all.

Otze now realized Sascha Anderson was a snitch and harbored a simmering rage against him for several years—until 1985, when together with original Berlin punk Colonel, he was able to burst in on Anderson at home in Berlin. Otze and Colonel tied Anderson up and turned his place over until they found some West German money—about 400 marks—to make up for the cash he had promised Otze back in 1983.

"This is for all the shit you put me through," Otze said to Anderson as he left with the money.

Anderson did not report the robbery to the police.

Otze may have gotten ripped off by Sascha Anderson, but he had pushed the envelope: everyone seemed to know that a band—*one of us*—had released music on a bona fide vinyl album, in the West no less. He quickly became an underground folk hero.

Otze and Schleim-Keim made the scene international. And between the embarrassment to the state of the release of Otze's music in the West and the increasingly alarming size and scope of the punk scene by that spring of 1983, it was just a matter of time before the shit really hit the fan.

22

In early 1983, Moritz Götze—Mita's friend and Jana's ex-boyfriend—had approached Siegfried Neher, the minister at Christus Church in Halle. The church already hosted a weekly meeting where punks could gather, drink beer, and talk, though as far as Neher could tell they weren't a very chatty group. There was more grunting than talking; most of what they wanted to say was scrawled on their clothes. Now Moritz wanted to put together a punk music festival and asked Neher to provide space at the church.

Neher was in his early thirties, with long hair, a generous heart, and a conscientiously open attitude. To the teens in his youth programs, he was known as Siggi. He'd learned guitar while fulfilling his military service in the nonweaponized *Bausoldaten*, and since his discharge in 1972 had continued to organize and play in church bands while he worked as a minister in a village outside of Erfurt. He had moved to Halle in 1979, where he found a vibrant scene orbiting the activist deacon Lothar Rochau. Siggi admired the way Rochau went out looking for people to join him, and the blunt way he spoke. Rochau would wade into a group of young people and cajole them into coming back to his church: "We're really doing things, not just standing around and bitching, we're thinking about how we can change this shithole of a country!"

Most of the forty or so members in Rochau's group, though, were in their late-twenties or thirties. Rock music was important to the cohesion of his group—but Frank Zappa represented the litmus test for his adherents. When a group of four punks went to Rochau's group one evening and were asked whether they knew Zappa, they shrugged, "Never heard of it."

The punks just didn't fit in with the older hippie types there.

The part of town where Siggi's church stood was populated by the families of workers from two nearby petrochemical plants. They weren't folks who were into Zappa, and it wasn't exactly a hotbed of environmental activity, either. There were none of the children of teachers or artists you might find in other parts of town. But the kids were nonetheless disaffected. And Siggi quickly felt a sort of connection to the punks who straggled into his church for this or that event. In Siggi's eyes the hippie types were somewhat pompous. The punks, by contrast, were far more open. But there was something more, something that had to do with his religious beliefs and his sense of duty as a minister: he saw punk as an existential scream, a desire to make contact with something that wouldn't otherwise react—and his mind kept calling up a passage of the Bible. Psalm 22: *My God, my God, why hast thou forsaken me? Why art thou so far from helping me, and from the words of my roaring?*

Siggi had always thought that Old Testament translations were too mild, written by hoity-toity people; in his eyes, the language in the Old Testament should have been raw, stripped—a scream; grammar and order would have gone out the window; people in anguish back then would have expressed themselves the same way the punks did now.

For dogs have compassed me: the assembly of the wicked have enclosed me.

That, thought Siggi, was a *punk* Psalm.

Wutanfall or Schleim-Keim could have written that, he thought, thinking of groups he'd seen at various church events in the last year. Müllstation, a punk band that practiced in the basement of Christus Church once in a while, could have written that.

Siggi said yes to Moritz.

And so, on Saturday, April 30, 1983, the evening before the annual official Mayday parades and festivities all over the country, East Germany was going to witness its first ever national punk festival.

23

Moritz Götze was something of an organizational genius, and even though there was no easy way to get information out in a country where the media system was completely locked down, he worked word-of-mouth networks to assemble a lineup of bands and to start the buzz about the concert among punks. He reached out to Jana and Mita in Berlin, who brought in Planlos as well as their own band, Namenlos. It would be the first ever public performance by Namenlos. Moritz was also able to get Wutanfall to come from Leipzig and Restbestand from Magdeburg. These bands in turn spread the word. By late April, hundreds and hundreds of people from all over the country were planning to come to Halle.

In early March, 1983, the authorities finally overcame deacon Lorenz Postler's fierce determination to continue to provide a meeting place for punks and succeeded in evicting the punks from Pfingst Church in Berlin by declaring the chimneys of the tower structurally unsound. All Open Work activities there were suspended with just one day's notice to pro-punk church leaders; other church officials had conspired against the punks to the point of letting security forces into the tower to photograph the *staats-feindlich*—subversive—graffiti and general mess.

The first Friday after the closure, March 11, would normally have been a punk meeting night. Instead, punks—many still unaware of the closure—were greeted in front of the church by uniformed and plainclothes officers checking identification papers. A surveillance vehicle was set up across the street with telephoto lenses sticking out. Several troop transporters full of cops were parked in the area, and a mobile police command center had been set up in a nearby grocery store. Police dispersed nearly a hundred punks who gathered in front of the church, hoping the doors might still miraculously open. After all, the doors had reopened the year before. But not this time.

There were, however, two upsides to the situation. First, as tensions had risen during early 1983, the punks had founded a *Punkrat*, or punk council. Up to then, organizational questions had been handled by church representatives like Deacon Postler. Now the punks could run their own affairs, creating groups to tackle issues, implement ideas, and solve problems. Among their first accomplishments was a proclamation stating, among other things, that "we" are faced more and more with "the alarming impression that almost the entire young generation, but not only them, are consciously or unconsciously deeply disappointed in our society." The punk council met the day after the closure of Pfingst was announced, vowing to continue activities.

And the second upside? With Berlin punks suddenly starved for a chance to hang out together, a huge contingent now planned to make the trip to Halle for the festival at Christus Church.

Namenlos had been practicing feverishly in the run-up to their first gig in public. But with the day of the show approaching, Jana worried that the police and the Stasi would try to keep fans and bands alike from reaching the festival. She figured they'd pluck punks off trains and ring the train station in Halle on Saturday to prevent any odd-looking characters from getting to Christus Church. So she rounded up a bunch of friends and proposed they go on Friday instead.

"We can have some fun," she said. "We'll already be there on the day of the show. And I know a squat where we can crash."

The plan worked. Or at least they thought so. They partied on Friday night and slept at the squat, just as Jana had promised. But a gang of punks couldn't swarm into town without attracting the attention of plenty of people who were more than happy to squeal to the police about it. And on Saturday morning, as everyone was still sleeping off their booze, cops burst in and emptied the building.

The cops took the gang of Berlin punks to the train station and put them aboard trains back to the capital. All except Jana. They knew from an informer that she had helped wrangle the bands, and they tried to squeeze her. They had also figured out she was from Halle. They told her they had reached her parents and her mother was prepared to come to the station with a change of clothes for her. Then Jana could stay in town, dressed like a normal person. Jana demurred. They stuck her on the next train to Berlin, alone, since her friends had been put on an earlier one.

I am not going to miss this concert.

It was the band's first real gig. And she was on a train heading the wrong way.

She knew Mita's mother and brother were planning to drive Mita down to Halle to watch her play, but she had no way to get in touch with them.

When her train stopped to switch locomotives at Jüterbog, a station between Halle and Berlin, Jana slipped out and waited for the next train heading in the opposite direction—back to Halle. She wasn't sure what she would do when the train actually arrived in Halle, with cops on the lookout for punks in general and her in particular. But she had to give it a try.

Back in Halle, the police had indeed poured into the train station to try to keep punks from getting to the church. The Stasi had an informant snitching on Siggi Neher as well as a few snitches placed among the young Halle punks themselves; they had learned of the Christus concert by February 11, 1983, when a punk informant described a meeting with Siggi that he had witnessed. But the Stasi had miscalculated the scale of the punk invasion, and the police weren't out in sufficient force to control the situation. Individual punks and small groups were detained or forced onto trains headed back to wherever they'd come from. But the cops seemed unsure what to do about the larger groups. Fortunately, most of the punks had come in groups—not to do things alone was something punks had learned the hard way in every town. The police had set up another line near the station exit, but again found themselves overwhelmed. Once out of the station, the masses of punks either walked or boarded trams to the church. They encountered one final police blockade right in front of the church itself. But there the police just tried to get the punks off the street and herd them into the fenced church grounds.

Across the street from the church stood a handsome old brick school with tall, pointed eaves; the authorities always worried that subversive activities at the church would somehow breach the school by osmosis. The geography classroom, which was at the top of the school on the side facing Christus Church, had been closed all week ahead of the punk festival as the Stasi assembled surveillance equipment. Pupils had been warned that the minister across the street—Siggi—was an enemy of the state. The school was empty on Saturday afternoon, except for the team in the geography room clicking away with their telephoto lenses sticking out the window, aimed at the Christus Church grounds below.

The church doors opened at four in the afternoon. The event was scheduled to go until eight. Siggi knew what the punks were like—that they spoke very differently from the average churchgoer, for instance, and that they could look outlandish. But this was something else. There were hundreds and hundreds of sullen black-clad kids, a few with full-on Mohawks. They barely uttered a word to Siggi beyond, "Beer?" They were from Berlin, Leipzig, Dresden, all over the country. Even if every punk in Halle was in the sanctuary, they would barely have registered in the middle of this hoard.

Then the concert started: Moritz and his band, Grössenwahn, took the stage—which was just the raised area of the altar. Siggi was surprised at the reaction to Grössenwahn, as out-of-towners quickly began shouting, "Get these assholes off the stage!"

When the better-known bands started to play, the church exploded as the punks, packed into the sanctuary, started to hurl themselves around and pogo up and down in a writhing mass of black. Siggi sat at the mixing board trying to make the rudimentary PA sound as good as it could given its low wattage, the tinny East German microphones being used, and the second-rate gear he'd been able to assemble. The music was relentless—two-minute song-bursts of anger, a sudden stop, then the band would hurtle into another one before the crowd could even catch its breath.

When Jana's train eventually pulled into Halle, she caught a break. There had been a big soccer match that day, and now the station was crawling with drunken soccer fans. This was not a subculture that looked kindly on punks. But for once it worked in Jana's favor as a bunch of them ringed her and started to tease her.

Using the soccer fans as cover, she managed to flee the station without any cops spotting her. Then she ran to the church.

Namenlos was already on stage when Jana finally arrived. They had played a couple of songs with A-Micha singing. Jana climbed up and took over the show.

Standing on stage, looking out at a churning sea of punks all pogoing and dancing and cheering, was an indescribable feeling, and the more crazed and euphoric they got, the more energized Jana got. She felt as if she were singing her soul right out of her body, screaming all the things she had always wanted to say, her rage glowing, the fire inside her stoked dangerously hot by her arrest earlier that day and the hours she'd spent trying to make it to this stage. This was all she had wanted to do—to express this perspective, this attitude, this philosophy that she and the band shared, to play their music loud and fast. Her need to freely speak her mind was so intense, so urgent, and now, here she was, with a room full of like-minded people bouncing off the walls. She felt . . . *understood*. She and her bandmates and her friends had always said the long-hairs were boring, just sitting around blathering for hours about this or that cause. That wasn't her style. She was a bomb-thrower, and that April evening she blew up the church.

Say it, speak it, shout it out loud!

Let the informant listen!

Police cars waited outside the church. That was nothing new. They often sat nearby when Siggi's youth groups gathered. But the police in the immediate vicinity had given up trying to hamper people entering or leaving the church.

The local residents, however, were horrified by the trail of degenerate youths in filthy, ripped clothing with fucked-up haircuts and offensive slogans scrawled on their jackets. One punk yanked his pants down and proudly walked around the churchyard naked from the waist down.

Even some of the church guests—particularly those from more hippie-like Open Work groups—almost fainted when they saw the scene. Hundreds of people jumping around like maniacs—pogoing—everybody smoking and flicking cigarettes onto the floor, one punk even took a piss in the corner of the church. All of this in the actual sanctuary, with the bands up on the altar. One thing impressed Siggi amidst the wild dancing: he had asked them to be sure not to damage the church's pipe organ or grand piano, and sure enough they made sure the church and its contents stayed intact. By the end of the night there wasn't a scratch on the piano or the organ.

To the uninitiated, the music sounded primitive, abrasive, even inept. "*Ein, zwei, drei, vier . . .*" and off the bands went, two minutes of breakneck chords and some word fragments screamed over the top. *Of course*, thought Siggi: when people find themselves in distress, in an emergency, they don't form perfect sentences, they just *scream*.

A line in one of Wutanfall's songs went:

Jauchegruben wie Elster und Pleisse
Wasserlos und stinkend nach Dreck und Scheisse

Cesspools like the Elster and Pleisse rivers
Waterless and stinking of filth and shit

Siggi and a number of other local clergymen he had assembled realized that while that could be dismissed as simplistic, it also represented a sweeping criticism of society, one they supported. Sure, by the standards of environmental activism it was almost banal, but it was also an aesthetic and cultural critique—an attack on the fundamentals of life in the East, a bloodcurdling cry that everything was wrong.

And then, of course, there was Jana screaming, *MfMfS . . . SS!*

No wonder the complaints poured in after the event. The local neighborhood association started a letter-writing campaign. Worse, the city councilman for the district surrounding the church dropped by to see Siggi, enraged by reports he'd heard about the concert.

"If you think you can come into my district and piss off the working people, you've got another thing coming," he told Siggi. "And that's no empty threat!"

It wasn't, either. Siggi and his family started to experience both discreet and open intimidation. After the festival, every night a police car idled in front of the rectory where Siggi lived, and the two-stroke engines of the Wartburgs did not purr quietly, they choked and coughed like a cheap lawnmower. Siggi's eight-year-old son was so scarred by all the threats and intimidation that he would need psychiatric help.

The regional church leadership also caught hell. And they didn't know what to do. Nothing of this scale had ever happened before. It was true that the punks were not church people; their music had nothing at all to do with religion and most of them considered themselves atheists. On the other hand, these kids represented a group in distress, they'd been beaten and oppressed, they were the castoffs of this socialist kingdom of heaven; *dogs had compassed them, the assembly of the wicked had enclosed them*; if anyone needed ministering, it was these kids.

Siggi found himself at the center of the same sort of battle that had engulfed the deacons who took in the punks in Berlin. The church was split between those, like Siggi, who wanted to make it work for outsiders, activists, and the downtrodden, and those who favored a more accommodating relationship with the government—which in its least insidious iteration meant hewing to a narrowly religious interpretation of the church's mission. As one government-friendly church functionary put it, "The church is there for everyone, but not for everything."

The problem was that, like most protestant churches, German Lutheran churches were quite democratic institutions. The Reformation itself had fundamentally democratic implications. First and foremost in a cosmological sense: the hierarchical system of mediation between parishioner and god had been abolished. But protestant churches were also democratic in a structural sense: taking the cosmological implications to their logical conclusions led to sects like Congregationalism, where any three people constituted a church, anyone could preach, and each congregation was fully autonomous. Even within the more rigid structures of the establishmentarian German Lutheran church, there was little the leadership—which routinely insisted the church was not oppositional and that churches were not places of opposition—could do to impose orthodoxy on its member churches or its clergy members.

Still, the pressure mounted on Siggi. The Stasi even tried to smear him by planting rumors that he was an alcoholic, in order to weaken his position within the church. In the end, however, church leaders found a kind of middle ground. Siggi was told that the church didn't want to hear any more complaints about alcohol abuse and noise pollution in conjunction with his work. Siggi was okay with one of those suggestions. He agreed to stop providing beer at punk meet-ups and at future concerts. It was BYOB at Christus Church from there on out.

As for the noise pollution, Siggi soon began to plot the next big concert at Christus Church, scheduled for Saturday, October 22, 1983. Little did he know that the bands who had played that first show would be shattered by then. And the Stasi would not take things so lightly next time. The festival in Halle in April 1983 had made the scene national, and that was perhaps even more alarming to the Stasi than the release of Schleim-Keim's music in the West. Otze and Schleim-Keim caused embarrassment; by contrast, a national network of punks with ties to the most troublesome churches represented a genuine threat, especially to a government as paranoid as Honecker's East Germany.

As spring turned to summer in 1983, the hysteria over punk reached the highest levels of government.

Chaos of Wutanfall in the band's Leipzig rehearsal space, 1982

III

Combat Rock

24

They came for Wutanfall first.

The Stasi's Department XX had been tracking singer Chaos intensively. A July 1982 report described a trip to Leipzig by a group of Berlin punks—including Colonel, Keule, Special, and Herne—to meet Chaos and other Leipzig punks. Reports in November 1982 detailed a trip Chaos took to Berlin with Wutanfall bassist Zappa, during which time he told Colonel and other Berliner punks about an upcoming gig in Jena, in the southern state of Thüringen. The reports also listed two other shows the band had played in Leipzig in the third week of November, and alerted authorities to the fact that Wutanfall had made cassette recordings of their rehearsals, which were then copied and handed around, facilitating the dissemination of their music throughout the country.

Another set of Stasi reports in early 1983 placed Chaos in Berlin for three days in February along with Wutanfall drummer Rotz and Ratte, who played bass in HAU, the other band Wutanfall guitarist Imad had started. In Berlin, the Stasi learned, the Leipzig punks had been setting up a Wutanfall gig for May 1983—not the sort of thing you could do over the phone in the DDR. They had also gone to Planlos's rehearsal space on Metzer Strasse, though the Stasi had been unable to establish what was discussed there.

Pressure had been steadily ramping up on Chaos. According to internal Stasi memos from late 1982, they considered Wutanfall the "favorite and best known" punk group: "Punks travel to their shows from across the entire country." As the band's singer, Chaos was viewed by authorities as public enemy number one—even though he never saw himself as the leader of the band, and music and lyrics were written by the whole band. Authorities paid attention to Chaos over and above other members of Wutanfall for another reason, too. But at the time Chaos would not have dreamed that anyone in his gang would be informing on him.

Still, he was often surprised at the details the Stasi interrogators revealed when he was hauled in. There would often be moments when he thought, *How could they possibly know that?* But then again, he reasoned, they probably had every place bugged.

Since finishing school in 1981, Chaos had been doing an apprenticeship as a carpenter, and his bosses there were also informing on him. Stasi officers regularly picked him up during work and hauled him down to the station *zur Klärung eines Sachverhaltes*, that is, to clear up some facts surrounding a case.

With Chaos, the initial approach involved physical violence and intimidation. But that just made him even more sure of his convictions—what kind of government wielded state-sanctioned violence against a kid who just wanted to dress weird and talk shit over loud music? An illegitimate one.

As time had gone on, the security forces had started to mess with his head in addition to the corporal punishment. They sought to demoralize him, to make him slip up and give them some piece of evidence they could use to throw him jail. Sometimes they would take him to the window during an interrogation and point out at another window across the way, in the pretrial detention center, and say, "Hey, look over there, that cell is reserved for you!"

By early 1983, he was receiving two summonses a week to report to police stations for questioning. If he didn't turn up for an appointment, they came for him. Usually at work.

During another trip to Berlin, he'd been picked up on Alexanderplatz, thrown in a car and driven all the way back to Leipzig, then thrown into detention. They interrogated him for seventeen hours straight that time, without breaks and without meals. Then they brought in a twenty-page summary of the talks and told him to sign each page to attest that it was accurate. He didn't care, he just signed them—it was all bullshit anyway.

After he'd signed, they picked up the stack of papers and ripped them up in front of his face.

"Let's start again from the beginning."

And they did.

After the second marathon interrogation, he couldn't even sign his name. He was trembling too much from fatigue and lack of food, water, and sleep.

They confiscated his ID papers and replaced them with a PM 12, a second-class ID that barred the bearer from traveling beyond his or her hometown. And while a PM 12 holder might be able to slip the police inside the country, it was impossible to cross any border. This was a serious blow for Chaos, who had already established connections to punks in Hungary. He'd found a lot of inspiration in his visits to Budapest, where the punks were further along than in East Germany—Hungarian punks were tolerated on the streets and even had clubs where their bands could play openly. Budapest was a place of refuge for Chaos, a place where he could get out from under the pressure of East German security forces.

Chaos was at the end of his rope. He finally snapped one afternoon in the back of an unmarked police car, lashing out as the officers in the front seat continued blathering at him.

"Shut your trap, you fucking pig," snarled Chaos from the backseat.

The atmosphere in the car suddenly changed.

They put a bag over Chaos's head and drove around for a while before dragging him out of the car and marching him into some woods—Chaos could hear the leaves and twigs crackling underfoot, and feel the soft forest floor.

Then, still hooded, Chaos was savagely beaten and kicked. He'd been hit and punched at police stations before, but nothing like this. When it was over, he was covered in hematomas, splattered with blood.

They took him, trembling and battered, into the Stasi stationhouse and made him sign a statement attesting that he had been well treated during his detainment. They had to move his hand for him as he signed.

The next day, Chaos turned up for work in a shocking state, scabs and swelling and deep bruises all over his body. Everyone could connect the dots: he'd been taken away by security forces, practically paraded through the workshop; he returned a bloody mess. There was no mystery as to what had happened.

After that particularly harsh beating, Chaos's parents became a bit more accepting of him and his side of the story—it seemed to them that maybe he wasn't the problem after all, maybe he wasn't some kind of hooligan. Still, they continued to think Chaos wouldn't have all these problems if he would just cut the crap—drop this silly punk thing.

"I'm not doing anything!" he told them, "I just play music and spike my hair up with shaving cream, OK? I just want to have my own brand of fun, that's all. That's no reason for them to beat me half to death!"

Other non-punks noticed, too. Chaos didn't have to say anything; the marks on his body said it all. For some people, that was the first time they'd come face to face with the ugly reality of what could happen if you strayed from the official path. With many punks, the brutality they encountered had served to harden their resolve and radicalize their thinking—now that same brutality made others wince, people at Chaos's workplace, for instance. It was impossible to ignore. Though most did their best. *They're not coming for me.* Chaos was struck by the silence at work. *Not my problem.* Ah, but not everyone looked away. The government's violence always had a boomerang effect.

None of that mattered for Chaos, though. Chaos was beaten down. Physically. Beaten down. Mentally. Beaten down. By the end it was an all-out terror campaign. They would kick in his door at three in the morning three or four nights a week, screaming at him as they stormed in. If anyone was crashing at his place, he'd be accused of harboring criminals. Grounds to take Chaos in for a night of interrogation.

And they started to come for him before every gig Wutanfall had lined up. They always knew. Sometimes HAU singer Stracke stepped in for him—Stracke had been practically a member of the band anyway, ever since the first rehearsals.

Things no longer felt the same to Chaos.

It had always been so fun—the little gang of punks against the idiot overlords. All the difficulties had just brought them closer together. But now he felt overwhelmed. Beaten down. The Stasi's strategy of degradation had worked.

As Chaos started to unravel, he felt he needed peace and quiet. His apartment had become a beacon for punks from all over the country, with people showing up and crashing there all the time; his apartment had begun to feel like an almost daily target of middle-of-the-night raids, his apartment . . . he needed *peace and quiet*. It was all too much.

He created a bulletin board for his front door, listing the apartment's hours of operation. He limited the opening hours and built in days off. Wednesday, for instance, was a day off. He didn't let anyone in.

"Sorry, but I'm off today."

The first time the cops turned up after that, he told them, "Sorry, but as you can see today is a day off." They just got more pissed off, more brutal.

He was done.

Chaos was done.

The best frontman in East Germany was done.

25

By late spring of 1983, Namenlos's Jana and Mita had squatted an apartment in East Berlin's Lichtenberg district. The place had no bathroom and they had to shit in a bucket. They often arrived home to find things missing or rearranged—they suspected it was the Stasi surveilling them and confiscating things because of the band, but they weren't entirely sure.

Officially, Jana had a job cleaning church facilities, but she was not going to work. She was supposed to start at seven in the morning, but since she and her friends tended to stay up all night, hanging out at each other's places, she constantly ditched. This was dangerous, because if the government could gather evidence that she wasn't working enough, she could be thrown in the slammer. Fortunately, by then she and A-Micha had become a couple and they had a plan. If they got married, Jana would no longer be legally obligated to work—in the eyes of the law, A-Micha would then be the breadwinner and Jana wouldn't leave herself open to getting arrested for not working. Jana and A-Micha got engaged and set a date for the fall.

Soon Jana and Mita squatted another apartment, on Stargarder Strasse, back in Prenzlauer Berg, not far from Mita's aunt's atelier. This apartment had been abandoned by somebody they knew—he'd been arrested and slapped with *Berlin-Verbot*, banished from his own hometown. There was no electricity in their new place, and the toilet was out in the staircase. The door had no lock and was almost always open. But the place was basically empty and the warm weather had arrived, so what was the difference. And besides, they had adopted a dog—a German shepherd they named Wotan— who could serve as sentry.

The summer of 1983 turned out to be the Summer of Punk—and a summer of resistance in general. After the closure of Pfingst Church to punks in March, the punk council had managed to organize several large-scale outings—the security organs' hope that rusticating them from Pfingst Church would be enough to break up the movement was proving illusory. Two hikes on the outskirts of Berlin drew nearly a hundred people each. Participants were later called in *zur Klärung eines Sachverhaltes.* The interrogators kept pressing them about one thing in particular—they seemed to think the outings included paramilitary training in how to attack the police.

On May 21, during a Free German Youth festival in Berlin, about thirty punks—including most of the members of Planlos and Namenlos—headed to the concentration camp at Sachsenhausen to lay a wreath. They had inscribed the bow on the wreath *Fascism never again–Berlin punks.* They asked Deacon Lorenz Postler to accompany them to Sachsenhausen, which was just north of Berlin and reachable by S-Bahn train.

The wreath-laying was a reaction to a new Stasi tactic: as authorities upped the fight against "negative-decadent" punks, one thing they tried was to portray punks as right-wingers. After all, Namenlos sang about Nazis, and authorities could use research about Western punk—in particular, the neo-Nazi skinhead movement—to support their assertion. A few skinheads were also starting to pop up in the East Berlin punk scene, too.

But the wreath-laying was also the kind of large-scale public action that freaked the government the fuck out. The fact that it was overtly political made it even worse.

When the group of punks arrived with their wreath at the Oranienburg S-Bahn station, they were met by a massive police presence and barred from leaving the station—the plan had obviously been leaked or overheard. It was a crazy scene: a group of youth battling riot troops in an effort to be allowed to criticize Nazism, which was the explicit philosophical enemy of the government whose riot troops were beating the kids. A-Micha ended up grabbing a cop by the throat in the melee. It was always a question of justice for him, and if the police were going to pick a street fight in order to hold the line for injustice, he would not hesitate to fight back.

The police eventually forced the punks back onto the platform, where they hopped on a train in the direction of the center of Berlin.

The punks thought they could outsmart the cops. They hopped off just one S-Bahn station away and tried to make their way back to the concentration camp on foot. Again, no dice—the police arrived as the punks were setting off through the fields. They gathered them up and once again forced them back onto a train.

Sitting in the S-Bahn, the punks came up with one last idea. They could try to lay the wreath at the eternal flame to the victims of fascism on Unter den Linden, the main drag that ran from Alexanderplatz to the Brandenburg Gate, past the national museums and the opera and Humboldt University. That boulevard was a showpiece of East Berlin, a stretch where tourists strolled. Would the authorities dare to arrest a group trying to lay a wreath to victims of fascism in front of tourists—potentially Western tourists? The answer was no. But first they had to get there.

The punks went in small groups, creeping from building entryway to building entryway, working their way from Marx-Engels-Platz S-Bahn station (now Hackescher Markt) until they had managed to get behind the memorial with the eternal flame. Finally, they all ran their fingers through their hair to make sure they were as outlandish looking as possible, with everything spiked up to the sky, and they ran to the front of the memorial. Two newlyweds were making their way out of the building, having just laid flowers of their own at the eternal flame. The groom was a security officer of some kind, wearing his dress uniform for their wedding day. He stared in disbelief as the disheveled punks rolled up, all Mohawks and ripped clothing. Nearby police stood helplessly by as the punks laid their wreath in full view of passersby and stood for a moment of silence in front of the eternal flame. When the punks emerged, they were immediately surrounded by dozens of plainclothes officers, and they were arrested when they moved away from the memorial. Still, news of their action spread fast, borne by punks and church-based activists across the country.

People both inside and outside the church also continued to secure space for punks. Minister Gerhard Cyrus let a band play at Galiläa Church one Sunday, announcing to the congregation, "When I am troubled, I sit in church and lament quietly. These young people here lament loudly." People started to leave as soon as the band had struck a few chords. Auferstehung Church hosted a two-day workshop on May 27–28, 1983, to which dozens of punks went. Local officials complained that "The disbanding of the punk scene in the Pfingst Church was a jumping-off point for resolving this phenomenon—the Auferstehung Church was not intended to become a replacement for that sort of riotous assembly!"

On June 5, Lothar Rochau, the deacon in Halle, staged a large protest against environmental degradation. Nearly two hundred people biked through town with posters, some wearing gas masks or scarves over their faces, and gathered outside the gates of one of the massive petrochemical complexes on the outskirts of town, where police attacked them with water cannons. Forty people were arrested and spent a night in jail. Rochau himself was arrested soon after, and the church hierarchy did not protest as he was tried and sentenced to three years for anti-state agitation, illegal contacts, and vilification of state organs. As sometimes happened with political prisoners, he was eventually bought out of captivity by West Germany.

Still, environmental activists did their thing with their signs and masks for a few hours and then it was over. Like visual artists and writers, political activists could melt back into anonymity after a demonstration. While politically focused activists might appear at first glance to have represented a more serious threat to the dictatorship, their protests were discrete events separate from everyday life. Punks, by contrast, because of the way they looked, represented active constant opposition any time they appeared in public. You couldn't spray hoses on punks and throw them in the slammer overnight to stop their particular form of protest. Because the next day they would just walk down the street again, embodying constant active protest, an all-encompassing protest tied to their very person and being. From the perspective of the Stasi, punk was a menacing outsider cult causing more and more kids to opt out of the preordained future the government had in mind for them.

On June 11, 1983, St. Michaelis Church in Karl-Marx-Stadt held another punk festival, inviting Namenlos and Planlos from Berlin to play, along with Leipzig's Wutanfall, with Stracke replacing Chaos on vocals. It was the first time a church in the city—about a hundred miles south of Berlin—had hosted a punk show. Otze and Schleim-Keim played, too, and they arrived just as Planlos were setting up their gear. Otze had a huge entourage with him, tough Erfurt punks, already drunk, and they stampeded into the place like wild boar. Planlos watched them come. They had played with Schleim-Keim a few times already and Otze was a regular in Berlin punk circles; the Planlos band members had begun to realize that a storm cloud of potential violence followed Otze and the Erfurt punks everywhere they went, threatening to rain blows at any moment. There was a spot on the grounds where everyone had been throwing their beer bottles. One of the Erfurt punks went over to the pile of glass shards.

"Hey, you're going to get hurt," people warned him.

"I don't give a fuck," he said.

He laid down on the jagged glass. When he eventually got up again, his clothes were ripped and blood dripped from the back of his pants. He danced, blood-spattered, when the band started to play.

Pankow took the stage wearing a T-shirt his girlfriend, Nase, had decorated for him with the words WENN UNRECHT ZU RECHT WIRD, WIRD WID-ERSTAND ZUR PFLICHT: When Injustice Becomes Law, Resistance Becomes a Duty. It was a quote from Rosa Luxemburg, a martyred communist activist, murdered in Berlin at the hands of a right-wing death squad in 1919. And even though Luxemburg's death was marked each year with official East German government commemorations, the rest of the band warned Pankow: *You could get thrown in jail for that.* He didn't care.

Karl-Marx-Stadt, which before the division of Germany was known as Chemnitz, had a population of about a quarter million but not a single punk band, though that wouldn't be true for long after the show.

For the rest of the summer, as the waves from these events rippled out, regional punk shows took place in churches all over the country. In two-bit towns like Eisleben, the excitement around a local band, Müllstation, was able to draw people from surrounding towns to a concert on June 18 in

Petri Church. When a punk in the town of Naumburg—a Stasi report put the number of local punks at eight souls in 1983—threw a birthday party, three dozen punks from *ten* different East German cities showed up. A whole new age cohort—a few years younger than the original punks—was being exposed to the music and philosophy. In many cases, these younger kids found something in punk that would stay with them through the end of the dictatorship—or perhaps more accurately, that would lead to the end of the dictatorship.

> Were you really born
> To be subordinate to it all?

It wasn't just a case of punks shouting that the world was fucked. There was something constructive happening, too, with all the events, the squatted spaces, the network of contacts—the punks were finding free space and beginning to create an alternative reality, their own reality, their own world. *The world is fucked.* Yes, they all agreed on that. The world was fucked. But there was something else, something far more powerful about what was happening. It was like the graffiti in East Berlin had said: DON'T DIE IN THE WAITING ROOM OF THE FUTURE. It was a call to action. *The world is fucked . . . and what are we going to do about it?*

That was the key.

What are we going to do about it?

Too much future was becoming more than a headache for the government; it was fast becoming an existential menace.

26

Planlos singer Pankow had been detained a lot more frequently lately.
At first he hadn't realized it was the Stasi—he'd thought the interrogators were normal cops. But he figured it out soon enough. They had taken Pankow for the type of personality they liked to recruit—open, talkative—and started a file to track attempts to convert him into an informant. They were right about him to a certain extent—he was open. The problem for them was that he was open about his aspirations for change. Pankow thought he could convert *them* rather than the other way around.

"It's a great country," he told them, "but we need to improve some things."

Pankow had never been interested in the West. Once he'd become a punk, he wasn't even interested in what was happening in Western punk scenes. Pankow was an East German punk through and through, and he saw his mission quite clearly: *We could do things differently here.*

The Stasi kept Pankow under constant scrutiny. Several of his neighbors on Marienburger Strasse had been enlisted to snoop on him. And they did so with gusto. On several occasions Pankow caught the baker's wife, who lived downstairs from him, listening at his door, notepad in hand. She filed reports with her Stasi handler listing things like visits from Leipzig and Dresden punks, plans she'd overheard about trips to meet up with the musicians in Wutanfall, and her personality assessments of Pankow: "Boehlke does seem to be one of the most sensible out of all of them."

The Stasi knew him so well that at one point, while he was messing around with his girlfriend, Nase, in some bushes one evening near Alexanderplatz, Pankow had heard a command: "Herr Boehlke, please come out of the bushes!"

They had recognized him by his *shoes*. Off to another interrogation.

By the time they finally asked him explicitly to become an informant, in the spring of 1983, he'd been getting detained and interrogated regularly for two full years. Pankow was taken by surprise at what he perceived as a change of tack.

"*Work with you*, what does that mean?"

The officer tried to cast it in the best light. There were criminal elements in the scene, and when a crime occurred, Pankow would just contact them, that's all.

"Rat somebody out? No way, I won't do that."

Never.

He felt that deep in his blood.

NEVER.

From that point on—once they realized he wouldn't become an asset—the Stasi set about taking care of him some other way. They regarded him as important. As with Chaos, the Stasi assumed that, as the singer, Pankow was the boss. They figured he was the frontman and thus the mastermind of the band, and since the band was the most prominent one in East Berlin, Pankow was basically a mastermind of the entire poisonous movement. But it didn't work like that. Not in the band—Kobs and Lade wrote most of the songs—and not in the DDR punk scene in general, which was stubbornly egalitarian, not hierarchical. The punks were nearly all at least fledgling anarchists, and they sought collective organization in everything they did. It was always about bottom-up politics, whether that meant how a band was run or how they wanted the country run.

In the end, Pankow made it easy for the Stasi.

During the summer, government-sanctioned publications held annual "press festivals" in various towns around the country. The day that Planlos, Namenlos, and Wutanfall had played in Karl-Marx-Stadt, *Neues Deutschland*—the flagship daily paper of the dictatorship—had opened its annual festival in the People's Park in Berlin's Friedrichshain district, just up the road from the punks' old hangout at Pfingst Church. The festival was more like a county fair than a professional convention, offering several days of exhibitions and entertainment open to the public. The year before, Dean Reed, a middle-aged American émigré popular throughout the East Bloc, had been a featured musical act at the festival; often called the Red Elvis, Reed had moved to East Germany in 1973 and alongside his music and film career had also established a personal relationship with dictator Erich Honecker. In addition to such state-sanctioned musical acts, there were often demonstrations of things like school children driving baby tanks, showing off the results of the military training that had been mandated in Eastern schools since the late 1970s.

The day he returned from Karl-Marx-Stadt, Pankow decided to go to the press festival—wearing his T-shirt with the Rosa Luxemburg quote: WHEN INJUSTICE BECOMES LAW, RESISTANCE BECOMES A DUTY.

You never knew who might be at one of these press festivals, and he had a vague plan to try to get on a soapbox and preach the punk gospel. It was not to be.

As he was walking toward the park, a police car pulled up beside him and a huge bull of a man stepped out—Pankow recognized him immediately. He was unforgettable because of his size, and Pankow had already encountered him many times on Alexanderplatz. The cop approached Pankow, picked him right off the ground, and threw him bodily into the back of the police car.

"So, Herr Boehlke!"

As they drove toward the detention center on Keibelstrasse, down near Alexanderplatz, the monster cop slowed down and pointed to a guy walking along the sidewalk.

"Check it out," he said. "I had that guy thrown in prison. He must be out again. And now it's your turn!"

"What?" said Pankow.

"Yeah, for that T-shirt? Three years."

Bullshit, thought Pankow. *I've been arrested a million times.*
Bullshit.

At the detention center they took his T-shirt and then interrogated him all day and into the night. During that time they broke into Pankow's apartment and searched it, and broke into the band's basement rehearsal space and searched that. Though the band was careful with lyrics—Pankow burned everything—there was one scrap of paper in the rehearsal space. It was the words to a song by Kobs that translated as "Smog and Soot." Luckily, a friend of theirs had been in the space at the time and heard the footsteps on the stairs. He shoved the scrap of paper into his pants just in time.

They threw Pankow in a cell overnight.

Pankow figured he'd be released the next day. After all, they couldn't keep him for too long without a formal arrest warrant. Though East German laws criminalized things that in the West couldn't be criminalized, the system was still a very legalistic one, and generally the security forces stuck to the letter of the law. For the most part, you couldn't just throw people in jail and hold them indefinitely.

But when the guards came for him in the morning, they didn't release him. They marched him out to a car, handcuffed. They drove Pankow to the back door of a hospital, removed him from the car, shirtless and handcuffed, marched him over to the building, and ordered him to stand against the wall.

A doctor emerged from the hospital door. He walked over to Pankow, made a fist, and bounced the fist off the top of Pankow's head. It was like something out of a cartoon. You could almost hear the sound effect: *Boing!*

Pankow nearly laughed.

"Fit for detainment," the doctor announced.

What the fuck? That was an examination?

The doctor signed a form and then Pankow was bundled back into the car.

Fit for detainment.

Maybe this isn't a joke.

At first, Pankow remained cocky back at the detention center, talking shit and acting the way he thought a renegade should act. But the longer it went on, the more he began to worry. Some of Pankow's closest friends, including Colonel, had already been imprisoned.

This could be serious.

Next they showed Pankow an arrest warrant: public disturbance, disorderly conduct, obstructing an investigation . . . and at the end was the proposed sentence: three years and eight months.

I'm going to prison.

"By the way, we'll make sure you serve your sentence up in Brandenburg, with the lifers."

Pankow, now twenty, knew he wouldn't last long among murderers.

The Stasi were not fucking around.

"Okay, this is your last chance: either you agree to work with us, or you're going to get three years and eight months."

I will never work with you, never.

He cried in his cell that night.

But he did not change his mind.

I'm going to prison.

And then, the next morning, they took him from his cell and released him.

Were they bluffing all along?

That wasn't actually the reason he'd been released, but it would be a while before Pankow would learn the real reason.

Pankow walked out of the detention center in just his ripped-up, splatter-painted pants and no shirt. He walked away from Alexanderplatz, the TV tower peering down at his pale, skinny, bare-chested body. He walked up Prenzlauer Allee toward the apartment on Marienburger Strasse that he was sharing with Nase. He was free.

When he reached his place, total chaos. They had rifled through everything and turned the place over. They had taken the photos he had of his friends, and they had taken the old pictures and posters he'd collected from illicit Western music magazines. But—he exhaled—they hadn't confiscated his records and cassettes. They were still there, and still intact.

But that was not the end of it.

27

A few days later, Pankow heard a knock at the door of his apartment.

Nase answered.

Stasi.

"We'd like to speak to Herr Boehlke," said one of the officers.

"He's not here," lied Nase.

They didn't have a warrant to enter the apartment, so they couldn't prove her wrong. But what if they had changed their minds and wanted to get him off the streets—maybe they had found out about the band's gig the next week? Pankow knew he was in a particularly dangerous spot: he had recently lost another job and hadn't been working—which made him *asozial*. They could jail him for that alone. He was at risk of going to prison under a pretext that had nothing to do with the band.

Fortunately, he'd finally been offered a new job—he just had to make it to the following Monday, then he'd be legally employed again. He was going to be operating the garbage press at Charité hospital, pretty much the worst job he could imagine. But better than jail.

As he furtively looked out the apartment windows, he saw suspiciously casual people standing around the courtyard, smoking cigarettes, not going anywhere.

Stasi, he thought.

He looked again a while later and the same people were still there.

Fuck.

More of them must have been waiting out in front of the building.

They are waiting for me to come out.

I'm surrounded.

Pankow decided to hunker down. Nase answered the door anytime there were knocks. She always said the same thing—no, haven't seen Herr Boehlke, no he's not here, no don't know where he is, no you can't come in.

But then his mother turned up at the door, red-faced and puffy-eyed.

"What is it?" Pankow asked after Nase let her into the apartment, "What's wrong?"

"Father's killed himself," she sobbed to Pankow.

She begged Pankow to go to the funeral, which would take place a few days later, over the weekend.

Since Pankow had left home in the fall of 1980, he had seen his father just twice. The first time, Pankow had been walking along the street in his full punk gear, buttons and anarchist As on his clothes, hair up to the sky, and he spotted his father on a passing trolley. The orange carriage rattled past and Pankow ran alongside banging on the window, his rage welling up. "Come out, you bastard!" he shouted, daring his father to fight him. Everyone on the trolley stared at Pankow as he ran and shouted and punched the glass— everyone except his father, who looked casually away and pretended not to recognize his son.

The next time—which proved to be the last—was near the subway station at Spittelmarkt. Pankow was walking with Kaiser, and said to him, "Hey look, that's my old man."

Kaiser didn't believe him.

"It's really him," said Pankow.

Pankow and his father did not acknowledge each other as they passed.

Now his mother was standing in front of him, crying, begging him to come to the funeral.

But the Stasi also no doubt knew that this father had killed himself, and they would be banking on Pankow leaving the building to attend the funeral. All they had to do now was wait.

After his mother left, Pankow and Nase sat glumly, trying to figure a way out. In the end, the plan they cooked up was surprisingly simple—almost comically simple. Nase went to see a friend who worked at a theater and got hold of a wig and some women's clothes.

On Sunday morning, the day of the funeral, Pankow put on a dress, high heels, a wig, and lipstick. He went down into the basement of their apartment building, which was connected to the next one down, and then emerged in the next-door entryway. Meanwhile Nase went out onto the street with a pack of cigarettes and sized up the situation. Pankow peeked out of the keyhole and waited for a signal from Nase, who was now standing across the street. If the coast was clear—or at least as clear as it was going to get—Nase would scratch her nose. If she lit a cigarette without scratching her nose, that meant Pankow should go back into the basement and hide. He waited. Then she scratched her nose. Pankow walked out in his dress and made his way to a nearby S-Bahn station. From there he rode to the family apartment in Pankow.

As he approached the building where he had grown up, he could see Stasi agents posted nearby. But either they didn't recognize him or they recognized him too late, and he managed to slip inside and up to his mother's apartment. Inside, all hell broke loose: this was his mother's worst nightmare, that Pankow would make a mockery of the funeral of his estranged father. Obviously he'd been unable to tell his mother of his plan in advance. His mother was already crying, his entire extended family was there, and here was Pankow, in drag.

"Oh, God! How could you! Have you lost your mind?"

Pankow quickly explained the situation and changed into normal clothes he had brought along—normal meaning his punk gear, which was hardly less provocative in the eyes of many of the rest of the family.

When they all walked out of the building, Stasi agents immediately surrounded him, grabbed his arms, and told him he was under arrest.

Pankow's mother fell to the ground, crying and screaming, begging them to let him attend the funeral first.

For some reason they relented, and said Pankow could go to the gravesite. They would take him into custody afterward.

At the end of the ceremony, as the rest of the crowd ambled toward their cars parked at the cemetery entrance, Pankow ran off through the grave-stones. Out of sight of the Stasi watchers, he hopped the cemetery walls and slipped into the surrounding woods of the Schönower Heide, an extensive forest on the north edge of Berlin. If he could elude authorities until the next morning, he could go straight to the new job at Charité hospital and—perhaps—avoid arrest.

On Monday morning, at eight o'clock sharp, Pankow slipped into the beautiful old brick hospital complex in the central borough of Mitte to start work. The garbage press was in a small room; in front of it were bags of trash and medical waste. Pankow had to load the reeking stuff into the press and then compact it all. Whenever the press filled up, Pankow opened the bay of a loading dock and a freight truck would come and cart off the dense block of garbage. Then he'd start loading the press again.

The first day it took him about half an hour to wrestle what garbage was there into the press; his shift went until four in the afternoon. So Pankow just sat there in the stinking room waiting for more garbage to arrive.

Then the phone on the wall rang.

"Hello?" said Pankow.

"It's Herr Breuer," a man said. It was the boss, head of personnel. "Come upstairs to my office."

Shit.

Pankow went up to the personnel office.

"Do you know who was just here?" asked Breuer.

"No," said Pankow.

"The Stasi," said the boss.

"Aha," said Pankow.

"Any idea what they wanted?" asked the boss.

"No idea," said Pankow.

"Well, apparently you're *political*—but I guess that's obvious from the way you look, isn't it?"

"Listen, I don't necessarily agree with what they think of me, but fine, I guess that's it," said Pankow.

"You know what?" interrupted the boss. "I don't agree with them either. I told them to get lost."

Pankow's new boss pushed a finalized employment contract across his desk toward Pankow. With that piece of paper, Pankow was legal again, employed, no longer subject to arrest for not working.

28

About a week later, on June 24, Planlos and Namenlos were scheduled to play a hometown show at the *Bluesmesse* in Berlin's Erlöser Church. Three months after getting thrown out of Pfingst Church, the Berlin punks were back in business, at least for one show.

The *Bluesmesse*—or "Blues Mass"—was a Berlin church tradition going back to 1979, when it started in nearby Samariter Church. A musician named Günter Holwas had approached the minister there, Rainer Eppelmann, whose obsession was peace and the demilitarization of youth culture and schools, about holding a concert in the church. Holwas had pledged to bring in a lot of disaffected youths, people who would not otherwise have been exposed to church activities. Eppelmann liked the idea; East Bloc blues rock had been the soundtrack to the DDR peace movement for years and a *Blueser*, or blues fan, was practically a synonym for a peacenik. For strategic reasons, Eppelmann decided to incorporate the music into a vaguely liturgical framework.

The Blues Masses quickly became a thing—several hundred people attended the first one on June 1, 1979, and by 1980 several thousand showed up whenever a Blues Mass took place, with a significant portion of the concert-goers traveling to Berlin from other cities. Authorities tried to shut down the Blues Masses based on public safety codes—the events were too crowded, they said—so Eppelmann arranged to move them from Samariter Church to Erlöser Church, a larger facility in a desolate corner of Lichtenberg that had extensive grounds to hold spillover crowds and information booths on various causes and discussion groups. The first Blues Mass held there, in November 1980, had attracted five thousand people.

By the time the punk bands were brought into the Blues Mass that summer of 1983, Rainer Eppelmann had become a focus of the state security apparatus. In 1982 he had issued a formal appeal for disarmament and for the elimination of military instruction in schools, and had managed to publicize the appeal in the West German media. He had also been a key figure in the campaign aimed at getting fellow pacifists to wear patches with the Biblical citation *swords into plowshares*, a campaign that infuriated the government in general and attracted the personal ire of Erich Honecker. The Stasi had stepped up their spying on Eppelmann, bugging his apartment, placing more informants around him, and infiltrating the events he organized, including the Blues Masses. They had even contemplated murdering him, though his connections to the West made them hesitate, as killing him might set off a potentially embarrassing uproar and threaten the precious international legitimization Honecker seemed to crave above all else. As with other rogue clergymen, the government had also tried to get the national and regional church leadership to discipline Eppelmann—to no avail.

Eppelmann had been chastened by the threats, but he had never been a rock-solid ally of the various outside groups inside the church anyway—his primary focus seemed to be self-promotion, particularly in the West. He was already notorious for showing up to demonstrations when the pictures were being taken and then buggering off before things got ugly with the cops; kids, including many punks, who got into hot water for signing his various petitions, also resented the fact that he himself seemed to be protected by his connections to the West while they took it on the chin. And now he seemed more craven. He had yanked the microphone away from musicians who tried to make provocative statements during Blues Masses. He had caved to pressure not to mention Poland and the Solidarity movement at his events. And the frequency of the Blues Masses had dwindled to just two per year.

The teeth had gone out of the events.

Which is exactly why Deacon Lorenz Postler thought it would be a great idea to integrate the punks and their music into the Blues Mass. He saw it as a chance to redefine the event, a changing of the guard. Enough with hippie passivity, punks were loud and aggressive, and far more radical. Eppelmann was very much opposed. But Postler—who, because of the Stasi's disapproval of his involvement with the punks, was still stuck in a studio apartment even though he had a wife and three children—won the day.

The scene at Erlöser Church that June of 1983 could hardly have been more different from the first big punk show in Halle. That had been a punk show pure and simple. It had also been inside the church. Here at the Blues Mass were what looked to be several thousand freaks and hippies, and the stage was outside in the churchyard, open-air. Jana watched as the hippies shook their long hair to a blues band playing before Namenlos. It sure as hell wasn't her thing, but then again Jana was too excited to pay much attention.

When Jana and Namenlos took the stage and ripped into their first song— *Mf... Mf... MfS... SS!*—the punks in the crowd surged forward and started to pogo. Many of the band's close friends were there and they sang along.

There were a lot of punks, but there were far more hippies, and unrest quickly spread through the crowd. Things started flying toward the stage— rocks and bottles and other projectiles.

A-Micha kept getting splashed with some sort of messy liquid—at first he thought the crowd was throwing tomatoes at the band. But no, it was bockwurst, which were exploding in greasy, watery bursts as they struck the stage and the band members.

"What is this shit?" people yelled from the crowd.

Most of the punks were bunched up toward the right side of the stage, a swirl of colorful hair, pogoing and shoving and loving the show. Toward the left of the stage were the older blues fans, most in the green parkas that were their uniform. In the middle, people started to skirmish. Fists started to fly.

Jana shrieked:

Minenfeld und Stacheldraht, damit sich niemand rüberwagt
Mauern und Elektrozaun, die tun uns hier die Freiheit klauen
Selbstschuss und ein Minenfeld, damit es uns hier gut gefällt
In unserem schönen Staat, in unserem schönen Staat

Minefields and barbed wire so nobody risks going over
Walls and electric fences, they're snatching away our freedom
Automatic firing devices and minefields so we like it here
In our beautiful country, in our beautiful country

More objects rained on stage. More shouts rang out. More fights erupted in the crowd.

Mita was loving it, reveling in the chaos. Her drums kept moving around, lurching away from her. She played on. Jana kept screaming lyrics and the band chugged on. A punk came out of the crowd and up on stage and danced alongside the band to offer support—and to block the projectiles whizzing through the air toward the band.

Namenlos played "Umweltlied," or "Environment Song." It went, in part:

Saurer Regen, toter Wald
Die Industrie vergast uns bald

Acid rain, dead forest
Industry will gas us soon

Finally, after four or five songs, a hippie climbed up on stage and addressed the crowd.

"Hey, you need to listen to the lyrics they're singing," he shouted. "They're saying the same things we say! Don't be like this! Listen to them!"

The situation improved somewhat after that, and the number of stones and bottles and bockwurst zinging past the band slowed. Still, it was a tough show, and Jana had to puff herself up and push quickly through the crowd afterward, trying not to betray the fact that she felt a bit crestfallen.

But then a girl came up to her as the next band, Planlos, was getting ready to start playing.

"That was so cool how you just kept going," she said. "That was so brave!"

"Thanks," said Jana.

For A-Micha, because of the animosity they had faced down, it had been the band's greatest show yet.

The gig functioned as a turning point for many in the crowd. A lot of kids were put off by the old blues fans' negative response to the punks and never returned to a Blues Mass; a lot of kids realized they might just be punks themselves.

Jana liked to think and write in images sometimes. As she looked back on the summer of punk, she saw communism as a building inside which a few people had managed to set up nice, comfortable rooms. Those people were Stasi people. And she pictured the lyrics of the band's songs as blows against the foundation of that building.

We're shaking the foundation.

We're a threat.

Jana wasn't so far from the truth. Longtime Stasi chief Erich Mielke was seething by this point. In fact, he now personally issued orders declaring all-out war on punk. *Härte gegen punk* was the command, which meant something like countering punk with relentlessness, severity. *Härte gegen Punk um Eskalation dieser Bewegung zu unterbinden*—Fight punk relentlessly in order to suppress the escalation of this movement. Mielke outlined the goals of his war on punk: to ferret out activities that could be punished with imprisonment; to identify and take action against the lyricists and composers of punk music groups; to find the connections between punks and the church, peace activists, environmental activists, "and other garbage," as well as any international connections the punks had. Finally, he wrote, "in the face of resistance, remove the kid gloves—we have no reason to treat these characters gently."

Mielke may have had enough, but A-Micha wasn't quite finished. To round out the summer of punk, A-Micha organized two more public actions. In July he took a group of punks to Oranienburg, where they had tried to lay a wreath at the nearby concentration camp in May. This time they put flowers at a memorial dedicated to anarchist writer Erich Mühsam, who was murdered at the concentration camp on July 10, 1934. The participants included other Open Work types in addition to punks—A-Micha had gotten to know more and more peace and environmental activists, in part because some of them were squatting in a building in Prenzlauer Berg near his own. Laying flowers to honor Mühsam was another moment when the different groups realized they shared goals, and older activists were forced to continue to take the punks more seriously.

Then on August 6, 1983, A-Micha rallied over 150 people to mark the thirty-eighth anniversary of the use of the atomic bomb on Hiroshima. Punks for peace. Many participants wore rubber masks, plastic bags, and goggles. And at the end of the unauthorized march they presented a plaque at Sophien Church in Mitte. A lot of these punks for peace were grabbed by the cops as they left the church grounds.

Interrogation time again.

Jana, Mita, A-Micha and their dog, Wotan, made their way safely away from the church, but at ten minutes to six they were nabbed near Alexanderplatz. They were held for several hours.

"The individuals were dressed as *punkers*," reported the arresting officers. "As a result of their decadent look an identity check was conducted. The individuals bore no resemblance to the photos in their identity papers."

The cops reported that they were mouthy, describing them as acting "fresh" and "provocative."

After so many arrests and interrogations, they were losing their fear; they knew this drill. If anything, they felt emboldened by the fact that the state seemed threatened by them.

This was getting fun.

29

On the morning of Thursday, August 11, 1983, Jana heard a knock at the door of her squatted apartment in Prenzlauer Berg.

It took a while for the sound to register. She and Mita had been out late partying the night before and had been in bed only a few hours. Mita had arranged to take the day off. Jana had simply skipped work again.

Today, Jana remembered, today they had scheduled a band meeting to discuss what to do if the Stasi came for them—or, as they had all pretty much acknowledged by now, *when* the Stasi came, not *if*.

MfS . . . SS.

"Come on in," called Jana groggily as the dog barked at the incessant knocking.

The door was never locked. In fact, usually their friends just came in without knocking. "It's open."

Nothing.

More knocks.

"I said it's open."

She didn't want to drag herself out of bed. She and Mita each had mattresses on the floor on either side of an old dresser they used as a sort of room divider. Mita was not stirring.

Jana just wanted to go back to sleep.

Wotan, their German shepherd, was now standing in front of the front door howling and growling and barking aggressively.

Jana finally stood up. The elastic band of her pajama bottoms was broken and she had to hoist them up as she staggered to the door. The dog ran to her and jumped around as she made her way to the door. She opened it.

Outside, two men and one woman. Obviously police of some kind, but in civilian clothes, not uniforms.

"*Kriminalpolizei.*"

Aha, police, criminal division.

Jana knew she didn't have to let them in, but then Wotan escaped her grasp and she scampered after the dog to try to calm him. The cops quickly slipped in before she could assert her rights and demand a warrant.

"You're going to have to come with us," they ordered. "*Klärung eines Sachverhaltes.*"

Mita had woken up by this point. Her face was covered with paint— someone had painted colorful geometric shapes all over her face at the party the night before.

Klärung eines Sachverhaltes? Jana and Mita were both struck by something when the cops said this. Normally you got a letter in the mail with the date and time you had to report to a police station when they wanted you to clear up some facts surrounding a case.

This is weird.

Then it began to dawn on them.

This could be about the band.

Their minds kicking quickly into gear, they asked to be allowed to take Wotan someplace where a friend could take care of him. If this was just to *clear something up*, then, well, they weren't being arrested, so the police shouldn't object to their looking after the dog, at least they hoped.

The cops pointed to Mita. She could take the dog to a friend's place.

The female officer and one of the male officers marched Jana out to an unmarked car and drove her to the detention center on Keibelstrasse, near Alexanderplatz.

They would interrogate her for the rest of the day.

Back at the apartment, the remaining officer told Mita to wash her face. When she was finished, she and Wotan climbed into another car and the officer drove them the few blocks down to Göhrener Strasse, to the Elias Church rectory, where A-Micha worked.

Mita stood in front and called up, trying to make sure as many people as possible heard her.

"Jana and I have to go down to Keibelstrasse to clear something up! Can someone come take the dog?"

Mita knew there were scraps of paper with lyrics, tape recordings of the band playing in their rehearsal space, photos, and all sorts of other potentially incriminating bits of evidence stashed around their apartment. She hoped that somebody would be clever enough to walk up there and get rid of it all. Maybe even A-Micha, if he hadn't yet been arrested.

A-Micha came down and took Wotan's leash. The officer did not recognize him.

"Okay, bye, have fun!" he said.

Then Mita got back into the Trabant. The officer started the little car with a puff of silvery black smoke and they rattled off down Prenzlauer Allee.

Take it all in, this could be the last time you see all of this for a while.

When they arrived at the detention center on Keibelstrasse, she snapped out of her reverie as they took her mugshots—front, both sides.

Then they gave her a piece of cloth and made her reach into her pants and wipe her crotch. They took the cloth from her with tongs and sealed it in a glass jar.

"We're taking a scent sample," they said.

Weird.

Then fingerprints.

When she asked to go to the bathroom, she was accompanied by an officer who didn't let her out of her sight.

Mita had never been through this before, despite being detained many times.

And then it was off to an interrogation.

Meanwhile A-Micha was still trying to figure out why exactly Jana and Mita were being taken in rather than receiving the usual letters. Namenlos bassist Frank had already been picked up, too, as had Kaiser of Planlos, whom the Stasi mistakenly thought played in Namenlos. It was two days before a major national holiday, A-Micha remembered. August 13 would mark the twenty-second anniversary of the building of the Berlin Wall and another year of successfully fending off capitalist aggression. The cops often rounded up punks before big public events to keep them out of sight and to confiscate their homemade buttons with embarrassing logos and phrases.

During his lunch break A-Micha took Wotan for a walk up to his apartment in the squatted building on Schliemannstrasse, just a few blocks from the church. A couple of punks from Erfurt were crashing at his place, and he needed to get them out of harm's way. He also didn't want them to see his hiding spaces for fear they would be interrogated. Once they were gone, he hid a few pieces of potentially damning evidence. There wasn't much—and he knew how to hide shit. A-Micha's best friend from elementary school—a guy he had even stolen and burned a DDR flag with—had been forced by his parents to go to work for the Stasi. The guy worked in a division that created spy toys for international operatives, things like books with hidden compartments to hide microfilm in for transportation across borders. A-Micha still trusted him, and he had taught A-Micha some great tricks, like removing a doorframe, creating a hiding space in the wall, then replacing the doorframe. Or digging holes beneath the floor stones of a building's basement and stashing things down there, always careful to re-smear the floor with coal dust and dirt.

After squaring things away at home, A-Micha went back to work at the church, scraping the old paint off the windowsills of the uppermost floor of the church building. A-Micha still felt there was a fifty–fifty shot that this was just the usual bullshit, a routine interrogation that would lead to nothing.

Shortly after three in the afternoon, A-Micha watched out the window as an unmarked Lada sedan pulled up. Two plainclothes officers got out and started looking around. A-Micha put down his palette knife and walked downstairs with Wotan in tow.

"Horschig, Micha?" asked one of the officers as A-Micha approached them.

"Yes."

"You're going to have to come with us."

A-Micha—and the dog—were put into the back of the car.

They drove to Keibelstrasse. A-Micha was taken inside, photographed, fingerprinted. As had happened to Mita, they handed him a piece of cloth and told him to shove it down his pants and rub it around. The scent sample was new to A-Micha, too, and like the others he began to realize that this might be serious.

They started to interrogate him just before five that afternoon.

This was a Department XX operation: *The breakup of the illegal punk music group Namenlos*, as the operation was described in Stasi records.

The shock and awe phase of the Stasi's war on punk was now underway.

The Summer of Punk was over.

30

A-Micha sat on a chair in the middle of the small room. The Stasi officer, a lieutenant, had his back to the window, silhouetted; it was difficult to see his face.

As part of a "procedure to investigate suspicious activity"—a particularly government-speak-sounding term, *Verdachtsprüfungshandlung*—"you will be subject to questioning."

A-Micha nodded.

"It is known to the investigative organ of the Ministry of State Security that on June 24, 1983, you appeared on the grounds of the Erlöser Church in Berlin-Rummelsburg. Comment on the circumstances of your activities there."

A-Micha was silent for a moment, then said, "I'm not prepared to make any comments on what I was doing on the grounds of the Erlöser Church."

He paused, looking at the stone-faced Stasi agent, then continued.

"I believe that first you are obligated to tell me why I am here being interrogated. I have nothing more to say."

The Stasi man started to show his anger, banging a fist on the desk, waving it threateningly in A-Micha's face. It was the first of many times that evening he thought he was going to be beaten.

"Let's try again," shouted the lieutenant.

It went like that until eight at night. Sometime after eight, A-Micha finally said, "Yeah, I was at the church, but I can't remember any crimes committed there."

The Stasi lieutenant: "What songs did you play there? Think carefully!"

When the lieutenant stepped out for a moment, A-Micha opened a light green folder on the desk and saw the lyrics of some of his songs typed out neatly.

Shit.

When the lieutenant returned, the interrogation continued.

"What songs did you and your friends perform on the stage on the grounds of the Erlöser Church? Answer the investigative organ!"

The Stasi man insisted the band had played seven songs. A-Micha said two.

"The investigative organ requests once again that you make truthful statements! What other songs did you and your friends perform on the stage at the Erlöser Church?"

The interrogation went on through the night. Eventually they had discussed five songs, the last of which was the MfS song—the one comparing the Stasi to Hitler's SS.

"You say the security organs of the DDR surveil the populace. On what basis do you make this assertion?"

Fuck it, thought A-Micha. He'd been heading for this moment since the day Major had been arrested in 1981.

"As far as I'm concerned, the populace is barred from the freedom of expression by the Stasi. Like me. I've been arrested even though all I did was openly speak my mind."

The Stasi officer sneered back: "What is your understanding of 'freedom of expression?'"

"I understand freedom of expression to mean the presentation of my own thoughts—and it doesn't matter whether those thoughts are for or against the interests of the DDR."

It was 4:30 a.m.

A-Micha was led to a prison cell, where he slumped onto the wooden slab that was the bed.

He was awoken about three hours later. Two officers entered his cell.

Finally, I can go home.

He knew they would need the consent of a judge to continue to hold him.

"You are being transferred," said one of the officers, "to a pretrial detention center."

They held up a warrant, signed by a judge early that morning: "Together with three other persons Horschig performed lyrics during a concert as a 'punk music group' that portrayed the societal conditions of the DDR as unfree and slandered the Ministry of State Security as a surveillance organ."

A-Micha was admitted to the prison in Pankow at 9 a.m. on August 12, 1983. Aside from his clothes, his only possessions were a cloth sack, four cigarettes, six safety pins, and a homemade button that said, in German, DESTROY WHAT'S DESTROYING YOU.

He would spend the next six months in pretrial detention in cell 59R, subject to daily interrogation.

31

After the scent sample, photographs, and fingerprints were finished, Mita was rushed around the building on Keibelstrasse and eventually seated opposite a Stasi officer in an interrogation room.

Stasi officer: "Describe the progress of your personal development to this point."

Mita: "I don't understand what this has to do with clearing up any facts of a case and as a result will not answer."

Stasi: "You are advised that for the assessment of the relevant facts of a case, under the criminal procedure regulations of the DDR, information about personal development must also be gathered."

Mita: "Despite this order I will not answer the question."

It's not like I'm a freedom fighter or something, I'm a drummer.

The interrogation continued.

Stasi: "What are your musical interests?"

Mita: "I like to play drums, which I taught myself to play. I own a drum kit."

Stasi: "In what form do you practice your drums?"

Mita: "I play alone mostly, or sometimes with other people. But I will not make any statement about other people."

Stasi: "In what public performances have you taken part?"

Mita: "Up to now I have appeared only in church spaces, where the freedom exists to do things spontaneously."

Mita explained that she had played at a Blues Mass.

Stasi: "What songs were performed by you and others at the Blues Mass?"

Mita: "I won't say anything about song titles, I have no comment. I have the right to refuse to talk."

Stasi: "Be advised that alongside the right to refuse to talk you have a civic legal duty to cooperate in the clearing up of a possible criminal offense. You are therefore asked again to answer the question!"

Mita: "I have no statement to make to the question posed."

Mita was interrogated three times that first day, August 11, 1983: from 10:40 a.m. to 1:30 p.m., from 2:30 p.m. to 8:00 p.m., and from 9:30 p.m. to 12:20 a.m.

Since the other band members were being simultaneously interrogated, their apartments were being searched, and other information was being brought to bear, the interrogators learned more and more specifics during the course of the day. The questions circled back, and the questioner kept adding additional info to show how much he knew. Mita realized the Stasi had apparently had observers at the Blues Mass. At one stage, her interrogator started to quote from lyrics of the MfS song . . . *SS!*

Stasi officer: "Why did you take part in the performance of the aforementioned song?"

Mita: "I took part in the performance of the song about the MfS by playing drums because I like to play music and I had the possibility to do that at the Blues Mass. And besides, the aforementioned lyrics are accurate."

Mita simply rejected much of the rest of the questioning.

Stasi: "It is further known to the investigative organ that you, together with other persons, performed songs with the titles *'Alptraum'* ['Nightmare'] and *'Friedenslied'* ['Peace Song'] at the Blues Mass. Comment on this!"

Mita: "I refuse to comment."

Stasi: "For what reason do you refuse to comment?"

Mita: "I refuse to comment about *that*. I have nothing more to say to the question."

Stasi: "What other public performances did you take part in?"

Mita: "I have nothing to say about that."

Stasi: "Why don't you have anything to say about that?"

Mita: "I have nothing to say about that."

Stasi: "Who among you wrote the lyrics of the aforementioned song?"

Mita: "I have nothing to say about that."

Stasi: "How did your hairstyle come about?"

Mita: "I have nothing to say about that."

Stasi: "Since when have you been living on Stargarder Strasse?"

Mita: "I have nothing to say about that. I'm tired."

Stasi: "Why do you refuse to answer even easy personal questions?"

Mita: "I have nothing to say about that."

At the end of the marathon sessions, Mita had to sign a typed, condensed transcript of the various interrogations, and then she was led to a cell to sleep for a few hours. Mita was still seven months removed from her eighteenth birthday—a minor.

32

The next day, August 12, Mita, too, was transferred to pretrial detention in the prison in Pankow. When she was admitted, she had in addition to her clothes—described as "ripped" in the official inventory—four marks and fifty-one pfennigs, and a pair of leather cuffs.

She was rushed upstairs, this way, that way, hands behind your back, *halt!* Mita was disoriented and trying to remember a few things her mother had told her to keep in mind if arrested.

This way, *halt!*

A door.

"Come in."

Mita and her interrogator shook hands.

"Guten Tag."

"Be advised," the officer began when her interrogations continued at the new facility, explaining the protocol by rote, "that preliminary proceedings as a result of urgent suspicion of criminal acts pursuant to Paragraph 220 are being initiated against you by the Ministry for State Security."

Paragraph 220 of the East German penal code was a legal holdover from the Nazi era. It functioned as one of several catch-all clauses frequently employed against what in the West would be called political crimes; the paragraph made slandering the system illegal—a malleably vague crime that carried up to a three-year jail sentence.

Mita had to repeat this back to the officer: "I have been advised that pre-liminary proceedings . . . "

Mita tried to remember her mother's advice.

"I want to ask who has been notified of my arrest," she said.

Stasi: "Your mother."

Mita: "And who will I be allowed to speak to?"

Stasi: "Also your mother, but that will be a while yet."

And then it began again.

Stasi: "For what reason did you, together with other persons, perform a song at a Blues Mass the contents of which warned the attendant audience to be wary of the Ministry of State Security?"

Mita: "The content of the aforementioned song is in my opinion simply a statement and not slander."

Stasi: "Why did you, together with other persons, publicly urge the audi-ence members to be wary of the MfS through the aforementioned song?"

Mita: "I publicly urged wariness of the MfS in the MfS song because if for no other reason you can be detained just for saying it. Because if you mention facts, suddenly, like me, your whole life can change. That does not constitute ideological freedom to me."

Stasi: "Who else took part in the performance of the song at the Blues Mass?"

Mita: "I will not comment on that."

And so it went, day after day. But never in a pattern that Mita could get used to or anticipate. For some stretches there would be interrogations all day every day, then suddenly they might not take her from her cell for a week. The point was to keep her on edge.

And night after night back in her cell, the worst food she had ever tasted shoved through a trapdoor, the footsteps of the guards in the hall, com-mands shouted through the door.

Mita spent three days in isolation, then had a series of cellmates. The sec-ond cellmate, Luise, had participated in a candlelight peace vigil in front of the U.S. embassy; she was in jail for only a week but sobbed inconsolably the entire time—she had small children on the outside and didn't know what would happen to them. Mita hated her third cellmate, Christa, a woman arrested on Alexanderplatz for standing around with a sign that said I WANT TO GO TO THE WEST. Mita suspected they put Christa in the cell just to piss Mita off. It worked.

By late August, the Stasi was trying to assemble a detailed picture of Mita's background and beliefs. In describing her childhood, Mita talked about how much she disliked the fact that she could be labeled an "enemy of the state" by leaders of the communist youth organizations just for speaking her mind. She went on to say that she wanted to be free to live the way she wanted to live as opposed to having to live according to rules and regulations and prescribed paths, and she wanted to dress however she felt like and wear her hair however she liked.

They began to press her for details of her connections within the church, asking her about events she had attended over the years and people she had met, asking who had arranged the Namenlos gigs and where the instruments had come from, probing, probing, probing, and Mita always parrying, never giving more information than the questioner revealed in his questions.

Still, the interrogators knew so much: they showed her photos of the Namenlos gigs in Halle and Karl-Marx-Stadt, they asked her about specific visits she had paid over the years to ministers and deacons in Berlin. They seemed to know everything about her and the band.

Then in late August, the authorities decided to give Mita—a minor—a psychological exam to decide whether she could be held criminally liable for her actions. They drove her in a closed prison van to a hospital on the outskirts of town, where she spent the day with a doctor, talking, playing clinical games, taking tests. The doctor determined that Mita had experienced an unusually high level of individual freedom in her household growing up. And despite an IQ test that established Mita had genius-level intelligence, the doctor described her as child-like and naïve, arguing that she wasn't able to understand the gravity of her situation. While acknowledging her "superb" intelligence, he argued that her intelligence was untrained and poorly developed. For various reasons, including her extremely anti-authoritarian upbringing, her personal development was *retardiert*—"retarded"—and her understanding of the world lagged approximately four years behind her numerical age.

Instead of a punk, the doctor wrote in his report for the Stasi, Mita was a "babypunk." Mita, the doctor concluded, should not be held responsible for her actions in a court of law.

After seven weeks in custody, Mita was released. And in December, the Stasi would officially drop the case against seventeen-year-old Mita based on the psychological assessment, though they maintained the veracity of the facts of the case—namely, that together with a punk music group Mita had slandered the state as well as the practices of state organs.

The Stasi continued to interrogate her three fellow band members and would take them to trial.

Härte gegen punk!

They would make the other three pay.

33

Like A-Micha and Mita, Jana hadn't been too worried when the police took her down to Keibelstrasse that morning of August 11, 1983. They all knew the day would come when they would be hauled in by *die Firma*, the company—another nickname for the Stasi.

When her interrogator began to pepper Jana with questions, she figured it was pointless to deny the basic facts. It wasn't that she shared A-Micha's compulsion to tell the truth—for A-Micha it was always ideological—but it was assumed that the Stasi had informers everywhere, including inside church-based events, so certainly they must have known about the gigs. Yes, she admitted, they had played songs at the Erlöser Church . . . *peace* songs, she said.

She figured if she gave a little she could avoid spending the next day listening to officers shouting "We know you're lying! We know you were there!" And then, she figured, she'd be released again anyway, since otherwise they would need a proper arrest warrant.

Like the others, Jana was interrogated all day and late into the night.

Stasi: "What about the way your parents live do you disagree with?"

Jana: "I would describe my parents as sticks-in-the-mud. Even though they are relatively young, they never go out, they just sit in front of the TV night after night. They've never tried to make anything out of their lives. And they expect the same of me."

During one of the breaks she heard a familiar voice wafting in the window. Was that . . . Kaiser, the bass player from Planlos? Sure enough, it was, she could tell as Kaiser started to lecture his interrogator on England and the history of punk, all full of enthusiasm. Kaiser was such a music fan, she thought, as his voice echoed and she tried to have a peek at the files on her own interrogator's desk while she was alone. Then she realized: *They got the wrong bass player! They think he's with Namenlos!*

At another point she heard a cough—through the window? out in the hallway?—that she recognized as A-Micha's. So he was here now, too.

The interrogation resumed.

Stasi: "Why did you become part of the 'punk scene' in the DDR?"

Jana: "What I'd like to say about that is that I feel very comfortable as a punk. I like to wear punk clothes because it's fun . . . And since, in my opinion, I am discriminated against by the DDR as a result of my outward appearance, a certain amount of aggression has built up inside me over time . . . I sing to let off steam . . . I'd just had it with all the harassment by the police and the Stasi."

After her long day and night of interrogation, Jana was marched to a cell, told to remove her shoelaces, and locked in for the night.

Early the next morning they unexpectedly presented her with the arrest warrant, and quickly marched her out to a van with six tiny cells built into it. She caught a glimpse of the other band members as she was shoved into the van—they had now apparently apprehended the correct bass player, Frank Masch. They were all driven up to the pretrial detention center in Pankow. It was difficult to tell how long the ride took when jammed into the tiny mobile jail cell, her knees aching in the dark.

Fear and panic were starting to seize her.

As the interrogations began again at the new facility, she began to worry about Wotan, the dog. The last she knew, the dog had been delivered to A-Micha, but A-Micha was now somewhere in this same prison.

"What happened to the dog—does somebody have the dog? Where is he now?"

Aha, her interrogator realized, the dog was important to Jana.

"If you cooperate with us, you'll be out soon enough and you can see your dog again," said the Stasi officer.

Jana was never going to cooperate, but the Stasi interrogator now continuously applied subtle and not-so-subtle pressure on her based on the dog. They'd found a soft spot in the otherwise steely eighteen-year-old, and they exploited it for weeks and then months.

Jana had a friend who'd been convicted of hooliganism a while back and had been sentenced to six months—that, in her mind, was still the worst-case scenario; there was no way she'd get more than that for some silly songs. But then her pretrial detainment stretched to three, four, five months, and she realized she was facing something more serious, maybe the talk of years in prison wasn't just bluster, maybe she really was going to be shut away for years. *Years.*

Her interrogations concentrated on the song lyrics. The words of the songs, who wrote which lines, who sang various parts. Nearly every interrogation covered the same material, but the interrogators always had more and more information. Jana, who had tried to reimagine the songs with lyrics about peace and pass those off as authentic, couldn't figure out where the additional details were coming from. Did they have recordings they were transcribing? Were her bandmates admitting things?

Prison was slowly crushing Jana's spirit. There was nothing to do, nothing to divert her attention from her immediate surroundings. A few times she called out through the ventilation ducts and was able to hear A-Micha's voice from the floor below—they exchanged an occasional *"Gute Nacht"* or "I love you"—but that was strictly verboten, and when she got caught she was thrown in an isolation chamber in the cold wet basement of the prison.

Jana had requested deacon Lorenz Postler as her designated visitor. That was denied. Since she had direct relatives, she had to designate one of them. She resigned herself to monthly visits from her mother.

Every few weeks, they moved Jana to a different cell. Her second cellmate had just tried to kill herself by slitting her wrists with the square end of a toothpaste tube. The woman cried all the time.

I can't take this.

I'm going to lose it.

And Jana did. One day she couldn't hold it inside any longer. She started throwing things around the cell and screaming—slamming chairs against the cell door, "Get me out of here! Let me out, you pigs!"

Down to the basement. Things were bad, but there was always something worse looming. Like this, the isolation chamber, cold and wet.

The only breaks were the interrogations, and since her interrogator didn't get physical or scream, she began to see him as a human being. Not that it changed her strategy. But as perverse as it seemed, she sometimes looked forward to the change of pace—march to the interrogation room, face the wall, hands behind your back, come in; a different room, a different face, a conversation, no matter how trying and fraught with danger.

And through it all, the dog, always the dog.

Wouldn't you like to see Wotan?

In the end, the Stasi figured out the real lyrics of six Namenlos songs that had been performed at the Blues Mass at the Erlöser Church. Among them: the MfS song and *"Nazis wieder in Ostberlin,"* or "Nazis back in East Berlin."

Then an odd thing happened: unbeknownst to each other, both Jana and A-Micha claimed to have authored all the songs in their entirety—each was trying to shield the other.

The Stasi decided to take both to a joint interrogation, where the two of them—in the presence of an interrogator—agreed to tell the truth about who had done what.

But then, on November 9, 1983, a new piece of evidence suddenly emerged. Somehow the Stasi had uncovered a seventh song, with the complete lyrics. And it was a cracker. The song was their *"Lied über die Staatsgrenze,"* or "Border Song."

Minefields and barbed wire so nobody risks going over
Walls and electric fences, they're snatching away our freedom
Automatic firing devices and minefields so we like it here
In our beautiful country, in our beautiful country

Where the fuck did they get that, Jana wondered. This was actionable material. The Stasi knew it. Jana knew it.

She was led to believe that bassist Frank Masch had coughed up the song lyrics as part of some kind of deal. In actuality, Frank shared A-Micha's urge to be honest about the material, and in the end, out of frustration, he had simply confirmed lyrics the Stasi had already figured out. There had been no deal: he would stand trial alongside A-Micha and Jana.

There was no way for Jana to know it then, but she would never see her beloved dog again. Wotan had long since been killed by the Stasi.

34

Jana, A-Micha, and Frank were cuffed and taken to court on February 2, 1984. The trial was closed to the public, but that morning Mita went and stood on the stairs inside the municipal courthouse in Pankow. She managed to touch Jana's hand before she disappeared into the courtroom with the others. A few other friends of the band had also gathered. They waved and shouted to Jana, A-Micha, and Frank as they passed by.

The months between her own release and the trial had been tough for Mita. In fact, she wished she'd never been let out. She had cried for weeks, overwhelmed with depression; she worried that people might think she had turned on her friends or agreed to become a Stasi informant in exchange for an early release.

Behind the closed doors of the courtroom, the trial progressed quickly, despite hectoring from pro-punk minister Georg Katzorke, of Elias Church, who had been granted admission to the trial. Eventually the judge ordered Katzorke to be removed from the courtroom. He refused to go quietly and had to be carried out.

Fortunately for the band, the Stasi had never been able to establish hard evidence that Jana had sung the offending "SS" in the "MfS song"—the rest of the song's lyrics were bad enough, but at least they escaped being accused of making a direct comparison between Honecker's security forces and Hitler's. Likewise, they had been able to convince the interrogators that "Nazis back in East Berlin" was about right-wing activity among youth, not a direct comparison of the East German Socialist Unity Party to the Third Reich's NSDAP. In the eyes of the authorities, however, there was another ideological problem with the song: "East Berlin" did not exist in government speak. The region was officially referred to as "the capital of the DDR," not merely a sector of a larger city.

The trial lasted just one day.

The defense lawyer limited his argument to protestations about Jana, A-Micha, and Frank's youth, impulsiveness and political immaturity. *They didn't know any better.* This wouldn't have been A-Micha's argument at all. He *did* know better—he just believed they should be allowed to say these things.

We are the people, thought A-Micha. *That's what this is all about.*

Jana tried to stand up and assert her right to defend herself, but she wasn't able to get a word in. After a while she sat back down. In the jumble of meaningless words she heard blathered, one stood out, one she heard often throughout that day: "decadent."

In the end, the three band members could do nothing more than snicker grimly among themselves—clearly the trial was a joke. Eventually A-Micha started openly laughing at the proceedings.

The trial adjourned in the afternoon. Jana, A-Micha, and Frank were split up again and taken back to prison. The next morning they returned and the judge asked them to stand as he read the decision. They laughed. Their lawyer poked A-Micha in the back and whispered, "Stop laughing! Now! Stop it!"

The verdict: *Guilty.*

Then came the prison sentences.

The accused Masch, Frank: one year.

The judge elaborated: even though Frank had asserted in court that he stood behind the band's lyrics, it was important to the judge that he hadn't sung or written them and had just played bass on the "so-called songs."

The accused Schlosser, Jana: a year and a half.

A-Micha, aka the accused Horschig, Micha: a year and a half.

By comparison, peace activists Reinhard Schult, prosecuted in 1979, and Hans-Jörg Weigel, prosecuted in 1980, received, respectively, an eight-month sentence and eighteen months of probation. Bärbel Bohley and

Ulrike Poppe, the founders of Women for Peace who had been arrested on December 12, 1983, were released after only six weeks, on January 25, 1984—by then Jana, A-Micha, and Frank had already been in detention for five months and their trial hadn't even begun.

Such a long time, thought Jana, *I'll never make it.*

And that was before she saw the prison—the notorious women's prison at Hoheneck, a facility for political prisoners built partially out of a sixteenth-century hunting lodge in Saxony, several hours south of Berlin.

Pretrial detention was one thing; Hoheneck was another. She knew that much. And she was afraid. *Will it be worse?*

It was worse.

Cash-strapped East Germany used prison labor to earn Western currency, forcing inmates—whether political prisoners like Jana, or common criminals—to work for international firms like Ikea, as well as a range of major West German companies. At first Jana welcomed the chance to get out of her cell. But she eventually drew a night shift, working eight hours through the night until 6:30 a.m., at which point she was sometimes forced to stay awake another hour for an official count of the inmates at 7:30 a.m. One morning, a guard got upset in the cafeteria during breakfast, which was served at the end of the night shift.

"Kommando 1, it is too noisy in here!"

The prisoners were marched back to their cells and told to stand and wait to be counted at roll call.

Fuck this.

Jana lay down on her bed. A couple of others did the same.

Let them come into the cell and count me.

When the guards announced roll call, the other prisoners went out dutifully. Jana and her cellmates did not. The guards locked the rest of the prisoners in a giant shower chamber and then used rubber truncheons to forcibly get Jana and the others out of bed. They accused Jana of inciting mutiny, but the other women insisted they had laid down of their own volition.

Still, Jana spent twenty-one days in isolation.

Hoheneck was worse than she had ever imagined.

35

Planlos, one of the last major bands standing, was collapsing in on itself. The band felt surrounded, paranoid, pressure seemed to be mounting all around; friends kept disappearing into prison, kept being deposited in West Germany, kept being drafted into the army. Everyone in the scene was convinced another guy, Schmitti, had actually been murdered by the Stasi—he had been run down in the street by a Wartburg sedan on his eighteenth birthday. He had told friends that his parents, both of whom worked for the Stasi, had warned him that he wouldn't live to see eighteen if he kept at the punk thing. The driver of the car was never apprehended.

During a recent detainment, Kobs had first heard about Stasi plans to liquidate the punk scene. *Härte gegen punk*, straight from the top.

After the Stasi raid on their basement rehearsal space on Metzer Strasse over the last summer, the band considered the space burned. No way could they continue to work on songs there with the kinds of lyrics they wrote—they figured the place was probably bugged now, and they knew the Stasi would redouble their efforts to get hard evidence against the band.

Some of their gear drifted a few blocks down the road to a squat on Fehrbelliner Strasse, just across Senefelder Platz from Metzer. The building was full of church activists. Planlos's gear would end up in the apartment of a guy named Aljoscha, who had both East German and Swiss passports and was a fixture in the social scene of bohemian Prenzlauer Berg. His place was a party hub frequented by a lot of musicians, including punks.

Interpersonal tensions created an even bigger problem for Planlos than the loss of their rehearsal space. At some stage after Pankow's release from detention back in June, his girlfriend Nase had told him that she had agreed to work with the Stasi in order to save his skin. She had been hauled in during his detention, interrogated, and, after being told Pankow would otherwise go to jail for three years, signed a written pledge to become an IM.

That's what saved me from jail!

It suddenly made sense to Pankow.

He was grateful. Beyond grateful. And of course, Nase wasn't really going to inform on her boyfriend or other punks. She wasn't like Pankow's meddling neighbors and never would be. Nase had agreed to be a Stasi source for only one reason: to spare Pankow prison. She figured that if she just told everyone in the scene that she had agreed to be an IM, nobody would discuss potentially sensitive information around her. That way, even if she came under pressure during meetings with her handler, she wouldn't know anything damaging. It was a smart way out. Basically, you burned yourself.

The problem was, you had to trust someone absolutely to believe that he or she would be able to function as a burned asset given the ferocity of the Stasi's efforts to crush punk. And while Pankow trusted Nase with his life at that point—after all, she had saved it—the rest of the band members didn't necessarily share his absolute trust. They understood she wasn't a willing aid to the Stasi, but there was too much risk.

They asked Pankow to split up with her.

Pankow refused: "She fucking saved me from prison!"

Tension rose.

The friction brought other issues to the surface as well. Pankow had always suspected that Lade still wanted to be the singer. Now, everyone on edge, paranoia overwhelming them all, Pankow began to worry that Lade was manipulating the other members to get rid of him so he could front the band again.

As the cloud of paranoia and mutual distrust continued to darken, Pankow remembered something else. Maybe for Lade, it wasn't just about being the singer? Back when Pankow and Lade had shared a squatted apartment, they'd had a late-night conversation about the future of the band. At that point, they'd had only one old mattress in the empty apartment, and they sometimes lay next to each other talking in the pitch-black room. They could talk seriously in that setting, but they also tried to crack each other up. And one night, Pankow remembered, Lade had suggested the band try to get an *Einstufung*—the government-mandated license that legalized amateur music groups and allowed them, among other things, to play in officially sanctioned venues.

Pankow assumed at the time that Lade was joking. He joked back about the idea of collaborating with the enemy: "Yeah, great idea! Cool, let's audition for an *Einstufung*!"

"Pankow, I'm serious," said Lade.

"Ha, ha," said Pankow, "Hilarious. But that's enough of that shit."

Lade began to talk about subverting the system from within, about infiltrating the state structures and using the system against itself.

"Are you crazy?" Pankow said, starting to get angry. "I'm not doing a fucking *Einstufung*. Never!"

Pankow never forgot Lade's final sentence at the end of the fight.

"Pankow, you're going to wind up in the gutter."

Pankow thought he knew what was behind Lade's attitude. Lade's home situation had been perhaps even worse than his own. Lade wanted to get out and make something of himself. In the fall of 1983, that conversation kept coming back to Pankow and, in his paranoia, he wondered whether Lade wanted to get him out of the band so he could convince the others to become licensed musicians. These were Pankow's best friends, and he was now questioning the foundations of their friendship.

The Stasi had already succeeded.

Finally, with the band at a standstill that fall, mutual animosity simmering and tempers flaring, Lade called a band meeting at Café Mosaik on Prenzlauer Allee—one of the Prenzlauer Berg cafés frequented by bohemian types. Lade was the only band member to speak. He gave Pankow one more chance: leave Nase because she's with the Stasi, or you're out of the band.

Fuck you guys.

Pankow got up and stormed out. It would be a long time before he spoke to any of the other guys again.

Planlos was dead.

By hook or by crook. The Stasi's plans tended to work, one way or another. Sometimes sowing suspicion and paranoia was enough. Sometimes it was more effective than having an IM. Sometimes you didn't even need an IM, or a committed IM. Sometimes suspicion and paranoia could be conjured out of thin air, using rumors or false clues, using threats real or imagined, real or intimated, real or fabricated.

The breakup hardly mattered anyway. Lade and Kobs were drafted into the army in November 1983. Pankow's draft orders followed a few months later. Kaiser had a medical deferment.

Lade told his mother he wasn't going to report for duty. He was going to go AWOL. His mother sobbed and begged.

You'll ruin the whole family.

Lade finally relented, and agreed to report.

Kobs, too, reported, to a National People's Army barrack north of Berlin.

At the gate to the base, a smiling major greeted Kobs: "How nice that you're with us now, Herr Kobs."

He knows my name?

This was the on-site Stasi agent.

Kobs soon learned that he had been assigned to a battalion for rehabilitating politically wayward citizens—about half the battalion had been busted trying to escape the country. There were also a few other punks.

Kobs's army experiences confirmed everything he'd always thought about the hypocrisy in the DDR. His unit was shipped up to the Baltic Sea coast at one point. They were officially tasked with helping build a new military port project. But the officers also wanted dachas built for themselves. So a portion of all the building materials and the heavy machinery was used each weekend to erect vacation homes for the bigwigs.

One day, Kobs received a letter from Lade.

In addition to telling stories of how awful it had been at his base, Lade wanted Kobs to promise one thing: that after the army they would pick up right where they'd left off.

Kobs wrote back. He promised.

But it was not to be.

36

The minor city of Weimar lies 140 miles south of Berlin. It is in Thüringen, one of Germany's least populous states. Even in Thüringen, there are half a dozen cities larger than Weimar; it has only around 60,000 inhabitants. In the early 1980s, it was a sleepy East German hamlet, soot-covered and gray.

Weimar may have been a provincial backwater, but it, too, had seen punk infest the local youth scene. There was something about the rush of rebellion—it was *fun* to provoke. Still, being a punk in a place like Weimar was seriously tough. In small towns, the police often knew kids' parents, and for kids who stuck out, there just wasn't enough space to be able to disappear the way you could in Berlin or Leipzig.

That didn't stop a group of six Weimar teens from carrying out a daring protest in the fall of 1983.

One of them was Grit Ferber, who had bright dyed-red hair and black fingernails. Grit was waifish and breezily social, quick to laugh and just as quick to make a smart-ass comment. Grit's problems with authority had started when she was thirteen, when she had dared to question her mandatory membership in a German–Soviet Friendship Society. Up to then she'd been a good little girl, and was in fact the officially recognized "spokesman" of her middle school class. Her grades were good, too: out of ninety kids in her middle school class, only the top three were chosen to enter a university-track high school—and Grit was one of them. But there she had continued to *ask questions*. She'd been brought up by her parents—a nurse and an engineer—to speak her mind, to say what she thought, but now that Grit had *different* thoughts, nobody wanted her to open her mouth.

Grit had fallen in with a group of black-clad punk friends: Holm, Andreas, Ulrich, Jörn, and Thomas Onisseit, whose older brother, Jürgen, played in a local punk band. Though none of them was religious, they'd met at church gatherings—gatherings that included music, cigarettes, and enough rotgut wine to get a buzz on.

In December 1981, most of the kids from the church group had attended the first real punk concert in the state of Thüringen, a performance by three bands in the crumbling Johannes-Lang-Haus, a church hall in Erfurt. One of the bands was Schleim-Keim, who blew the roof off the place. Almost literally. The local minister sweated and pleaded with the crowd to stop pogoing because he feared the ceiling might collapse. The Weimar teens had never seen or heard anything like Schleim-Keim's Otze: wearing his EAT SHIT T-shirt, Otze played drums, spat, and barked insanely hostile lyrics about spies and cops with an incandescent rage that ignited the church hall.

The group of friends began to experience the usual punk problems— aside from constant harassment from the local citizenry, all five of the boys were expelled from school. Grit was allowed to continue, but was ordered to attend a meeting with a school administrator only to walk in and find Stasi men there instead.

"If you continue to do this—" they began. Grit waited for them to say she'd get kicked out of school. But they didn't. What they said was "—you'll end up in jail."

Grit had been slated to graduate in spring of 1983, hoping to go off to university afterward. Instead, she was damned as "politically immature" at her graduation ceremony, called to the podium last, shamed, and then denied entry to university. In the fall of 1983 she began a training program to become a gardener in the city's cemeteries—it was the only option open to her.

Grit lived a little outside the central part of town, and by 1983, whenever she walked into town she'd be stopped along the way.

"Ah, Frau Ferber, show us your papers, please."

"Why?" she asked the police officers. "You obviously know who I am."

Eventually they revoked her national identification card and replaced it with a PM 12. Up to then, neither Grit nor the rest of her friends considered themselves very political. But they started to develop a feeling in their guts that certain things were very wrong with their society, and this feeling slowly morphed into something like political sentiment—the kind of political sentiment most people were afraid to speak aloud.

And so, as the cold of autumn settled on Weimar in 1983, the black-clad gang—Thomas and Ulrich, eighteen years old, Grit, also eighteen, and Jörn, Holm, and Andreas, all still seventeen—began to think about taking action.

All we do at the church meetings is sit around talking. We want to do more than just sit there, talking.

They all felt that the church groups were doing too little.

Let's do something concrete, something public.

It's not like they were trying to destroy the country singlehandedly, but they wanted to push things along, they wanted something to happen. It drove them nuts that everyone complained but never openly. That hypocrisy made Grit and Thomas and the gang sick.

Let's do something concrete, something public.

Risk assessment fell to Grit. As they sat together and brainstormed things they could do, she would figure out the penalties they might incur if caught.

Hmm, if we do that, we could get five years. We should think it over. Maybe it's not the best idea.

Then in September 1983, Thomas had brought a new book to share with the group. He'd bought it in a local bookstore. The book, *Zürich, Anfang September*, was by a Swiss author named Reto Hänny and had originally been published in the West in 1981. The edition Thomas bought had been republished by a DDR press called Volk und Welt. The book told the story of the protests, riots, and police violence that followed the Zurich city government flip-flopping on a pledge to convert a former opera house into a youth center.

Apparently, Thomas had realized, the East German censorship agency saw the story as illustrating the evils of the West. DDR officials had obviously seen it as a chance to show how Western youth were suppressed.

They're too blind to see any parallels to their own situation.

The rest of the group found the book equally fascinating, and they kept going back to pages about the slogans protesters had spray-painted on walls around Zurich. Then suddenly they realized, *We could do the same thing here!*

They had tried to reach out to likeminded people in other parts of the country to create a nationwide event of some kind. But that sort of thing was tough with no reliable or secure means of communication. Scattershot word-of-mouth messages made coordinating things with any precision virtually impossible. Who could you trust? But here was something they could do locally, for now, to make a statement at the very least, to move forward, to show up the fangless church groups sitting around talking, talking, talking.

This is it.

This is action.

Public action.

Rummaging through the basements of their apartment buildings, they turned up a few used spray cans. They began making little runs that same month. Different groups of three or four of them went out in the dead of night, wearing gloves. A couple of them sprayed jagged anarchist circle-As here and there as another kept watch. There was never a plan of attack—they just wandered the mute, blackened streets. At the end of each run the sprayers dropped the empty paint cans into the sewer system, taking home no hard evidence of their activities.

The message during those first few weeks was merely implied: *We are here, motherfuckers, we are here.*

On Thursday, October 6, the eve of the thirty-fourth anniversary of the founding of the DDR, a national day of celebration, of parades and speeches, they set out again to festoon the facades of the city with slogans that would make the following day worth celebrating *for them.* These would be cries of protest, war cries—even if awkwardly scrawled and dripping.

The six of them crept through the center of town, aimed the spray cans, and left their statements for all to see in lurid orange letters, obscenely slithering, awkwardly scrawled on the walls of this little town:

STRIKE BACK

BE REALISTIC, DEMAND THE IMPOSSIBLE

DEFEND YOURSELF

ACTIVE RESISTANCE

They also sprayed a word that had already become a sort of shorthand political slogan throughout the East Bloc:

SOLIDARITY

It was a great night, full of adventure, punk-rock action, and real rebellion instead of *blah blah blah*. And, truth be told, they were more than a little proud of themselves. Before they dropped the paint cans into the sewer, they added one last message:

YOU WILL NEVER FIND OUT WHO IT WAS

That turned out to be wishful thinking.

The police started hauling people in the next morning, Friday, October 7, the national holiday. The six sprayers' recent activites were an open secret among their peers. But by Monday, over a hundred people had already been questioned and still nobody had squealed.

As the six sprayers were quietly congratulating themselves at a café on Monday afternoon, their confidence boosted that they would get away with it, everything was about to change for them. But the information that would break the case wasn't being coerced out of some casual acquaintance of theirs. It came from Jürgen Onisseit, Thomas's brother. And Jürgen wasn't at the police station at all. He was in the Stasi's local headquarters, sitting across the desk from one of their hated operatives. Jürgen was a punk, too, but this was no interrogation. The Stasi man's face was familiar to Jürgen: he was, in fact, Jürgen's handler. Jürgen told his Stasi handler that Ulrich and his friends were responsible for the graffiti. He didn't mention his brother Thomas's name, but it was obvious Thomas, too, would get caught—he was one of Ulrich's closest buddies. Afterward Jürgen took a clutch of East German marks and left. It would be many, many years before anyone in the punk scene—or the Onisseit family—realized what Jürgen was: a paid Stasi snitch.

By Monday evening Thomas, Grit, Ulrich, and Holm had all been arrested. They spent the night being interrogated; the next morning they were marched out to an unmarked van with the same six tiny cells inside. They were unable to see each other and ordered not to speak. The van started up and drove around for—who knew how long? They lost all sense of orientation after the first few turns in the windowless van.

Finally the van lurched, made a few tight turns, and stopped.

They had arrived. Somewhere.

Uniformed guards pulled them out one by one, all handcuffed except Grit. This pissed Grit off, since she considered herself every bit as threatening as any of the boys.

The four of them found themselves inside a loading bay of some sort, with the bay doors shut behind the van so they couldn't see outside at all. They were marched through a door that led from the loading bay into an adjoining building. They were separated.

Grit had to strip. She was given a full body search in a room full of male and female guards.

"Bend over," they said.

"Spread your legs," they said.

Her clothes and belongings were taken out of the room.

They presented her with a form to sign—something about wearing institutional clothing. She was still naked.

"I don't want to sign this," she said. "Let me have my own clothes back."

"We've got time," laughed a guard.

She feared that if she had to stand there naked much longer she might start to cry. She didn't want them to see her cry. She signed the paper and the guards slowly handed her a tracksuit-like prison uniform and a pair of underpants that were far too big for her. She put the clothes on. They marched her to a narrow cell. The first thing she noticed was the window. It consisted of a few opaque glass bricks that let in an anemic trickle of light but didn't allow her to see out.

Each of the three boys was also given a blue tracksuit and then thrown into an isolation cell before eventually being transferred into cells they shared with two other prisoners.

When Ulrich entered his cell, the two other prisoners asked what he was in for.

"It's political," he told them.

"We're all *political* prisoners," said one of his cellmates with a tone that added, *you fucking idiot*. "This is the Stasi joint."

So this was Thüringen's central Stasi prison, in Erfurt. The only contact Ulrich or any of the others would have with the outside world for the next five months would be the sound of the bells of Erfurt's cathedral.

After five months of incarceration and interrogation during pretrial detention, a trial was held in February 1984. The entire state of Thüringen was on lockdown during their court appearance, with the train stations and city centers of Erfurt and Weimar as well as many small towns heavily patrolled by armed security forces.

It was for all the world like a terrorist trial. The four punks were marched into the building and down the halls through a gauntlet of machine-gun-toting guards. Even in the courtroom itself, guards stood posted with machine guns at the ready.

Thomas, Ulrich, Grit, and Holm were also joined in court by the other two co-conspirators, Jörn and Andreas, who, unbeknownst to the other four, had been arrested in November, a month after the first four.

They'd been told time and time again in prison that they would not get less than a year and a half. But in the end, Thomas and Grit got six months, and Ulrich and Holm were sentenced to five months. The other two defendants, Andreas and Jörn, who'd been arrested a month later and released again in January, got lesser sentences, equal to the time they had already served. They arrived back home after the trial feeling guilty and uncomfortable about their seemingly preferential treatment.

This was a common Stasi tactic—leniency gave off the stench of a dirty deal, of treachery.

Is Jörn an informant?

The suspicion was typically enough to bust up a circle of friends.

Sure enough, Jörn was ostracized from the scene immediately, a situation that did not improve when his former buddies got out of prison. Before long Jörn disappeared to Berlin, slipping off the grid and living illegally in a derelict building in Prenzlauer Berg, among the many punks who had taken up similarly tenuous, invisible lives inside the physical borders of East Germany but somehow outside the DDR.

But there was another consequence of the ordeal: the gang of Weimar punks weren't afraid anymore. One of the main sources of fear of the Stasi was the *not knowing*.

After half a year of prison, they now *knew*.

And they knew they could endure.

Swooping down on Grit, Thomas, Ulrich, Holm, Andreas, and Jörn in October 1983 was supposed to send a message to the opposition scene. But in the end, because of the resilience of these six punks, the Stasi inadvertently provided the opposite example.

They survived . . .

Why can't we?

We can.

STRIKE BACK.

We will.

STRIKE BACK.

STRIKE BACK.

STRIKE BACK!

37

Despite the arrests of Namenlos, the implosions of Wutanfall and Planlos, and the other police actions in motion against punks nationwide that fall of 1983, anticipation had still been running high for the second national punk festival, scheduled for October 22 in Halle's Christus Church. The legend of the first festival, back in April, had spread far and wide in the DDR.

City authorities were determined not to be embarrassed a second time. Siggi, the minister—and *enemy of the state*—had been leaned on to cancel the event. Church officials had been asked to intervene. All to no avail. Siggi wasn't backing down, and his congregation wasn't going to force him to.

Unbeknownst to Siggi, though, the live-in maintenance man at his church had been informing on him. As a result, the Stasi had very detailed information about the planning of this second festival. This time the secret police were determined to smash it.

The Stasi had devoted a major and six underlings to run the operation, in conjunction with the *Volkspolizei* and the Transport Police. A three-page Stasi memo outlined a nine-point plan to subvert the event, complete with the streets and tunnels they planned to blockade to prevent anyone reaching the church, and the plans for fake speed traps that would be set up along incoming highways to filter out punks.

As October 22 approached, Department XX's Operation Decadence was well underway.

Once again, the geography room in the school opposite the church had been closed all week. Once again, the pupils had been warned about the enemy of the state operating behind the church walls. This time, in fact, students all over Halle were warned. Of course, for some kids, anything that bothered the authorities that much just had to be cool—whatever the hell was going to happen at Christus Church sounded adventurous and conspiratorial, and it further piqued their interest in punk. In fact, for exactly that reason, hordes of very young teens planned to make their way to the festival, and not just from Halle. They wanted in on the scene and—perhaps—out of society.

On the Thursday before the festival, all known Halle punks and their associates were issued summonses. Those who didn't accept the invitation to come down to the police station for a chat were picked up and driven there. After they were interrogated, more than a hundred were issued orders not to attend the upcoming "criminal event" at Christus Church. They had to sign papers stating that they would comply with the orders. The major in charge had already cabled Stasi offices in nearby cities and towns like Erfurt and Eisleben and ordered them to undertake similar measures against their own punks, and to hinder any from traveling to Halle.

Otze and Schleim-Keim warranted their own telegram to Erfurt police from the Stasi.

Some concert-goers were clever enough to travel to Halle a day or two in advance, but by Saturday morning, train stations all over the country bristled with extra transport police, all on the lookout for punks. Recognizable punks who showed up in stations in Berlin, Leipzig, Magdeburg, and elsewhere were detained and questioned until their trains had departed. Groups were chased from the platforms.

Yet somehow, punks still scurried out of the trains arriving in Halle on Saturday. They had not, however, ever seen the likes of the barriers between the station and Christus Church. Transport cops at the Halle train station were rounding up punks as fast as they could, pushing them back into their train cars until the trains chugged off again. Some groups were accompanied on their trip by an officer who collected all their identification papers and wouldn't relinquish them again until they were back in their hometowns.

It would get worse.

For out-of-towners who managed to slip the grasp of the transport cops at the train station, the Stasi and police had set up checkpoints on the streets leading from the station to the Christus Church. The side streets were choked with troop transports—the kind used to cart off large numbers of detainees. Baton-wielding cops lined some of the routes to the church; anyone who tried to get through was attacked and beaten.

For locals, the situation wasn't much easier. Cops occupied public squares in the city and ringed tram and bus stops. In the morning hours leading up to the festival, a few kids who looked "normal" were able to reach the church. Some local punks tried wearing costumes, putting overalls and hats on to try to blend in as ordinary workers of the district. Others took taxis straight to the church gate and managed to avoid getting nabbed. But most either were sent away or faced batons or arrest.

As the festival start time of 1 p.m. approached, even the "normal" kids— not outwardly punk—who tried to get to the church had difficulty. At the tram stops near the church, groups of Stasi officers and cops surrounded any young people who hopped off—*Papers, please!* Without an address in the immediate area, kids had a choice: leave the area or be arrested.

Groups of punks began straggling into the church. Some were bruised or even dripping with blood. One had grabbed a police officer's cap as a trophy when he'd braved a line of batons.

Like animals at the slaughterhouse, thought Siggi, surveying the battered teens who had made it into the church.

What amazed him was their reaction. Despite the respect they had shown at the first festival—making sure the organ didn't get damaged, for instance—he feared they would want to break things after being attacked. But all they wanted to do was dance, to pogo and writhe around—they vented their aggression on the dance floor, while a band thrown together spontaneously from the few musicians who managed to get to the church knocked out some rough chords at breakneck speed.

Though originally Siggi had expected as many as a thousand people, in the end, only about a hundred and fifty people managed to reach the church.

A group of Berliner punks had written a short theater piece about being a punk. Not all the players had reached Halle, but Siggi went onstage and explained the situation. Volunteers came forward to read the roles so the piece could still be performed.

In the opening scene, two punks discussed their troubles with their parents. One said to the other, "But what can you do about it, eh?"

The other replied, "I left home, squatted a place of my own."

The conversation continued with the two punks bemoaning the way all decisions were made for them. Too much future.

"You're nothing more than a marionette," said one.

"I want to live the way I want to live, not the way they have planned for me."

Later in the play, in a scene set in a squatted apartment, a punk described a recent interrogation: "Same as always, they asked about people I'm supposed to know . . . some punk is supposed to have spray-painted Nazi slogans on a wall."

Another punk, pissed off, said, "They must be crazy. First we're not allowed to lay a wreath at the concentration camp, and then we're supposed to be Nazis."

In another scene, a punk was stopped by the police, asked for his papers, beaten with a baton, and told he was being taken to jail. When he complained that he hadn't done anything and that they couldn't just take him into custody, the cops said, "You're about to see what all we can do."

And outside the church that day, the punks really had seen what all the police could do.

The second national punk festival was a bloodbath. But the Stasi's actions also had a boomerang effect. For many of the younger kids entering the scene or thinking about it, this was the first time they'd been threatened by the police. And the first time they'd seen cops beat the shit out of other kids. It was the kind of thing that made you question your society in a fundamental way.

One young Halle resident, fourteen at the time and not yet a punk, couldn't believe what he had witnessed. *Putting that kind of effort into preventing music from being played? That's just crazy.*

But that fourteen-year-old knew one thing now: he was going to be a punk.

And he was definitely not alone.

Major, shortly after her expatriation

Kaiser (left) and Lade (at drums) rehearsing, ca. 1981

East Berlin punks at Plänterwald, ca. 1981

Punks on Alexanderplatz, ca. 1982

Rosa Extra in Prenzlauer Berg, 1982

Keule, Colonel, and Esther Friedemann, ca. 1982

Hand-printed poster for the first punk festival at Christus Church in Halle, 1983

Planlos (left to right: Kaiser, Micha Kobs, Lade, Pankow) in Karl-Marx-Stadt, 1983

Mita Schamal and Jana Schlosser in Leipzig, ca. 1983

Christiane Eisler / Transit Agency

Mita (middle left) and Jana (middle right) of Namenlos, ca. 1983

SUBstitut Archive

Police photo of
A-Micha, 1983

SUBstitut Archive

A-Micha (at left) and deacon Lorenz Postler (at right,
with beard), 1983

SUBstitut Archive

Mita (left) and Conny Schleime, ca 1982

Pankow, singer of the band Planlos,
ca. 1982

Otze of Schleim-Keim, 1983

L'Attentat, ca. 1984

Poster for the Church from Below, ca. 1988

Stasi surveillance photos of Speiche, undated

Private archive of Paul Landers

Karoline Bofinger

Feeling B, ca. 1984: Paul Landers (left),
Aljoscha Rompe (middle), Flake Lorenz (right)

Die Anderen (in the second row
at left is Toster)

Private archive of Jörn Schulz

Wartburgs für Walter (left to right: Jörn Schulz, Ina Pallas, Bernd Hennig) in Poland,
November 1987

Mathias Schwarz

Illegal album by Re-Aktion taped
over an official release on the
state-owned record label, Amiga

Punk festival at Erlöser Church, April 1988

Paul Landers of Feeling B (head of table, at right) and Tatjana Besson of Die Firma (standing behind Landers) at a planning session at the squat Eimer, 1990

Buildings being razed in Prenzlauer Berg in the late 1980s

Ratte, bassist of HAU and L'Attentat, on a train to Berlin, 1983

IV

Rise Above

38

On the last night of 1983, Elias Church in Prenzlauer Berg hosted a punk gathering and somewhat subdued New Year's party. The event had originally been planned for September, but no church had agreed to let the punks congregate within its walls at the height of the Stasi crackdown. Now, on New Year's Eve, a sandbox was erected in front of the Elias altar and punks lit candles for all of their friends who couldn't be there—all those in prison, in the army, or sent away.

The original punk scene in East Berlin lay in rubble, still smoldering from the attack by Stasi chief Erich Mielke. Major was gone. Three members of Namenlos were in pretrial detention being interrogated, desperately hoping their case would proceed to court. Planlos were being rehabilitated in special army units reserved for the politically suspect.

In Leipzig, four punks—including Ratte of the band HAU and Connie, a seventeen-year-old punk who had always looked up to Jana and Mita of Namenlos—had been busted for spray-painting FREEDOM FOR JANA, MITA AND A-MICHA! on city walls. They'd been held in pre-trial detention for three months and then sentenced in November to seven to ten months jail time. During the trial, Connie's father wore ripped jeans and an old vest in court, trying as best as he could to look like a punk—his silent way of supporting his daughter. Stracke, the singer in HAU and, for now, Wutanfall, had participated in a candlelight vigil in protest over his friends' arrest and himself been detained, along with forty others; he was released at Christmastime after more than a month in detention. Chaos had dropped out of Wutanfall after being savaged by the authorities. In Thüringen, six punk teens were sitting in prison for spray-painting anarchist graffiti; Otze of Schleim-Keim would also soon spend four more months in Stasi prison in 1984.

Circles of big-city punks had been broken up by other means, too. They'd been sent to work in distant villages. They'd been banned from travel to other cities—Berliners couldn't go to Leipzig, and vice versa; known Dresden punks couldn't go to either of those cities. Some punks were simply banned from the central boroughs of their own cities. Still others were expatriated to West Germany—in Halle, for instance, the number of people shown the door in 1984 more than quadrupled the number booted in 1982. The concerted action against punk in 1983 and 1984 far exceeded that undertaken against any other opposition group since the installation of dictator Erich Honecker in 1971.

But it was too late.

Punk had taken hold even in the smallest villages of the country.

The number of punks was already growing again; more sympathizers had been drawn in by the huge events throughout 1983. By the time Namenlos, Planlos, and Wutanfall had been neutralized, the tremors they'd caused had already rippled out. Countless other kids had already felt the reverberations and knew something was happening, knew the government was scared, knew they didn't want to die in the waiting room of the future. For every band the Stasi smashed, it seemed as if ten more cropped up.

Even in Berlin, in the midst of the crackdown, a second generation of punk bands had already formed. And outside Berlin, in the hinterlands, the scene boomed with the aftereffects of the Summer of Punk. The Stasi could congratulate itself on having silenced the loudest and most dangerous voices of the punk scene. But they underestimated the reverberations those voices would have. Kids—especially younger kids, who had only been on the fringes of the scene and witnessed the excitement but not the consequences—were still captivated by the public *fuck you* that punk represented.

Marcus Hugk was fourteen in 1983, living with his parents in Adlershof, a neighborhood just beyond Plänterwald, where Marcus had first seen punks the year before. Being around punks gave Marcus a whole new mental framework, and he was determined to contribute something concrete to the scene. Which is how he hit upon the idea of starting a band. He wanted to play songs that disregarded the structures an official music evaluation committee would approve of. He wanted to sing lyrics that defied state ideology.

Fuck the pigs!

Fuck the FDJ!

Too much future!

Marcus, his friend Bernd Hennig, and a few other punk teens began with a children's guitar and a homemade amp they cobbled together, and used whatever else they could scrounge up until Marcus was able to grab a few drums from his father's workplace—his dad was an official musician employed by the Interior Ministry.

The new combo recorded some songs on a hand-held cassette player and wanted to pass the tape around to their friends. Now they needed a band name.

And it had to be a good one.

Well, they thought, *punk* was often translated as *Abfall* in East Germany— *garbage*, in essence, which in German could also be called *Müll* . . .

They also wanted their friends to know how cool they were.

What would make us sound like bigshots?

International!

And of course, *international* was also a pun on the communist anthem that every East German child learned as a Young Pioneer.

Aha! What about Internationale Müllabfuhr?

International Garbage Removal.

Perfect.

Next came a graffiti campaign to get the word out about their band.

The first time they sprayed the band name on neighborhood walls, it took an awful long time. Not to mention the amount of space—and spray paint— they needed to write *Internationale Müllabfuhr*.

Let's just use the initials: IM.

Several times over the course of two weeks the band members went out and sprayed *IM* on walls in areas where punks hung out. They also tagged their own school.

That was a mistake.

Those two letters had already set off alarms in state security circles. IM was the abbreviation the Stasi used to describe a snitch in internal documents—short for *Inoffizielle Mitarbeiter*. IM was a secret designation. The general public used the slang term *Spitzel* to describe Stasi snitches. Was an insider spray-painting the neighborhood walls of Treptow and Adlershof? That seemed crazy. But it stoked the surveillance state's paranoia.

Officers from the Criminal Division turned up at Marcus's school and began to pull students out of class. Kids who looked like trouble. Kids who looked like agitators. There were a few kids whose look put them under immediate suspicion: punks. Their outward appearance alone told school administrators and police—and everyone else—that they refused to be slotted into officially sanctioned society.

Haul them in.

The police escorted Marcus, Bernd, and the other members of the band to interrogations where they were joined by some "colleagues" from the Stasi.

The police had photos. They had the recordings of band's songs. They even had some scraps of paper with lyrics handwritten by the band.

Bernd explained during questioning: "Our lyrics are just nonsense and jokes. We were just having fun. We didn't think anything of it. And we didn't know it was illegal to get together and make music without an amateur band license."

The interrogation kept circling back to one central question: Whose idea was it to spray the abbreviation IM?

"Was it the CIA?" they shouted. "Was it the West Germans?"

Eventually the interrogators realized that the band's use of IM had nothing to do with the Stasi's own internal use of the same term. They confiscated Marcus's cassettes. One of the band members was sent to juvenile work camp.

Even though the rest of the boys weren't sent away, the hours spent in dingy holding cells being told they might not be released weighed heavily on them. Marcus and his buddies were just kids, after all. The Stasi officers had demanded the boys renounce the punk community. The boys weren't about to do that. But they did give up the band.

Marcus and his school friends were just one of dozens of groups that formed in 1983 and 1984. Some, like IM, were short-lived; others became driving forces in the underground, thorns in the side of the dictatorship as it struggled to deal with what must have been absolutely incomprehensible: the reconstitution of the punk scene in the wake of the Stasi-led crackdown. Bands like Feeling B, Aufruhr zur Liebe, der Demokratische Konsum, die Firma, Happy Straps, Klick & Aus, Betonromantik, and Ornament & Verbrechen all started in Berlin in 1983. They would be among the underground's heavy hitters for years. Many more were to come.

Within a year of the crackdown, even the Stasi would have to concede that the movement had not only reconstituted but expanded. And then what could they do?

39

Aljoscha Rompe was already in his mid-thirties in 1983. He had a degree in physics. One of the few ways to be cleared for university was to prove your ideological maturity with an additional stint in the National Volks Army, and Aljoscha had served extra time in the NVA prior to his studies. It was during his time in the army that Aljoscha first ran afoul of the Stasi. In early 1972 a snitch told the Stasi about comments Aljoscha made at a party in the barracks—comments about how to democratize the DDR. He got in trouble again later that year for setting up an illegal club in Berlin, where he held not only discos but political discussions.

In 1978 Aljoscha spent three months in police custody while being investigated for "subversive agitation" as a result of his role in the production of a satirical calendar put together by a group of underground artists. During his incarceration, he was interrogated eighteen times; his lawyer also had to file a complaint after a police dog was let loose in Aljoscha's cell in the middle of the night.

Also while in custody in 1978 Aljoscha received notification that his biological father, whom he had never known, had died. The news came with a surprise: his father had been a Swiss national. His mother, a committed communist who left her husband and moved to East Berlin when Aljoscha was just one year old, had never told him; her second husband, Robert Rompe, was an Eastern academic, functionary, and member of the communist party's Central Committee from 1958 until the collapse of the DDR.

Aljoscha was still in detention when he applied for a Swiss passport, without telling his mother or stepfather since he knew they would disapprove. He got the passport in 1980, which allowed him to go back and forth to the West whenever he pleased. Aljoscha took advantage of his new status by applying to study at the Free University in West Berlin—not because he wanted to get another degree but because he wanted to get financial aid. Soon he was living off a West German educational stipend while still based in the East.

By the early 1980s, Aljoscha was a well-known figure in bohemian circles—and bars—of East Berlin. He was raucous and hyper-social. He had a lust for life that infected those around him. And he had a sort of existential restlessness that constantly got him into interesting places.

The Stasi cultivated informants around Aljoscha and surveilled him and those around him until the day the agency closed its doors in 1990. Aljoscha's own stepfather became an IM.

Aljoscha worked for *VEB Studiotechnik*—the People's studio engineering enterprise—and spent several years driving officially sanctioned bands around the country to play at state-sponsored festivals and youth clubs. But he was getting fed up.

Then he discovered punk.

Aljoscha got to know Planlos when the band was still rehearsing at their basement space in Metzer Strasse 14—that is, before the Stasi searched the place. Aljoscha had also had an apartment in Metzer 14 for a while. By the time Department XX moved in on Planlos in the summer of 1983, Aljoscha had squatted an apartment on nearby Fehrbelliner Strasse. He offered to let Planlos use his new place, a huge attic space. It was in pretty rough shape, but he had already "soundproofed" it for the legendary parties he threw: he had lined the parts of the walls and roof that were intact with old mattresses. As for the parts that were bombed out, there was nothing to be done. Electricity came from a cord Aljoscha had strung from his roof to the roof of the building across the street, where he had tapped into a live wire. For his parties,

Aljoscha cooked up huge vats of spaghetti, punk bands played, and everyone got blasted. His building also housed a number of other likeminded people, including Günther Spalda from Rosa Extra and Carlo Jordan, who would later play a key role in underground environmental activism.

The more Aljoscha listened to the punk bands that practiced at his place and played at his parties—in addition to Planlos, a band called die Firma had begun working at his apartment and others soon followed—the more convinced he became that he could do the same thing. He had already sung in a hard blues band, even if it had never developed into anything serious.

All he needed was a band.

40

Aljoscha's band arrived in the form of two teenagers: Paul, an eighteen-year-old bleached-blond guitarist, and Flake, a gangly sixteen-year-old keyboard player, both brought in by Alexander Kriening, a drummer who had already been playing with Aljoscha for a while. Kriening had been in the punk scene for years: he used to jam with Planlos bassist Kaiser back in 1980, before Planlos existed.

Paul Landers knew Kriening from hanging out with him at the punk meeting spot in Plänterwald. Paul had grown up in a neighborhood so close to the Berlin Wall that police patrolled the area day and night, often with dogs, and even children needed special permits to visit friends in some of the buildings closest to the border.

For Paul, the Wall wasn't something he bristled at, it was just his daily reality: *If I lived in the desert I'd see sand, if I lived in the Arctic I'd see snow, I live here and I see the Wall*. Paul's father was a professor of Slavic languages and his mother, a Russian teacher; both were heartfelt believers in social-ism but also somewhat disillusioned about how things worked in practice in the DDR. Still, Paul and his family knew life could be far worse than in East Germany—they had spent a year in Russia and had seen food short-ages there. After taking a strict approach bringing up Paul's older sister and not liking the results, they had left Paul in peace when he started to dress funny and to attend Blues Masses and punk shows at Berlin churches. That spring of 1983, Paul was living in a squat on Invalidenstrasse and finishing up an apprenticeship in communications engineering. He was handy with electronics—he'd converted a radio into his first guitar amp and built his own guitar effects.

Kriening asked Paul to come meet Aljoscha on the afternoon of Thursday, March 31, 1983. Paul waited for Kriening and Aljoscha at Senefelder Platz in Prenzlauer Berg. Paul was shocked when Kriening showed up with a balding old man in jeans, a T-shirt, and a leather vest.

Who the hell is this?

Together they went to a bar. To call the old man—Aljoscha—an enthusiastic drinker would be an understatement. Aljoscha went to order drinks for everyone, but Paul, who hadn't been to a bar before, was nervous and claimed he wasn't feeling well.

"In that case," Aljoscha said, "you need an herbal liqueur."

He had Paul drink a shot of an East German version of Jägermeister to settle his stomach. After two hours in the bar, happily buzzed, the three of them wandered over to Aljoscha's apartment. The longer they hung out, the more Paul began to see past Aljoscha's age. Aljoscha was a font of ideas, and they had even begun to write a song when Aljoscha started riffing on a lyrical idea Paul had thrown out.

The next day Paul wrote in his diary:

Yesterday I was in the underworld, together with Kriening. We went to a musician's place, the guy was bald in front, had curly hair in back, wore a purple scarf, disgusting, pointless yammering, laughing, totally wasted, but he has an amazing apartment. A punk band rehearses there.

The second time Paul went to Aljoscha's place, a few days later, Lade from Planlos was playing drums in the attic apartment. Paul could hear the racket from the bottom of the staircase. He was hooked, he was in.

Kriening had brought in Christian "Flake" Lorenz, too. Flake was sixteen and looked even younger. They'd known each other for several years, had met at a concert at the school Kriening attended with Flake's older brother.

Kriening knew something important about Flake: he had just gotten an electric organ. Kriening knocked at Flake's parents' apartment one afternoon and asked him to join the band.

"What am I going to play?"

"Well, actually, bass. We don't have a bass player and you can play the bass tones with your left hand."

Yep, Flake could do that with his new organ.

The next day Kriening returned, this time with Aljoscha. Flake, too, was taken aback at his age and his odd look and attitude. Aljoscha giggled the whole time, and acted like Flake's parents' place belonged to him, tromping around and then carrying the organ out of the place and down the stairs, with Flake trailing behind.

The organ was too heavy to carry back to Aljoscha's place, so Aljoscha flagged down a car and convinced the driver to schlep it to Fehrbelliner Strasse. Flake followed on foot, and by the time he arrived in the strange, sprawling attic, his organ was set up alongside the other musical equipment in the living room.

Flake could not believe his eyes. The apartment was like nothing he had ever seen. It was like some sort of music studio, except that the roof was crumbling and open to the sky here and there.

Incredible!

Aljoscha pulled out a bottle of apricot brandy and they began to chat. Aljoscha quickly downed a whole tumbler of brandy while Flake nursed a small splash of it—he'd never drunk hard alcohol before. Then Aljoscha made a casserole, ever the good host.

Flake just sat there with his mouth open in amazement.

The second time Flake went to Aljoscha's place, Paul was there. The whole band was there: Aljoscha, Paul, Flake, and Kriening. They jammed at ear-splitting volume, with the windows open. Flake couldn't understand any of the lyrics Aljoscha shrieked and warbled, sounding tortured, twitchy, out of breath.

Still, it was a band. Well, sort of. For the initial few weeks it was more like a party, people coming and going and drinking and playing music and drinking and drinking.

They dubbed the band Feeling Berlin, then quickly shortened it to Feeling B. From his years as a roadie, Aljoscha seemed to know everyone—musicians, promoters at official clubs, bar managers. One of his friends was André, the singer in a heavy blues-rock band called Freygang. André was a long-haired old warhorse who kept running afoul of authorities and having his performance license revoked and reinstated and revoked again. He invited Aljoscha to test out Feeling B during a break between Freygang sets at an official club on the rural outskirts of East Berlin the night of May 14, 1983.

It did not go well.

When officially licensed bands played at official clubs, they typically had to play multiple sets, filling an entire evening from seven to midnight. Feeling B was slated to fill the biggest break, the one during which Freygang would be fed dinner by the club. But by the time Feeling B got their chance, the band was wasted. Aljoscha had kept ordering rounds of beers and vodka and orange juices, and the young guys were not able to keep up. They were also nervous about playing in front of an audience for the first time. Feeling B sounded horrible when they took the stage, and almost from the first note they played, beer glasses started flying toward the stage. They managed to stick it out for about fifteen minutes. To make matters worse, Paul and Kriening got picked up by the cops on the way home on Kriening's moped. They were taken to a rural police station and interrogated from eleven at night until three in the morning. Kriening also took punches to his gut and face.

When Paul eventually made it home, he scrawled in his diary: what he had always dismissed as tough-guy tall-tales about the police turned out to be true.

The next Feeling B show was during the day at an insane asylum in Berlin's Lichtenberg neighborhood, kind of a public rehearsal in front of the inmates. Aljoscha had arranged it with a guy he knew who worked there. The bands Rosa Extra and Die Firma came along. Then Feeling B played another gig, this time with Rosa Extra and Wutanfall in a church—just before the summer crackdown on the major punk bands.

But while the Stasi was preparing to hammer the hardcore punks during that summer of 1983, Feeling B was on vacation. Aljoscha had taken the entire band to Hiddensee, a narrow island in the Baltic Sea and his place of refuge since childhood, when he'd started going there with his parents.

"Hiddensee is the most beautiful spot in East Germany," Aljoscha told the boys. "The Greek isles have nothing on this place."

And Hiddensee was where the band really came together.

Aljoscha convinced a friend with a car to drive the four band members to the ferry that went to Hiddensee—cars were not permitted on the island itself. At the ferry they loaded their rudimentary gear onto a wooden cart they could wheel by hand, and made their way across to the island. You needed to be able to prove you had accommodations to board the ferry, but Aljoscha was able to talk his way through nearly anything, and managed to get everyone across despite his plan to sleep open-air on the beach.

On the island, the band pulled their cart to one of the chalky cliffs on the ocean side and unloaded. They hooked up their jerry-rigged amp to a car battery, Kriening tipped over the cart to make a bass drum, and they were ready to jam around a campfire. The beach party scene on Hiddensee was magical.

The island had its share of bigwigs, but Aljoscha knew who was with the Stasi and who was okay. He knew the areas where noise wouldn't carry, and where they could sleep without being spotted. The island was considered a border area, so doing illegal things carried some risk of being charged with attempted defection. But the island's only cop—Officer Gruber, everyone knew his name—rode a loud Schwalbe moped, which you could hear from miles away since there were no other motorized vehicles. Something about the place had always attracted freaks and fun-seekers. The campsites and cafés were crawling with scenesters from the Berlin underground. Hiddensee was a giant playground for cool kids, and Feeling B staged impromptu concerts on lazy afternoons or around a campfire at night, everyone drunk and dancing while the band basically rehearsed.

Feeling B started to go to Hiddensee every weekend, all summer, adding on whatever days Paul and Kriening could skip work. Flake had just finished school and would start his apprenticeship in the fall. Other Berlin bands, like their friends in Die Firma, came to visit. They were amazed at the scene and the fact that Feeling B staged electrified concerts in the woods or on the beach, sheltered from prying eyes and ears by chalky cliffs.

Every weekend party, party, party, playing music together and drinking in bars and cafés. At closing time they bought bottles of wine or cases of beer to take out—a last couple rounds to fuel an all-night party in the woods and to soften the ground below them when they passed out, illegally roughing it in some hidden spot Aljoscha had found, no tent, no sleeping bags, not even a tarp.

Still, even sleeping in bushes, all this fun cost money.

Once again, Aljoscha had a plan: earrings.

Huh?

Earrings.

Aljoscha had realized that metal hoop earrings were not readily available in East Germany but were highly sought after. Using his Swiss passport he crossed into West Berlin and bought spools of silver-plated copper wire. With pliers, the band members learned to twist the wire into hoops and create rudimentary clasps. Some of the hoops they decorated with colorful bits of fabric or beads. Soon, they could make a pair of earrings in four minutes. The material for a single pair cost next to nothing when Aljoscha bought it in bulk, and they found they could sell them for twenty East German marks. The band could simply sit at a café without a cent in their pockets, eat and drink all day, and, by selling earrings to tourists, finish the day full and fucked-up with a huge wad of cash. They took boxes of their earrings to beaches, campsites, and concerts. They sold like hotcakes.

They pooled the money in a band slush fund that Aljoscha kept. He suggested they should try to buy a band vehicle. Sometimes if Flake said he wanted an ice cream, Aljoscha would hand him a fifty and not ask for the change. By the end of the summer, nobody was sure how much money Feeling B had saved, but they figured it must have been thousands.

In September, Feeling B played a punk wedding party together with die Firma at a church in Johannisthal. Church officials got nervous about the racket and threatened to shut down the party several times.

But instead of continuing down that well-trod path—occasional gigs in churches—Feeling B was about the take a major detour, one that would change the whole punk scene.

41

On October 27, 1983, Feeling B auditioned for an *Einstufung*, the government performance license bands—even amateur bands—needed to play in public legally.

Another friend of Aljoscha's had set the whole thing in motion. The guy, Arnfried Schobert, had been part of an officially licensed blues-rock combo that also toured in the 1970s as East Berlin's Pink Floyd tribute band. Definitely not punk. But despite Feeling B's weird polka-punk sound and the punk background of the younger members, Arnfried urged Aljoscha to audition for an amateur license—it was the only way forward, he said.

Once again it was a case of Aljoscha knowing people in the official music world, and of the band playing by their own rules.

Why can't we get an Einstufung?

The word *Einstufung* means evaluation—in this case, a rating given by a cultural commission. There were five ratings, from the worst—*Unterstufe*—through *Mittelstufe, Oberstufe, Sonderstufe*, and the best of all, *Sonderstufe mit Konzertberechtigung*. A band could also fail to qualify at all. The various levels reflected the commission's assessment not just of the individual musicians' talent level and the quality of their songs, but also their political maturity—the extent to which they complied with government notions of music and, especially, lyrics. All five ratings came with the government seal of approval, and the practical difference between them lay primarily in how much a band got paid. The concert business in East Germany was unique:

a venue could let a band play only if the group was legally sanctioned with an *Einstufung* and had a corresponding tax ID number—the number was necessary for payment, and the band's stamp of approval was needed to keep club and bar managers from getting fired or worse. Bands were paid an hourly rate for shows that generally were billed for five hours, providing music from seven to midnight. The rate did not vary based on how many people turned up, but on what level *Einstufung* the band had. *Unterstufe*? Four marks fifty an hour per musician. *Sonderstufe*? Seven marks fifty an hour per musician.

Despite allowing the acts to earn a little money, the *Einstufung* ratings were for amateur bands only. And in order to audition for one, band members had to be able to prove they had jobs—*real* jobs, unrelated to the band. Luckily the members of Feeling B were covered. Paul, for instance, was working as a boiler technician at a library near his parents' apartment. Flake was an apprentice toolmaker. Aljoscha was ostensibly a full-time student in West Berlin. Kriening presented the only problem: he was working as a janitor, but he'd been called up for army service and failed to report. The band just had to hope Kriening's army records didn't get cross-checked by the commission.

The afternoon of October 27, Feeling B went to the Kulturhaus in Berlin's Karlshorst neighborhood, feeling nervous and excited. Their confidence built as they watched other bands audition in front of the commission.

Wait, we're better than them.

Feeling B took no chances, changing potentially contentious lyrics, adding extra songs, and creating a blow-out performance in the empty hall. They projected Super 8 film clips of their Hiddensee adventures behind them, and they put a block of dry ice in an old laundry machine basin and mounted it atop a ladder so the band was swathed in dry-ice fog.

The commission sat with the band afterward and passed judgment from behind their table, consulting their notes: "First, the singer needs to learn to sing more clearly and work on his microphone technique. Second, the guitar player must not fall to his knees so often."

The verdict: Feeling B had passed, and would receive an *Einstufung* at the *Sonderstufe* level—the second best rating.

With their *Einstufung* in hand, Feeling B became trailblazers of a new way forward—soon enough, many more bands followed them into this new gray area, officially sanctioned as amateur musicians. Their status represented a concession to punk on the part of the government. Or did it? Kids who considered themselves true punks did not see it that way. They saw it as a government attempt to defang the scene by dangling the possibility of legitimacy, to co-opt the scene, to kill the scene by hugging it to death. They saw it as a new front in the dictatorship's war on punk. The Stasi had tried the stick; this was the carrot.

After all, was it really possible to use the official power structure against itself—to undermine the system from within? The first generation of punks certainly hadn't thought so. They rejected the entire system. *Destroy what's destroying you*. Feeling B now seemed to have a foot in each camp. After getting their amateur license, they continued to turn down gigs at special events put on by the Free German Youth. But they never explicitly said they *refused* to play state-sponsored events, just that they couldn't fit them into their schedule. And they did play in officially sanctioned concert venues all over the country.

No more churches for Feeling B.

They would find they weren't welcome in the church-based scene anymore anyway. The punks who'd been targeted by the Stasi crackdown considered anyone who submitted to the government for approval a traitor, a turncoat.

Verräter!

But then again the members of Feeling B didn't see themselves as very political. They didn't have any songs like Namenlos—*MfMfS . . . SS!* They considered themselves more about having fun than about politics. Or maybe having fun *was* their politics. Polka-punk, party-punk, whatever you called their music, it certainly wasn't politically strident. They weren't counterrevolutionary agitators; Feeling B were more of a guerilla party troupe. They were happy to live their dreams despite the system—music and booze, partying and traveling. They were happy to live their dreams *within* the system. Shit, they'd received a *Sonderstufe*, the second best rating.

Despite that rating, the concert payday for amateur bands wasn't worth much. The real money, Feeling B would find, was in the inflated travel costs they were able to bill venues. Even with that money, the band continued to depend financially on selling earrings and handmade T-shirts and jackets everywhere they went. Their DIY business thrived as they began to take punk to the people, spending their weekends playing hole-in-the-wall youth clubs in every godforsaken village in the DDR.

The boys in Feeling B approached it all with an innocent sense of fun, in part because they could—they had never encountered much trouble and now could live semi-legally as itinerant musicians, continuing to pool their money for band use.

Without the need to show official employment again until they had to renew their *Einstufung* a few years down the road, they began shifting into the expanding gray areas of the economy, becoming less dependent on day jobs and less fastidious about even working day jobs at all.

This corresponded with a general change in East German society: the overarching importance of having an official job was fading. One reason first-generation punks feared not having jobs was a spike in the prosecution of *asoziales Verhalten* cases starting in 1978 and peaking from 1979 to 1982. The incidence of criminal charges for not working decreased from 1983 on—by 1985 the number of prosecutions had dropped to just 40 percent of the number it was in 1980. And the drop in prosecutions of youth as *asozial* over the same period was even more dramatic, down in 1985 to less than 5 percent of the number in 1980. With fewer arrests being made, the fear of not having an official job diminished sharply as the decade wore on.

The members of Feeling B compared their *Einstufung* to a driver's license: you paid attention to the rule book during the test, but out on the open road you could drive as fast and as crazy as you wanted. To the band, the *Einstufung* represented a kind of independence, a kind of freedom. And they intended to make the most of it.

The day after Feeling B passed their *Einstufung*, Aljoscha took the band's collective pot of money and bought a used Trabant. Since people had to wait years to take delivery of a new car in the East, used cars were expensive.

They really had sold a shitload of earrings that past summer.

Aljoscha began to use his contacts to put together a busy schedule of gigs, sometimes several per week.

As far as Feeling B saw it, their new status—with wheels and a license to rock—proved that anything was possible, even in East Germany. The opportunities were there.

We may live in a dictatorship, Paul thought, *but it's a dumb one. There are holes in it. And we can operate in those holes. We can live our whole lives in those holes. And live well.*

With his Swiss passport and the chance to see the West, Aljoscha had come to hate it. He often talked about the way money ruined people. Paul and Flake shared his distaste for the West, even if they didn't have Aljoscha's direct experience. In that regard they were typical DDR punks, for whom the West was never a goal or ideal.

In the East, Aljoscha and the boys could now hop in their car and head off to one big continuous party that they were always the center of—wherever they turned up, shit got crazy. Over the next year Feeling B finished just a handful of concerts intact. Seven to midnight was just too long for them to stay sober enough to perform—or at least for Aljoscha to stay sober. He finished nearly every show falling off the stage or babbling incoherently or simply passing out on stage, forcing the others to take on vocal duties and play long, improvised passages to pad the shows.

The young band members knew they could be better if they weren't drunk all the time. And they knew that Aljoscha was a liability at times. But they never contemplated kicking Aljoscha out. Feeling B was meant to be a party, and Aljoscha was the life of the party. And besides, the last thing they wanted was to be like one of the inert professional bands of the official East German rock scene.

Taking punk to the people wasn't always easy in 1984. There were pockets of punks at most shows—but not always. One night in the cafeteria of the applied science college in Wismar, up on the Baltic Sea coast, the audience turned ugly. About a thousand students had been looking forward to an evening of dancing to conventional covers, and instead were confronted with Aljoscha's shambolic, warbling antics, the band's crazy rhythms, and

Flake's childlike Casio tones tinkling alongside Paul's angular guitar riffs. Beer glasses started flying at the stage. At first the band was defiant. Paul and Flake shouted, "Come on! You can do better than that!" But the crowd got too angry, too violent. The band switched over to playing blues shuffles to protect themselves and to appease the student mob.

For Aljoscha, part of the point of any performance was to do something unusual, something jarring even, but always with the aim of instigating fun, of pushing the party along. One night they played naked. Some nights the band distributed balloons filled with jello and told the crowd to throw the balloons at them if they didn't play well enough. And they *never* played well enough. They knew it themselves, but they didn't care. It was all about partying.

The band would spend another summer together on Hiddensee in 1984, again roughing it, selling earrings, and, of course, partying like it was the only thing that mattered in life. And for them, it *was*. They had succeeded in making it so.

For the next five years Feeling B became the soundtrack to the longest-running party in the DDR.

42

Since the closure of Pfingst Church and the Stasi crackdown in 1983, both the punk community and Berlin's Open Work had been without a home base.

Thanks to an original punk named Herne, the punks had found a new meeting place at the very end of 1983: Erlöser Church, in Rummelsburg, the spot where Namenlos had played their last gig prior to their arrest.

The space wasn't in the church itself but down in the basement of a side building at the back of the church grounds, up against the raised S-Bahn tracks, a building that had once housed a small church hospital. And you couldn't really call it a building. The only thing left of the structure above ground was a brick stoop and the top of the foundation. Everything else had been destroyed during the war. But the cellar, or *Keller* in German, was still mostly intact. Punks called their damp, musty new subterranean home alternatively the Leichenkeller, which means corpse cellar, or the Profikeller, after the building that had been above it, which was named after a doctor—a Professor Fischer—who had once practiced there. A number of other original punks, including Kaiser from Planlos, whose medical waiver had saved him from being conscripted into the army, began to hang out at the Profikeller.

Herne had been thirteen when he was first drawn to punk, in 1977. He and his brother Mecki, a year and a half older, saw a punk at the school they attended in Köpenick—she was a few years older, with crazy blue hair. They didn't really get to know her, but they were impressed. Really impressed. She was just so fucking cool.

Her name: Major.

Herne's first year at the Profikeller, 1984, was a lonely one. His brother was in jail and many of his closest friends were gone. Herne kept the place going with an eye on the eventual return of his friends. He figured the original gang of Berlin punks would be returning en masse by the middle of 1985 after serving in the army or in prison.

While he waited, Herne took to writing letters to any address he could get his hands on that had to do with punk. He sent letters to punk-rock labels in West Germany and Dischord records in Washington, D.C. In many cases, their replies managed to slip through state surveillance of international post and reach Herne.

By far the most important contacts Herne made were to punks in Poland. Again it started by an almost random mailing campaign to punk bands in Warsaw, several of whom wrote back. Because of the Solidarity uprising, it was still illegal for ordinary citizens to travel between the DDR and Poland, but Herne quickly figured a way around the regulations. He registered one of the Warsaw punks as his cousin—there was virtually no way to check the veracity of a claim like that back then—and, as relatives, they were granted visas to visit each other. Soon he had other Erlöser punks also registered as cousins of various Polish counterparts. Polish punks were several steps ahead of the East Germans: the Polish punk band Dezerter, for example, played in front of 20,000 people at the open-air Jarocin festival in Warsaw in 1984, only a year after martial law had been suspended; Karcer would play the main stage at the same festival the following year. The audacity of the Polish punks—and all they were able to get away with—began to exert a major influence on their new friends in East Berlin.

As more of the original punks returned, Herne started to set up shows at the Profikeller on Saturdays. It was a lot of work. Once he had lined up a band, he had to visit band rehearsal spaces around East Berlin in order to collect the instruments and amps he would need. All of this using public transport. And then, of course, he had to get boatloads of beer. But word spread—first in Berlin, then slowly throughout the country—and the concerts eventually became the beacon that had been missing since the closure of Pfingst Church.

One thing he and everyone agreed on at the Profikeller: there would be no bands with *Einstufungen*. For some Erlöser punks, it was a practical issue: *those* bands, like Feeling B, had plenty of opportunities to play in other venues, including official youth clubs. For others, it was ideological: *no fucking way*. Those bands had been co-opted by the same regime that sent A-Micha and Jana and Mita to prison for their lyrics, the same regime that jailed Herne's brother.

No fucking way.

The moment you permit your thoughts to be censored, you've made a compromise—a compromise that is not necessary.

Another original punk who kept the fire burning while the first generation was largely banished from Berlin was Speiche, the willowy kid who had helped spray-paint the phrase OVERTHROW THE POLICE STATE in Grünau back in the day. Speiche was now seemingly everywhere all the time. He was active in Erlöser and in Open Work, and he worked at Zion Church, up on the roof mostly, one of several punks hired as laborers by Carlo Jordan, the environmental activist who lived in the same squat as Aljoscha and who, as a certified engineer, was supervising renovation and upkeep of the church.

Speiche was hyper-social, a hub connecting many people and groups. For that reason, some suspected he might be a Stasi snitch. But this suspicion was also partly a result of the Stasi's own strategy for dealing with Speiche: unable to turn him, the Stasi tried to burn him. During interrogations of other punks, they planted the idea that Speiche worked for them; they also had snitches spread rumors about him.

Speiche eventually had keys to seven different empty apartments, most deserted by people who had left the country. He held classes in these places, training all sorts of people in self-defense—punks, women's groups, gay groups, activists and outcasts of all stripes. And as neo-Nazi skinhead violence gradually became more of a problem in coming years, he became a key figure in the organization of *Antifa*, or Anti-Fascist groups.

Speiche had always had the feeling that he would be willing to give his life for freedom. And even though his dream had been of a peaceful world, a world of brotherhood, where everyone could live their life as they wished and love one another, Speiche—unlike many of the people in the environmental movement, for example, who tended to be older or more hippie-influenced— had no qualms about fighting violence with violence. Especially skinhead violence.

But in 1984 that battle was still mostly in the future.

43

On one of the first days of September, 1984, several months before Namenlos guitarist A-Micha's prison term was set to end, officials took him out of his cell and drove him to Karl-Marx-Stadt.

He was taken to an office and set in front of a Party official.

"Horschig, Michael."

"Yes."

"So, let me see here . . . you wish to leave for the West?"

"What?" said A-Micha.

This must be some kind of trick.

He had never filed an application to vacate his citizenship, to leave.

"No," he said. "I do not wish to go to the West."

"What is there for you here?" the official asked A-Micha. "Why don't you just go to the West?"

A-Micha refused.

On September 4, 1984, he was released from Naumburg Prison.

He was five years into his ten-year countdown to the end of the DDR and he was free again.

Jana, Namenlos's singer, remained in the women's prison in Hoheneck. But now that her fiancé was free, A-Micha became her designated visitor. He came to see her and subtly explained what had happened to him.

Jana understood.

Two months before her own term was over, they drove her to the same transport point and asked her if she wouldn't really rather emigrate. Jana vowed to become a good citizen, and said she wanted to marry and have children with A-Micha.

The truth was, they wanted to change their country, not leave it.

I will not let them defeat me.

Upon her release, A-Micha and Jana moved into a squat on Schliemannstrasse in Prenzlauer Berg. Mita was living nearby in a place she had squatted on Gleimstrasse.

The punk council—originally formed at Pfingst Church, now based at Erlöser—and Open Work had started to facilitate the squatting of apartments, particularly in the crumbling nineteenth-century buildings of Prenzlauer Berg and Friedrichshain. There were nearly-entire buildings squatted on Lychenerstrasse, Schliemannstrasse, and Dunckerstrasse in Prenzlauer Berg, and on Simon-Dach-Strasse in Friedrichshain. The punk network maintained a catalogue of empty apartments various people had spotted, serving as a clearinghouse for would-be squatters and helping them get into the places.

With the loss of monopoly control over housing, and the increase in gray-market economic activity, the dictatorship was slowly losing its ability to define the future.

Almost as soon as Jana was released and reunited with A-Micha, the two of them wanted to put the band back together. They didn't have any problem with the fact that their original bass player, Frank Masch, had confirmed some song lyrics late in the pretrial detention process—at the end of the day, they all stood behind their songs and their right to sing them. But Frank had applied to emigrate in the meantime, so A-Micha and Jana felt his goals were different from theirs now, and they worried he could end up compromising the band.

Perhaps, they thought, Kaiser from Planlos, whose bandmates were still off at the army, would want to work with Namenlos? Kaiser had spent a lot of 1984 with Mita, the lone member of Namenlos spared a long jail sentence. A-Micha and Jana met up with Kaiser and Mita and asked them. They agreed. They wanted to keep going, to keep making music, to keep fighting.

The building where Jana and A-Micha had squatted housed just one last "normal" person among the punks and freaks: an eighty-two-year-old woman who, mercifully, was hard of hearing. The new band lineup started using an empty apartment in the same building as a rehearsal studio. They checked in with the old woman to make sure it wasn't going to be a problem.

"Do you hear the music? Does it bother you?"

"*Ach nein*, all I hear is a bit of a vibration," she said. "Actually, it's nice to be able to tell there are other people around."

Namenlos was back.

Kaiser recognized something in A-Micha when he came out of prison: A-Micha was interested in music and playing in the band and all, but at the end of the day it almost didn't matter to him any more what he was doing as long as it was fighting the system. A-Micha could just as well have organized an army. In fact that might have been more to his liking. For A-Micha, this was a war. And he would never stop fighting. *Never.*

He would also *never* contemplate playing footsie with the government the way Feeling B was and others soon would be. As he saw it, the government had tried to kill the scene with repression and infiltration; when that tactic appeared destined to fail, the government added another strategy—integration, co-opting the scene by creating wiggle room within the amateur band license system. There wasn't enough wiggle room in the whole of the DDR to incorporate A-Micha's rage.

A-Micha started hanging out at Erlöser Church, too. Alarmed Stasi reports, which included information provided by several snitches planted in punk circles, document the activities "Anarchie-Micha" undertook in the Profikeller: he organized an anarchist circle, an environmental discussion group, a group to study history. He held lectures on the Makhno Movement, an anarchist insurrection of farmers and laborers in the Ukraine led by Nestor Makhno that, during the Russian Revolution, amassed a militia of 100,000 infantry and cavalry and established an independent anarchist society before being violently suppressed by the Red Army.

The tenor of things at Erlöser Church changed with A-Micha's return. What had been a loosely organized bunch of punks mostly getting drunk and hanging out in a basement became highly organized and highly active. The government also regarded it as highly threatening: A-Micha's Stasi file, titled *Schwarz* or black, was administered by the specialized counter-terrorism branch of Abteilung XX, the AG XXII. A-Micha was seen by the dictatorship as a terrorist, just as he had predicted in his song *"Der Exzess."*

Namenlos made a triumphant return to Halle's Christus Church in December 1984, playing to hundreds alongside Otze and Schleim-Keim, Paranoia from Dresden, and the Berlin band Betonromantik, at a two-day oppositional workshop. Jana was a little fearful of singing the lyrics that had sent them to prison—she was on probation for two years after her release and could have been tossed back into the slammer at the drop of a hat. Fortunately everybody knew their songs and the entire crowd sang the lyrics, a rough-hewn chorus growling and howling about Nazis in East Berlin. This led to one of the first brawls between punks and skinheads, who made up a small portion of the audience. Most DDR skinheads had started out as punks and still had connections to the scene; they were drawn to the shaved-head look because in some ways it was even more provocative than a Mohawk. As the decade wore on, the skinhead scene began to evolve from a bunch of thrill-seeking brawlers into actual neo-Nazis. At that December 1984 concert in Halle, for instance, some skinheads wore *white power* patches. The fistfights in Halle hinted at the future—to an eventual break between the punks and skins, a break fraught with violence and at least one murder.

Namenlos began to play regularly at events set up by any and all of the oppositional political groups, whose ranks were now heavily stocked with young punks. The band got people dancing wildly, pogoing, every jump and stomp and lurch a blow to the regime and its increasingly futile attempts to control every facet of life.

44

B y the mid-1980s, Open Work in Berlin had become an autonomous, self-governing operation. It was welcoming to people who didn't necessarily consider themselves punk when it came to fashion or music, though most of the participants subscribed to a similar anarcho-punk philosophy, whether or not they wore Mohawks.

The problem in Berlin was that while punks now had a place to hang out—the Profikeller—Open Work still had no permanent home in the city. Pfingst had wanted to get rid of the punks, but condemning the bell tower apartment had ended Open Work altogether.

With the new level of organization and activity that came with the return of A-Micha and others, Erlöser-based activists built bridges to other groups throughout the city and the rest of the country—peace groups, environmental groups, and rights groups, as well as Open Work communities in other cities—and pushed for a new, permanent home for Open Work in Berlin.

What the Berlin chapter of Open Work wanted: a church building with an intact roof where they could pursue their mission of serving the city's outsider community and fighting the society that created outsiders. They wanted a building that would be open every day, with room enough for concerts, workshops, and parties.

What the Berlin chapter of Open Work had: an infrequent café night featuring readings, discussions, and exhibitions in the punks' cellar on the grounds of Erlöser church, and very infrequent larger-scale events on the side—like a two-day political workshop and punk music festival in October 1984.

Then, in September 1985, Open Work convened a general meeting in a rented church space. At that meeting, attended by nearly two hundred people, the idea of squatting a church first started to percolate. Squatting was by now such a normal part of how the underground operated that it seemed only natural to solve another space issue by simply grabbing it, carving it out, making it theirs.

Action.

Still, it initially looked as if squatting might not be necessary. For one thing, there were a lot of empty church buildings in Berlin. For another, the large number of people who turned up for the general meeting seemed to give Open Work leverage. So representatives of the Open Work community began to negotiate with church leadership for a home base.

In the rush of enthusiasm that followed, the Erlöser gang was eager to keep people updated on those negotiations. This led in the fall of 1985 to the publication of an underground newspaper—the first such publication in East Germany. Called the *mOAning Star*, its initial core staff included Kaiser and other first-generation punks. The title combined a reference to a British labor union paper—the *Morning Star*—with the letters *OA*, which were the initials of Open Work in German: *Offene Arbeit*.

Open Work eventually took the strategy of declaring itself a congregation, albeit one made up almost entirely of nonbelievers and governed strictly by direct democracy, with no hierarchy whatsoever. Despite initial optimism that the church would provide a home for the new "congregation," by the end of 1985 Open Work would be denied space at fourteen different church buildings where it requested access. It galled the activists that Zwingli Church, near Warschauer Strasse S-Bahn station, had recently been ceded to the state library system as an auxiliary storage facility under a ninety-nine-year lease while Open Work couldn't get space despite their roots within the church.

But the Erlöser crowd didn't give up easily.

For one thing, they now had their own publication.

When it was first conceived in 1985, the *mOAning Star* was supposed to function as an in-house info sheet on negotiations for space, and also—since it initially looked like space w ould be quickly forthcoming—a way to inform readers about the event schedule at the new venue. But as the hunt for space dragged on, the *mOAning Star* instead became a satirical political newsletter that took pride—punk pride—in being provocative, undiplomatic, and downright disrespectful in its coverage.

The key figure behind the *mOAning Star* was twenty-two-year-old Dirk Moldt, who functioned in essence as the editor in chief—at least as much as anyone did in such an anti-hierarchical context. Dirk was also the paper's political cartoonist. He had grown up in an atheist household, and his first exposure to the church had come when he started to attend Blues Masses at Samariter Church as a teenager. He immediately loved the fact that the events were filled with freaks. But Dirk soon began to question the hippielike ethos that dominated the Blues Masses. What he initially thought he had found in the long-haired blues crowd he found in punk instead. There was something about the punks—they were funny, for one thing, and they were all about *action*. He started to go to punk shows as often as he heard about them, and though he didn't affect a punk look, his affinity for punk and anarchism continued to deepen. When Namenlos and Planlos played the Blues Mass at Erlöser Church in the summer of 1983 and were initially shouted down by the blues fans, that settled things for Dirk. It was all about punk for him from then on.

The *mOAning Star* very much embodied the punk spirit. For one thing, the paper reflected the grotesque humor that had drawn Dirk, among others, to the punks in the first place. Also, unlike subsequent underground publications, the *mOAning Star* was most definitely not intended for Western media consumption. Unlike some other activist groups, Berlin's Open Work activists did not cultivate contacts on the Western side of the Wall. If anything, the Erlöser Church gang—both the all-punk group and the more heterogeneous Open Work—tended to look eastward, building ties to Poland and Hungary and Czechoslovakia.

Editorially, the *mOAning Star* operated independently of the church, but it did benefit from an important church privilege: with the addition of an official stamp that said "for internal church use only," the paper was shielded from government legal action. Of course, it was still dangerous to be associated with such a project. There were no bylines and no masthead. In addition to providing the protection of anonymity, the lack of attribution and leadership structure suited the Erlöser crowd's radically democratic approach.

Under Dirk and Kaiser, and with contributions from the Erlöser punks as well as the lay deacons Lorenz Postler and Uwe Kulisch, the *mOAning Star* became an important underground paper, distributed as far afield as Dresden, Halle, Jena, and Karl-Marx-Stadt, and eventually sharing production facilities—and Dirk, as political cartoonist—with the *Umweltblätter*, a famous underground environmental newsletter that was founded in 1987. From initial print runs of just a few dozen copies, the *mOAning Star* reached a thousand within a few years.

By October 1985, A-Micha had also gathered a staff—including Jana and Kaiser—to publish another political newsletter, the first of which was called *die Un/freie Gesellschaft*, or the *Un/free Society*. At around the same time, other Profikeller punks started a fanzine called *Alösa*, a Berlin-accented spelling of Erlöser that allowed for anarchist *A*s in the design. The outbuildings of Erlöser Church were now the source of three uncensored publications, all shielded from shutdown by the "for internal church use only" stamp.

They had done it again.

Create your own world, your own reality.

DIY.

Revolution from below.

45

When Pankow was discharged from the army in late 1985, he didn't miss a step. He had been to the Profikeller before his conscription and was still friendly with Deacon Postler, and it felt natural to him to return. But Pankow didn't necessarily fit in the same way he had before his military service. He no longer dressed so outlandishly or wore a punk haircut. A younger generation of punks had come along while he was in the army, and Pankow didn't know any of them. Still, he joined A-Micha, Kaiser, and Speiche, who formed a sort of inner circle at Erlöser. And Pankow soon got to know Dirk Moldt, too.

Other aspects of Pankow's life were a mess.

Pankow was still deeply in love with Nase, who had saved him from prison by agreeing to collaborate with the Stasi, then burned herself as an asset by telling everyone. Despite pressure from his band mates, Pankow had stuck by Nase just as she had stuck by him, and they were still together when he had to report for army duty. Pankow was crushed when he arrived back home and found she had moved on.

Pankow had come home from the army with the idea of founding a new band. He settled his differences with Kaiser over the breakup of Planlos, but the breakup still haunted him. He felt oddly inhibited now. Somehow he had lost the courage to sing, to front a band. The demise of Planlos—the animosity, the distrust that the Stasi had managed to cultivate—had been so traumatic, and the shock of being chucked out by his friends was something he had never recovered from. Now the person for whom he had drawn a line in the sand—Nase—had abandoned him, too.

Still, Pankow wanted to make music—up to then it had been his means of taking ownership of his life, the way he wrested control of his own future. He started talking to Kaiser and Dirk Moldt about forming a band. In this new outfit, Fatale, Pankow did not sing. He decided to hunker down behind the drum kit. Dirk would play guitar. Kaiser would play bass and sing, or they could find another singer. Pankow wasn't going out front anymore.

Although the new band provided a way to connect to other people, in some ways Pankow found himself less animated by music, less passionate about it. Limiting the scope of his activity to being in a band no longer seemed sufficient to him. He wanted to do things at a national or international level, to be part of something much bigger. So in addition to putting together Fatale, he got involved in a number of other efforts. He joined Open Work's fight for space and he joined a punk theater group that was also operating out of Erlöser Church. He joined peace groups and groups liaising with the Polish opposition. Slowly he began to shift more and more of his energy into straight-up political activities.

Fatale eventually found a frontman in Herne's older brother Mecki, who was now out of jail. Mecki had briefly tried singing in a project with Imad from Wutanfall, and was friends with other Leipzig punks. The Stasi kept close tabs on him.

With the Fatale lineup set, the band rehearsed for a few months. They sang about everyday problems and the environment, they railed against consumption and production-line work, and they delved into more pointedly political topics, too.

The first Fatale gig would be in early 1986 at an Open Work benefit concert for an agrarian commune in a village called Hartroda, in the southern state of Thüringen. The Hartroda commune had been founded in 1978 to serve adults with disabilities. One of the cofounders, Matthias Vernaldi, was nineteen at the time but due to a physical disability he had always lived at home; he was rarely able to meet up with other people his age and yet he didn't share the same ideas about life with his straitlaced parents. East Germany had services and facilities for school-age kids with disabilities, but most adults with disabilities felt marooned, typically forced to live either with their parents or in nursing homes intended for the elderly. Vernaldi and a group of friends—some with disabilities, some not—decided to establish an alternative. For that they immediately attracted the attention of the Stasi, who started "Operation Parasite" to monitor them. Despite the scrutiny, they eventually managed to get hold of a farm with a wreck of a farmhouse on it. They lived off of much of what they produced—vegetables, eggs, pigs—and brought in a little money selling fruit and wool.

Pankow found the Hartroda commune magical. They were doing out in the open what many punks were trying to do furtively in Berlin and other East German cities. They had disengaged and struck out on their own, pursuing collective goals and a lifestyle that suited them. Vernaldi and his friends had created their own world, their own reality. Their fundamental philosophy was similar to the punks: as Vernaldi used to say, you had to make the best out of whatever the situation on the ground was, and not wait around until everything was just right. You could wait forever for that.

Don't die in the waiting room of the future.

Maybe communities like this could be the building blocks that could be scaled up to a societal level, the cells that could form an entire organism? Though a lot of the punks espoused some sort of socialist anarchism, they themselves often weren't entirely confident about the chances of success for such a system on a society-wide level; it just seemed like the most attractive blueprint in the abstract. But here was a functioning, concrete model.

Pankow and Kaiser and A-Micha, Jana, and Mita weren't the only key players from the first generation who kept charging forward. After singer Chaos left the Leipzig band Wutanfall in the wake of his extreme harassment by the Stasi in 1983, the band fused with HAU. The new band included guitarist Imad, who had quit Wutanfall for HAU; Stracke, the HAU singer who had replaced Chaos in Wutanfall; and, upon his release from prison for spray-painting FREEDOM FOR JANA, MITA AND A-MICHA, bassist Ratte.

Ratte represented the government's worst nightmare: totally unfazed by his prison stint, he put his leather jacket back on as soon as he walked out of the prison gates and went straight back to punk, to activism, to ignoring the laws he deemed unjust, to fighting a regime he considered illegitimate.

In the end, the only original and continuous member of Wutanfall—drummer Rotz—left the band, so they decided to change their name. They became L'Attentat, and the new band proved as incendiary as Wutanfall. In addition to playing Wutanfall songs like "Leipzig in Ruins," and *"Bürgerkrieg,"* or "Civil War," L'Attentat had strident new songs, too. *"Friedensstaat,"* or "Peace Nation," was a send-up of official government rhetoric on security through militarization. *"Kinderkrieg,"* or "Children's War," was a bitter commentary on military training in schools. "Demonstration" had a couplet that translated "Freedom of thought is guaranteed, but if you try to use it you get hauled away."

L'Attentat sang about taboo subjects and used explicit terminology—the Wall, the Party—that even other non-licensed punk bands might have had second thoughts about using. All of this over an intense, menacing hardcore sound.

The lyrics of another tune, *"Ohne Sinn,"* or "Pointless," translated as:

I'm old enough to go it alone
I don't want to see all this shit anymore
The way you rob me of my future
And ask me to fight for things you no longer believe in yourself

When the members of Wutanfall and HAU joined forces to form L'Attentat, they had sat together and all agreed: we will say exactly what we think, even if that means we go to prison. Ratte, who had been to prison, knew what that meant. Stracke, too, had been detained for a month and knew the potential gravity of what they were agreeing to. But they fully backed the band's determination to be open, not to mince words. Stracke loved the sense of liberation. If he was interrogated and asked whether he was opposed to the state he would just say, "Ja."

Go fuck yourself.

L'Attentat also sought to foster a sense of community around the band, to build a sturdy network. On holidays like Mayday or Easter the band created photo collages with greetings and fun images, printed them as black-and-white photos, and sent them to hundreds of people. They mailed out invitations to their gigs and parties, again using a darkroom to copy the flyer in the form of a photo. They knew the mass mailings would attract attention from security organs. That was part of the point.

We are here, motherfuckers.

Leipzig now had a space comparable to the Profikeller at Berlin's Erlöser Church: the Mockauer Keller, also a basement on the grounds of a church. Like the Profikeller, the Mockauer Keller became a buzzing hive of activity, information, and communication. In early 1985 L'Attentat played a gig there that embodied their sense of community. Namenlos came down from Berlin, Paranoia from Dresden, and it felt as if the whole punk family was represented, the whole country. Unfortunately it also proved to be the final show by that lineup of L'Attentat.

Once again it was the singer they came for first.

In the summer of 1985, L'Attentat vocalist Stracke was arrested—again—and held in pretrial detention—again. This time, however, Stracke went to trial after two months of detention. He was sentenced to one year and seven months for illegal Western contact and vilification of the regime. He had sent an article about Eastern punk to a West German fanzine.

Stracke wondered why L'Attentat guitarist Imad, who had also written for Western fanzines, hadn't been picked up. But he wouldn't have believed the real reason why: Imad had served up Stracke to the Stasi just as he had doomed Chaos back in 1983.

Like everyone in L'Attentat—or at least, as they had all vowed—Stracke wasn't worried about going to jail. Punishment was not a disincentive to Stracke; he would obey the law if and only if he deemed it legitimate, just, fair. Stracke felt confident in the fact that what he did, and what he was doing with the band, was right, and that the laws under which he was guilty were wrong. He even said so in court, just as he had said he would when the band rebooted. Was he opposed to the state? *Ja.*

Stracke was eventually ransomed from prison by West Germany. By the second half of the 1980s, political prisoners were becoming an ever more valuable source of Western currency for the Honecker regime, another export product, like blood supplies—which were also siphoned from prisoners.

L'Attentat, meanwhile, reconvened with yet another singer, Perry. The band still had no clue that Imad was betraying them from within.

This second incarnation of L'Attentat played the benefit concert for the Hartroda commune together with Fatale in early 1986. The gig was the start of two ongoing relationships—one between punks and the commune in Hartroda and another between Fatale and L'Attentat. Both bands were deeply involved in the Open Work scenes in their respective cities, and they went on to play many gigs together, helping to further unify the Berlin and Leipzig punk scenes.

Otze had also kept Schleim-Keim going. The original bass player had been conscripted into the army in 1984, around the time Otze himself spent four weeks in Stasi detention. When Otze was released, Schleim-Keim started up with a succession of bass players, two of whom turned out to be Stasi snitches. The band shape-shifted on stage, too. Otze sometimes played guitar instead of drums, and several other people joined the band over the course of the years. In part this was because Otze was living like a nomad, with no fixed address and without so much as a change of clothes or a toothbrush.

The band remained a sensation. With their second bass player, they started playing a new song, *"Prügelknaben,"* which means "Baton Boys," as in the kids who get beaten by police batons. The song included the following lines:

Wir wollen nicht mehr, wie ihr wollt
Wir wollen unsere Freiheit
Wir sind das Volk, wir sind die Macht
Wir fordern Gerechtigkeit
Wir sind das Volk, wir sind die Macht

We don't want it the way you want it anymore
We want our freedom
We are the people, we are the power
We demand justice
We are the people, we are the power

The phrase *Wir sind das Volk*—"We are the people"—from Otze's new anthem would be heard again in a few years, echoing through the streets of East German cities.

46

Meanwhile Feeling B were inspiring a new generation of bands, bands that were not mainstream but did not draw the same line in the sand that the more political punks did when it came to getting amateur licenses and performing in official youth clubs.

One kid who orbited Aljoscha and Feeling B was Olaf Tost. He went by the nickname Toster and was a relative neophyte when it came to the punk scene.

Toster had seen punks at Alexanderplatz when he was fifteen and sixteen, in 1980 and 1981, but his musical socialization had been in the blues scene—he had even played guitar in a teenage blues band.

Still, Toster respected the punks because they were so *blatant* about everything. Like a lot of teens who encountered punks back then, he was shocked at the guts they had to flaunt their disregard for societal norms like that—the safety pins and homemade jewelry made out of beer tabs, the obviously controversial slogans scrawled on their clothes, the hair. You sure as hell couldn't go to a Free German Youth meeting looking like that. Which meant they *weren't*. They weren't going.

Toster had encountered problems at school for much more minor fashion transgressions. A few years back he'd found an old camo jacket with a German flag patch on the shoulder. The camo wasn't the official National Volks Army pattern and the flag didn't have the hammer, compass, and ring of rye of East Germany. When he wore it to school he got into trouble immediately. From then on he'd been known as the kid who flew the West German flag.

It's so easy to fall onto the wrong side of things, he thought.

And yet, there were the punks, strolling around like fucking aliens, getting hassled and beaten by cops and good citizens alike, and turning right back up again in public. Toster knew only one punk personally: a school friend who went by the name of Dafty, who had played in a few short-lived bands and knew everyone in the punk scene, including Paul Landers of Feeling B.

Toster found himself casting about, feeling as if he was falling between the cracks, politically disaffected but also put off by what he saw as propagandizing by church-based peace activists he encountered. He was also dismayed at how *uncool* the hippielike peace activists were. Toster felt the same anxiety as any teenager of the era—it really felt as if the end of the world would come during his lifetime. Nuclear armageddon. *Boom*, done. He didn't know how to deal with it.

Neither side is going to get me. Not the church people, not the pseudo-communists. I'm just going to do my thing, and party.

Dafty volunteered to show Toster around the punk world.

Once Dafty had introduced Toster to some punks, Toster realized one of them might be able to help him with something. He had been trying to get hold of an effects pedal for his guitar—he'd painstakingly saved up the 150 Western marks he would need, but the pedal wasn't available in the East. When he met Paul Landers and heard about Aljoscha—with his Swiss passport and freedom of movement—a bell went off in Toster's head. This Aljoscha guy could get the pedal for him.

Toster eventually went over to the squat at Fehrbelliner 7 to ask Aljoscha personally. He could not believe the scene—it was more bohemian than anything he had ever seen. Aljoscha agreed to get the pedal and Toster forked over the cash—an absolute fortune at the time. But Aljoscha dragged his feet. Toster stopped by a couple times a week to gently remind him. After a while the ritual of hanging out at Fehrbelliner 7, drinking wine, meeting more and more people, and becoming part of the scene became more important than the original mission. By the time Aljoscha finally procured the pedal, Toster was travelling with Feeling B to their shows.

Dafty, like so many first-wave punks, had been shipped off to an army unit in 1984 for reeducation. By then, though, Toster had entered the world of Feeling B. And Feeling B was doing *exactly* what Toster wanted to do. Toster came to see the band's amateur performance license—the *Einstufung* that allowed the band to play openly, in official venues—as a strength. The church punks, Toster reasoned, were preaching to the converted. But when Feeling B went into some backwater town and brought the noise in an official youth club, they were playing to kids who had no idea this kind of thing existed. Besides, the youth clubs had *real* stages and *real* sound systems. Toster didn't want to be a dissident and he didn't want to leave; he did want to play music. And the Feeling B model allowed you to make a living playing music.

Soon Toster started a band of his own.

Toster's band, die Anderen, or the Others, would lend their name to a whole new genre of music in East Germany—their name became synonymous with the gray-area bands that auditioned for amateur band licenses and yet thought of themselves as operating outside the realm of official music. These bands soon came to be lumped together and called *die anderen* bands, or the *other* bands; that is, the outsiders.

47

I n the 1980s, rent on an official apartment in Prenzlauer Berg cost about fifty East marks a month. You could get twenty freshly baked bread rolls for one mark. But one blank cassette cost twenty marks.

Still, cassettes had several advantages. First and foremost, although expensive, they were at least available. And cassettes could be easily duplicated. In Russia, many big factories or institutions had devices to cut vinyl records—the idea was to allow for the distribution of patriotic songs and speeches on special occasions. In such a big country, it was perhaps more efficient to allow local production of such stirring recordings than to distribute them from a central manufacturing plant. The upshot was that in the Soviet Union, with so many devices sitting around, adventurous musicians could make and distribute flexi-discs on materials considered waste—the USSR was awash in illegal records cut on things like X-ray photographs. The DDR did not hand out machines capable of copying vinyl. Shit, copying *paper* was virtually impossible in the DDR, hence the use of home darkrooms to copy flyers as black-and-white photos.

Cassettes were also a "fast" media. A band could record direct to cassette and have a finished product—playable in almost any household in the country—as soon as the last note subsided. Then it was just a matter of copying it from one tape to another. Sure, this had to be done in real time, but it was at least *possible*.

Flake from Feeling B had a cousin in West Germany who sent him a nice tape deck as a gift. For a time, nearly all the recordings in Prenzlauer Berg were made on that deck. But while lots of bands and musicians recorded on Flake's tape deck, Flake's own band Feeling B was one of the few bands that didn't bother with recordings.

Feeling B were in a unique situation, one made more complicated by their *Einstufung*. On the one hand, they were the most widely known and most frequently performing punk band in the country. But on the other hand, they actually didn't want to advance their "career." It wasn't just that they objected to making music for the sake of selling it—after all, they could have given it away. Because of their *Einstufung*, they had to be careful not to become *too* successful. They didn't want to end up in the horrible wasteland of professional Eastern bands. Nobody in the scene—even those with aspirations of living as musicians—wanted that sort of Eastern success.

The most adamant opposition to the idea of Feeling B making recordings came from Aljoscha. To him, a Feeling B concert was a unique event, a happening, and anything that detracted from that would be a mistake. Feeling B, to Aljoscha, was all about the fun of being there, together; he wanted the active participation of an audience, not the passive ears of mere listeners.

But for the rest of the scene, cassettes were a lifeblood. In a society where the state maintained an iron-fisted grip and official monopoly on mass communication, tapes represented an alternative grassroots form of media, a shadow system free from government oversight and censorship.

There was no distribution system for unsanctioned cassettes. People simply passed them around, traded them, re-taped them. Once it had been the Pistols and Crass and X-Ray Spex; now it was also Eastern bands, or even some unknown DDR musician's basement tapes. No official media acknowledged the existence of these homemade recordings, much less reviewed them.

As the scene grew, bands began to put artistic covers in the cassette boxes, copy their tapes in larger quantities, and even encourage people to order tapes through the mail. Bernd Jestram and Ronald Lippok of the first-generation punk band Rosa Extra started a cassette-only record label called

Assorted Nuts, which was based in a squatted apartment in Friedrichshain. As musicians, both Jestram and Lippok had already moved into the gray areas that opened in the wake of Feeling B in the mid-1980s, Bernd with the band Aufruhr zur Liebe and Lippok with Ornament & Verbrechen. When the two of them had trouble getting hold of enough tapes for their label, they scrounged up officially issued cassettes by artists like Mireille Mathieu—the French crooner whose music was licensed for sale by Amiga, the state-run record label—and recorded over them.

Jestram was expatriated in 1986 and ended up in West Berlin. But illegal labels soon sprang up all over East Germany: Klangfarbe in Karl-Marx-Stadt, Zieh-dich-warm-an in Dresden, Trash Tape Records in Rostock, Hartmut in Leipzig, and in Eisleben a label called Christus—named for the church in Halle that had hosted that first-ever punk festival in 1983. In Jena, a label called Hinterhof Productions released twenty-two cassette albums by fifteen different bands during the late 1980s. There were also countless homemade tapes recorded and handed out by bands themselves.

Not all of the bands producing cassettes had been coopted by the *Einstufung* process. On the contrary. Christus was basically the house label of the unlicensed original punk band Müllstation. Hinterhof Productions issued tapes by Sperma-Combo, die Fanatischen Frisöre, and hardcore rejectionists Antitrott, among other decidedly "negative-decadent" bands. Trash Tape Records released tapes only by bands without an *Einstufung*. Sample of lyrics from one of their bands, Virus X:

Wir brauchen eure Normen nicht,
Ihr wisst ja nicht mal selbst was richtig ist.
Wir werden euch niemals vertrauen,
Wir wollen uns unser Leben selbst aufbauen

We don't need your standards,
You don't know yourselves what's right.
We will never trust you,
We want to make our own lives.

Or take a 1985 tape by the band Re-Aktion, out of Potsdam, which contained material that was downright Namenlos-like, including incendiary screeds against the police. A typically explicit Re-Aktion couplet:

Say good-bye to the Party,
Shout *opposition!*

This shadow media system changed the game. Suddenly underground music that bypassed the state-run media could find a larger audience than ever before. The scale of underground tape distribution grew to be staggering—by 1988 three quarters of all music released in the DDR originated outside the state-controlled media system.

Things were changing in a broader sense as well. *Glasnost.* Since the ascension of Mikhail Gorbachev as leader of the Soviet Union in 1985, the signals coming from the East had changed. Right from the start, Gorbachev broke taboos when he admitted to economic problems in the USSR. And he just kept going, deploying the word *glasnost* to describe his reform goals— a word that up to then was most familiar as the term dissidents used to describe their demand for *openness* in court proceedings.

1986 proved a landmark year: Gorbachev made concrete policy changes based on glasnost in March; in November he told Soviet satellite states that they had a sovereign right to self-determination, indicating his unwillingness to continue to meddle in their domestic affairs; and in between those two developments, the biggest nuclear disaster in history occurred at the Soviet power plant in Chernobyl. For East Germans, Chernobyl provided a concrete example of the hypocritical, dishonest leadership of their country. DDR news outlets trivialized the potential consequences of the massive radiation leak; it was only from Western outlets that East Germans were able to learn the scale of the disaster.

In the wake of Chernobyl, A-Micha of Namenlos collected signatures for a petition on nuclear policy reform. He intended to forward the petition to the East German parliament. Two other punk bands, Vitamin A, from Magdeburg, and Müllstation, from Eisleben, specifically addressed the

Chernobyl disaster—Vitamin A organized a rally during a local workers' festival, and Müllstation collected signatures for an anti-nukes petition that was similar to A-Micha's.

Two members of Vitamin A were jailed.

On March 27, 1986, just weeks after Gorbachev formally introduced his policies of glasnost and *perestroika* at the 27th Congress of the Soviet Communist Party, the official youth radio station of the DDR, DT64, launched a new show called *Parocktikum*. The show was initially broadcast for one hour on one Thursday a month, but soon extended to two hours every Saturday. The host, Lutz Schramm, began to play songs from gray-area bands whose tapes he collected. Suddenly listeners across the entire country heard bands that operated outside the official record label system, even if the only bands DT64 dared to broadcast did have amateur-band licenses.

As a later Stasi report would lament, looking back at these developments, "Amateur licenses are easily procured . . . which has fostered an independent scene in Berlin . . . a scene also propagated on youth radio . . . as a result, the number of punk sympathizers has risen."

Many bands that had operated entirely outside the system came in from the cold at this point and auditioned for an *Einstufung*. The old-school Dresden punk act Paranoia evolved into the amateur-licensed band Kaltfront; former Planlos members Lade and Kobs formed the Goth-influenced Cadavre Exquis; die Zucht, from Leipzig, became die Art. When Toster's buddy Dafty returned from the army, he, too, secured a license for his new band, die Drei von der Tankstelle—the Three From the Gas Station. More and more bands began to make tapes and send them to Schramm at DT64.

Even so, this new development did nothing to bridge the divide within the scene: while some bands submitted cassettes to the host of *Parocktikum*, others refused on principle to enter the state-run media world in any form, even through the side door of the radio show. To them—the rejectionists—this was just another example of the state trying to coopt the scene. If anything, DT64's tacit approval of gray-area bands only intensified the philosophical battle within the scene.

For people who thought like Toster, frontman of die Anderen—people who wanted to make a living as a musician and find an audience for their music—access to the national airwaves spurred them on. Groups in the *anderen bands* scene could make a name for themselves on government radio and pack official venues, but that also allowed them to unleash their own sometimes politically unsavory sentiments on live audiences. Even if the lyrics weren't as explicit as straight-up rejectionist bands like Namenlos and Re-Aktion, it didn't take a genius to read between the lines of a song like *"Scheissegal"* by Kaltfront:

> *Was ihr sagt ist mir egal*
> *Was ihr denkt ist mir egal*
> *Was ihr wollt ist mir egal*
> *Scheissegal*
> *Es hat keinen Sinn zu warten*
> *Ich passe nicht in das Klischee*
> *Ich habe keine Illusionen*
> *Ich glaube nur, was ich sehe*

> I don't care what you say
> I don't care what you think
> I don't care what you want
> I don't give a shit
> There's no point in waiting
> I don't fit into the cliché
> I have no illusions
> I believe only what I see

48

For the hardcore punks, the political punks, the ones who refused to seek amateur licenses or work with the government in any way, 1986 became the most active year since 1983. Things were really taking off.

On the third weekend of June, thousands of youths—the Stasi's conservative estimate claimed 700, including 280 punks—descended on a small town in Thüringen called Rudolstadt for a three-day church-sponsored festival billed as Jugend 86, or Youth 86. Pankow's band Fatale played, creating a major draw for Berlin punks, alongside Schleim-Keim, L'Attentat, and other bands. Local authorities proved unable to control the situation, and punks had complete run of the little town of 30,000.

A Stasi follow-up report mentioned not only the unlicensed bands and the distribution of unauthorized publications, but also the fact that groups of punks left the church grounds and created commotions in town.

After the festival, one concerned citizen complained in a letter to city officials that he and his wife had gone to the market on Friday evening and noticed other townspeople walking home with looks of confusion and disgust on their faces. The man and his wife soon realized why: in front of a grocery store they saw "so-called punkers," whose "appearance cried out revulsion and rebellion," the citizen reported, "and instilled terror." That same good citizen had also overheard a conversation in town in which another older citizen claimed that the police "were *afraid* to intervene."

Afraid.

Of the punk hordes.

And maybe, just maybe, they *were* afraid—punks certainly hadn't faced the obstacles in Rudolstadt that they had in Halle back in 1983.

The Stasi noted with alarm the extensive network of contacts and communications between punks in cities like Halle, Magdeburg, Dessau, Erfurt, Karl-Marx-Stadt, Leipzig, and Berlin, but where were the lines of baton-wielding cops? Where were the orders to keep punks from boarding trains to Rudolstadt? Where were the rows of police trucks to haul away detainees? Sure, the Stasi accumulated information about Jugend 86 and the tenor and content of discussions during the festival, but was that going to help tamp down the rising tide of open revolt?

One of the bands that had played Jugend 86 was a newly reformed Internationale Müllabfuhr, or IM—called IM 86 for the Rudolstadt show. IM's guitar player, Bernd Hennig—now eighteen, going by the nom-de-punk of Boris Becker, and a regular in the Profikeller—put together the new version around a female vocalist named Cabi. After Jugend 86 the group quickly renamed themselves Kein Talent, or No Talent.

Boris Becker, it turned out, had been manipulated into informing for the Stasi—into becoming an actual IM. During conversations with the Stasi that had begun when he was significantly underage, Boris had declared himself opposed to any form of violence in the exercise of power—he believed that people's support for any system should be won over, they should be convinced, not cowed. His handlers considered him idealistic and saw that he was extremely loyal to his friends. They used it all against him. Boris was led to believe that he could *help* his friends. If he just gave the Stasi information about this or that, they wouldn't have to haul other people in for unpleasant interrogations. He could even prevent things that might get people sent to jail, they told him. And so, as Kein Talent became a regular draw at the Profikeller and Boris attended all sorts of other meetings and concerts there, he relayed some details to his handlers.

A punk named Reimo played drums in Kein Talent. Reimo also played in another combo, called Antitrott.

Antitrott represented a new trend—the arrival in East Berlin of scads of kids from elsewhere in East Germany. Antitrott had been founded in

Frankfurt Oder, a small industrial river city on the Polish border, northeast of Berlin. Like East Berlin, Frankfurt Oder had some nice old buildings and cobblestone streets; like East Berlin, many of those buildings and streets were in grim condition, and there were lots of ugly new apartment blocks, smokestacks, and wide open fields of mud where other buildings had been razed or destroyed. The population of Frankfurt Oder was under 100,000, so the city's few punks really stood out.

Reimo had started Antitrott with singer and guitarist Thomas Kremer and bassist Jörn Schulz upon their return from mandatory army duty in 1984. The boys had been conscripted during early attempts to break up the punk scene. They returned from the army angrier and more determined than before. Initially authorities had sought to coopt them into the new gray areas opened up by Feeling B, offering a musical mentor and trying to get them to rehearse in the basement of an official youth club. Instead, Antitrott found an isolated storage shack and worked there—until the place burned down. Then they broke into an empty building on the outskirts of town where the electricity was still on and practiced there. Until they got caught. After that they practiced in a waterlogged basement.

Antitrott's music was ferocious. When they played their first live show at a church in Leipzig on New Year's Eve, 1984, the crowd went fucking crazy.

The band quickly developed a national reputation. They played at churches all over the country, headlining things like a peace workshop in Karl-Marx-Stadt. As the band played to bigger and bigger crowds, authorities began to make things difficult back in Frankfurt Oder—they were constantly detained and interrogated, and their parties were raided. Jörn became paranoid, often peeking out the window to see what cars were outside his place, what conspicuously inconspicuous agents were standing around. One night in 1986 he was on his way home on the back of a friend's motorcycle when they were pulled over. They didn't have their wallets. Jörn's friend told the police he would go get his papers if they gave him a minute to grab them at home, just around the corner.

"What about me?" Jörn asked.

"Not you, Herr Schulz," a cop replied. "We know who you are."

The fact that the police in Frankfurt Oder recognized him by sight set off a new set of alarm bells in his head.

I've got to get out of here.

Soon after that Jörn fled.

Although it was illegal to change places of residence without permission, Jörn crashed with a girl he knew in Berlin named Ina. He never returned to Frankfurt Oder or saw his family again while the Wall was still standing. Instead, he and Ina squatted an apartment together in Friedrichshain, briefly married, and started working together on songs that would eventually form the basis of another band, Wartburgs für Walter. Kremer, Antitrott's singer and guitarist, was already dating Tatjana, a member of the Berlin band die Firma, and playing in a side project with her; Kremer soon followed Jörn to Berlin. Reimo, the band's drummer, was the last to make the move.

As the decade wore on and the legal obligation to work was no longer rigorously enforced, more and more people simply left the provinces and made for Berlin—or other cities where they could disappear and find their way in the cracks opening up, in the increasing amounts of free space being carved out of society in the big cities, in the squats, and in activities outside the official economy, like making clothing and jewelry for private sale.

By the second half of the 1980s, Esther Friedemann, the girl who had been jailed in 1981 for spray-painting anti-Wall graffiti, was making so much money selling hand-sewn clothing on the black market that she was able to buy a used Russian luxury car, a big fat Chaika GAZ. She made occasional trips to Czechoslovakia to buy fabrics, she used sheets and mattress covers from East Germany, and she repurposed materials from pre-War pieces she was able to get her hands on. For an investment of five or ten marks in materials, she could make a piece she could sell for a hundred marks. She hawked her fashions both to ordinary people, especially up on the Baltic coast during summer months, and to artists and officially sanctioned musicians who wanted out-of-the-ordinary clothing. In addition to Robert Paris, with whom she'd been jailed, Esther's circle of friends included a round-faced, Mohawk-topped kid named Sven Marquardt, an aspiring punk photographer who made money selling his compositions as art postcards up at the Baltic beach towns.

Another source of off-the-books income in the late 1980s was smuggling. Despite the heavily fortified wall dividing the city, the two Berlins still functioned like border towns, even if it was a uniquely intimate and dangerous border they straddled. As in any border town, the discrepancies created opportunites for adventurous traders. The unlicensed punk band Der Demokratische Konsum, for instance, ran Russian military jackets to West Berlin, and had their runners—low-level diplomats—and other contacts in West Berlin buy Western porn magazines with the money; the porn mags were then traded to Russian soldiers in the East for more jackets, and round and round it went. They made so much money that some people in the scene assumed the members of Der Demokratische Konsum worked with the Stasi because of the way they lived—they were known for going into bars, often themselves dressed in Russian military gear, and ordering bottle after bottle of East Bloc champagne. At one stage they had three beautiful Tatra cars, outlandish shark-finned Czech sedans that looked like giant sci-fi versions of VW Beetles. The band was able to exist in a parallel world—which was, after all, the aim of many punks.

Another guy, Siegbert Schefke, found a gold mine in classical sheet music. He had Western family and friends bring over record albums, which he could sell in the East at an astronomical markup. He used some of the windfall to buy sheet music, which was very cheap in the DDR. He sent the sheet music back across the border, where it would be sold to piano and violin teachers at prices far cheaper than those offered by West German sheet music publishers. The West German teachers saved money and Schefke made a mint. Siegbert Schefke was no punk, but he was best friends with Carlo Jordan, the environmental activist and construction engineer at Zion Church. And he was wired into the scene enough to have Feeling B play his birthday party one year. Schefke ended up recording interviews with DDR punk bands and arranging to smuggle their music over to West Berlin for broadcast on a show called *Radio Glasnost*, a program devoted to the voices of protest inside East Germany and intended for Eastern ears. Schefke was ten years older than many punks—he was twenty-seven when, along with Jordan and others, he became a co-founder of the *Umweltbibliothek*, or Environmental Library, that opened in the basement of Zion Church in

September 1986 and led to the on-site publication of the most famous East German *samizdat* periodical, the *Umweltblätter*, or *Environmental Pages*.

Schefke became a well-known figure to punks: Speiche, who worked for Jordan on the roof of Zion Church and was also involved with the Environmental Library, called Schefke "Media Siggi" because of all of the amateur-journalism operations he undertook. In 1989, Media Siggi would be the only journalist able to film the swelling street protests in Leipzig—his footage of the demonstration on October 9, 1989, which was smuggled out and broadcast on West German TV the next day, was seen throughout East Germany and is credited with helping to snowball the number of protesters during the final weeks of the dictatorship.

But in 1986 Schefke was still new to the underground scene. Three key experiences had led to his strident anti-government convictions: he had been kicked out of university for a year because he had signed a petition against the stationing of nuclear missiles in East Germany; he'd once had books he'd bought in Hungary confiscated at the East German border; and he had realized while serving his mandatory army service that he would never be willing to fight to defend the DDR. When he had finally finished his studies in 1985, he started working as a construction-site manager. It wasn't long before he lost the job after getting detained at a political demonstration. By then he had accumulated so much money from his exploitation of the illegal border trade that he decided to risk not working to focus full-time on his primary goal: regime change.

You idiots just made a full-time revolutionary out of a nights-and-weekends revolutionary.

He loved pissing off the authorities, and he was sure that helping punk music get played on *Radio Glasnost* pissed them off. He was also convinced that the best way to effect change was to get attention for things happening in the opposition scene. In his mind, that was the way to make underground activity reverberate, the way to make the East German masses feel the ground shaking beneath the dictatorship.

Antitrott (from left: Reimo Adler, Thomas Kremer, and Jörn Schulz), ca. 1986

V

Burning from the Inside

49

By the end of 1986, Berlin's radical Open Work participants had set their sights on the following summer, when East Berlin's Lutheran Church leaders planned to hold a national conference in Berlin from June 24 to June 28, 1987, hoping to attract tens of thousands of East German participants as well as international guests and media. Open Work wanted to stage a shadow event, an anti-event: the Church Conference from Below.

In reality it was a last-ditch plan. Berlin's Open Work was dying—or really, being killed by the church itself. Open Work had been shut out of every church space in Berlin. Morale was flagging as Open Work's top goal— free space—seemed to slip further and further from their grasp.

But the official church conference inadvertently provided a perfect way to leverage support.

For several years church leaders had been wheedling the government for permission to stage a national conference to coincide with celebrations of Berlin's 750th anniversary in 1987. It would be the first large-scale church conference in East Berlin since the building of the Wall. There had been quiet negotiations since 1984, and the church proved willing to sacrifice a lot in exchange for permission to hold the event. At an institutional level, the church seemed willing to pull the rug out from under groups the government found politically troublesome. Church officials had engineered the cancellation of a peace workshop scheduled for 1987, for example, as well as the Blues Masses. When environmental, human rights, and peace groups operating in churches around the country were denied inclusion in the national conference, it was seen as such a betrayal that Berlin's Open Work had little trouble finding supporters for an alternative conference.

Walter Schilling, the minister who had created the Open Work concept in the southern state of Thüringen fifteen years before and was still an active figure among what the government considered the rogue elements of the clergy, went so far as to write a rousing essay in support of an anticonference.

"Many will probably take those who demand and work toward a Church Conference from Below for imbeciles who just want to vent their frustration, who just want to disrupt and endanger the official church conference or even the relationship between the state and church," wrote Schilling. "People make problems because they themselves have problems—and at the same time, hope." Behind the rebelliousness, Schilling heard screams for personal autonomy and self-determination, for love and solidarity, for a purpose in life, for happiness. He also wrote that such problems could not be dismissed as merely youth problems, that they were in fact societal problems—which made them problems for the church, too. "What good does it do the church to maintain its own little world if the cost is its soul?"

The punks had seceded from society, finding refuge in squats and churches and creating their own world; now Open Work in essence planned to secede from the church, which had gotten far too chummy with the government in the run-up to its national conference.

There were barriers. Space, for one. The point of the church's concessions to the government was to sideline political groups and silence opposition, and Open Work—that fetid slop bucket of faithless punks and freaks, that rabble-rousing radically democratic cesspool—was seen as the worst example of such groups. There was no possible way the organizers of the official national conference would submit to Open Work demands aimed at disrupting the conference they had been working on for years.

It didn't matter.

The concept for the anticonference began to solidify in March 1987. Concrete planning sessions began in April, followed by seven more sessions before the event itself. Starting with barely a dozen people, the planning group soon ballooned to a hundred and fifty, including participants from ten other cities. Within Berlin, the planners included large contingents from the Environmental Library and the Initiative for Peace and Human Rights, as well as people from the many small groups working out of city churches, such as peace groups from Pankow and Friedrichsfelde. On tap at the alternative conference: indoor and outdoor concerts, including an open-air headlining show by Antitrott with Kein Talent as support; readings; a play; photo and art exhibitions; discussions on such topics as East European opposition movements, Jesus-as-anarchist, and the political situations in South Africa and Nicaragua; information booths on environmental issues, the Environmental Library, and anarchism, among other things; and even a do-it-yourself printmaking stand where people could make posters with slogans like "We demand space for Open Work."

The organizers expected to be able to attract about two thousand guests.

Any revolution needs to be financed and Berlin Open Work had found a champion in Schilling. He actually broached the topic of how to finance the conference before the issue occurred to organizers, and then Schilling volunteered to lend the Berliners 10,000 marks. A major hurdle had been cleared before they even realized it was there—now they could buy supplies, among other things. Two people stepped up to handle the finances for the conference. One was a guy named Silvio Meier, who like the members of Antitrott and countless others had recently made his way into Berlin's underground scene from the hinterlands—in Silvio's case, from Quedlinburg, a medieval town in Saxony-Anhalt, just north of the Harz Mountains. The other was Fatale guitarist Dirk Moldt, who also oversaw the publication of the *mOAning Star* newsletter. For years afterward people called Dirk "Millionaire Moldt" because of the finance role he played in the event.

Discussions at planning sessions created friction between the aggressive, action-oriented Open Work mob and other mostly older activists, who were steeped in a tradition that sought dialogue. The punks sometimes grew exasperated at what they regarded as endless waffling over every detail. At one meeting, Wolfgang Rüddenklau of the Environmental Library, then thirty-five, was leading a committee discussion aimed at hashing out a procedure for procuring a few thousand bockwurst to sell during the Church Conference from Below. Finally a punk named Matze stood up.

"That's enough," he said. "I'll take care of the fucking bockwurst."

The organizers had volunteers, financing, and bockwurst. What they still lacked was a location. They notified the church of their intentions during a regional synod meeting in late April and demanded a centrally located church with extensive outdoor space.

The response from church leaders: radio silence.

On May 14, 1987, Church Conference from Below organizers invited church leaders to the Environmental Library's basement space and broke the news: if the church did not provide a centrally located building with extensive outdoor space, Open Work would squat one during the official church conference. Then they asked the church leaders to get out.

Open Work was betting that the church leadership would blink when faced with this proposal. After all, what would church leaders do if a church facility actually was squatted? Call in the police to empty it by force? During a national church conference, with international representatives and media in attendance?

Good luck, assholes.

The church took the threat seriously. Rainer Eppelmann, the minister at Samariter Church who had initiated the Blues Masses, figured his church might be the one targeted for squatting. He told a Church Conference from Below organizer that he would indeed call in the cops if they tried to stage the alternative conference at Samariter.

Still the church leadership did not budge.

The clock was now ticking as the official church conference was just weeks away.

50

n June 1987, U.S. president Ronald Reagan was scheduled to stop in West Berlin during the celebration of Berlin's 750th anniversary.

The history behind the date of the anniversary was highly dubious. It was ostensibly tied to the first appearance of the name of the city in court papers—in 1237—in the course of a legal dispute between the church and a member of the local gentry over tithing. But as one underground newsletter in East Berlin remarked, 1987 was actually the 50th anniversary of a Nazi celebration of the city's 700th anniversary. Prior to a 1937 celebration cooked up by the Nazi propaganda machine, the year 1237 had never been regarded as significant, since the known existence of settlements on the site preceded that date by centuries. Yet for some reason the date was resurrected in the 1980s. And once it was, the anniversary was—inevitably—taken up on both sides of the Wall, since neither East Berlin nor West Berlin was going to cede any aura of historical legitimacy to the other side.

West Berlin authorities were so concerned about the potential scale of anti-Reagan protests that they brought in additional police reinforcements from West Germany, putting 10,000 cops on the street in full riot gear in the run-up to his visit. Municipal sources said it was the biggest security operation in the city's history.

It's easy to forget now, but under Ronald Reagan's presidency, the chance of a shooting war between the US and the USSR seemed more tangible than at any time since the Cuban missile crisis. The world lived in the constant shadow of a genuine existential threat: total nuclear annihilation.

By the 1980s the possibility that humanity could be vaporized in a matter of minutes occupied a dark but prominent place not only in individual consciences but also, especially in the West, in pop culture. Not surprisingly, given the fact that their country was bristling with missiles and nukes and regarded as the likely flash point for World War III, West Germans seemed to have the most angst of this sort. A couple of huge international pop hits by German artists brought home the point. At first blush, Alphaville's "Forever Young," for instance, seemed to be a sweet ditty about typical teen yearnings. Except for one little thing: the reason we might remain forever young was because we could all be fried in a global blast of mutually assured destruction. Or take Nena's "99 Luftballons." One minute a couple is holding hands as they watch their balloons float into the sky; the next minute an early warning system picks up the dirigibles and triggers an all-out nuclear exchange. Then there were all the British bands with songs on the topic, many of them hits in West Germany and across Europe. Ultravox's "Dancing with Tears in my Eyes" chronicled a couple's final minutes on Earth before it goes up in flames; the Smiths's "Ask" suggested the bomb would bring us together in a common destiny as radioactive ash; the Police's "When the World Is Running Down, You Make the Best of What's Still Around" described life in a fallout shelter; Kate Bush's "Breathing" was narrated by a fetus with a somewhat improbable knowledge of fission reactions and their aftermath. There was Anne Clark's "Poem for a Nuclear Romance," the Sisters of Mercy's "Black Planet," the Cure's "A Strange Day"—the list goes on and on.

This was the bleak reality of life while Reagan held the nuclear launch codes.

On June 11, 1987, despite rain, tens of thousands of protesters took to the streets of West Berlin. Demonstrators torched cars and smashed store windows. Police fought back with tear gas and batons.

"Reagan is a murderer and a fascist!" the demonstrators chanted.

Feelings for Reagan were no warmer in the East.

Kids in the East had also grown up with a genuine sense of fear that the world might actually come to an end during their lifetime. That it probably would, in fact. For some, this fueled nihilistic feelings—one reason Toster from die Anderen, for instance, never got deeply political was because he stopped giving a shit. *Forget changing the world, let's have a party.* To Toster, the posturing, especially from Reagan, was like a pissing contest—but one that affected the whole world. And while Gorbachev had raised hopes a little, the future still looked dim with the tough-talking Reagan in power in the U.S.

On June 12, the day following the protests in West Berlin, Reagan delivered his speech at the Brandenburg Gate, with the Berlin Wall as a backdrop. Police sealed off the entire Western district of Kreuzberg in order to contain protesters they feared would overwhelm the modest audience assembled at the site of the speech.

In front of the Brandenburg Gate itself, a hand-picked crowd provided a made-for-American-TV audience for the lame-duck, Iran-Contra-scandal-ridden president. Estimates of the crowd size varied, but even the highest estimates were under 50,000. (Kennedy had drawn half a million.) Many of those present had been bused in; many had connections to the Allied military communities. Gorbachev's star had long since eclipsed Reagan's in both Germanies, and there was little interest in, or West German media coverage of, the speech.

The previous week, at nearly the same location as Reagan's speech, David Bowie, the Eurythmics, and Genesis had headlined open-air shows on three successive nights as part of anniversary celebrations. Each night a couple thousand East Germans had tried to approach the Brandenburg Gate from the east in order to hear the music; for Reagan, they didn't bother.

"Mr. Gorbachev," Reagan intoned, "tear down this wall,"

And nobody on either side of the Berlin Wall gave a fuck.

51

Two days later, organizers of the Church Conference from Below met in Halle for the last major planning session prior to the event. The group still had no reason to think the church would provide space. The Berliners had determined they would squat Pfingst Church, the old punk hangout in Friedrichshain. It seemed perfect, with an enclosed yard and several useful indoor spaces.

The following week, just days before the official church conference was to kick off, Open Work held one last round of negotiations with church leaders in Berlin. Somehow, in a moment of indiscretion, the name "Pfingst" slipped out of the mouth of one of the Open Work organizers. If anything, though, church leaders seemed relieved—at least they knew that the target wasn't one of the churches they themselves planned to use as part of the official conference. They decided to take temporary formal control of Pfingst and hand it over to Open Work peaceably to avoid the embarrassment of having it squatted.

Starting on the morning of June 26, 1987, organizers of the Church Conference from Below readied Pfingst, setting up stands and PA systems, loading in supplies for the café and bar. The Church Conference from Below opened its doors at four. Right away, almost a thousand people entered the grounds. The official opening took place two hours later, with a greeting to "friends and foes" and a speech from a young woman who attacked church, state, and party leadership and told participants that the two-day event would demonstrate the need to tackle things from the bottom up, from below.

The number of attendees continued to grow. Friday night, organizers held a general meeting, which was mobbed. Because of the unexpectedly large crowds, the church ended up giving Open Work a *second* church facility in order to avoid any potential unpleasantness—Galiläa Church, a few blocks away, would absorb overflow and host additional events on Saturday.

On Saturday, the day of the main event, as many as four thousand people were on the grounds of Pfingst Church at any given time. There was dancing and partying and punk rock, but the political impact was real: thousands of people had participated in the various workshops and discussions, with some individual events drawing huge crowds—Saturday night's general meeting attracted one thousand four hundred participants, for instance.

A government report offered a sneering description of the meetings as "completely chaotic, almost anarchic." There was no leadership, everyone lobbed criticism, and the working principle was described as "democratic." This last word reads in the report like an epithet, a curse. *Democracy*, the lowest of the low.

In the pre-dawn hours of Sunday, June 28, 1987, Dirk Moldt's work was finally done as the Saturday night revelry wound down. Millionaire Moldt stashed a denim sack filled with over 15,000 marks in notes and coins earned from concessions, and then went to savor a few drinks and bask in the sense of accomplishment as volunteers on the cleaning crew began to tidy up.

Overall attendance at the anticonference had surpassed six thousand, tripling expectations.

Six thousand!

It had been a smashing success.

Organizers who had been in a state of despair over Open Work's prospects prior to the conference suddenly had a euphoric sense of purpose and solidarity, even a feeling of power. The momentum was not fleeting, either, as the Church Conference from Below led immediately to the founding of a permanent Church from Below, replacing Open Work in Berlin and becoming an umbrella that fostered collaboration among disparate groups—from punks to peaceniks, from the Initiative for Peace and Human Rights to the Environmental Library, from teenage miscreants to aging freaks.

The Church from Below saw the causes of the various groups as inter-related: when you talked about peace you couldn't ignore human rights or environmental issues, or the structure of society for that matter. It wasn't about one or the other, it was about all of it at the same time. It wasn't about reform, it was about wholesale change. *Destroy what's destroying you.* The Church from Below reflected the aggressiveness and unconventional style of a punk-inflected organization—in fact, A-Micha and Kaiser advised the Church from Below on how to organize itself, based on their experience in Erlöser.

From then on the Church from Below held general meetings every two to three months, enabling them to maintain active contacts nationwide. The Church from Below created a deep and extensive root structure for what-ever was going to grow out of the underground. And as the Stasi began to pay more and more attention to the new network, they made the same mis-take they had when trying to break up the punk scene a few years before: they sought to identify leaders and focus on undermining them. The Stasi assumed every organization had a top-down structure like the Stasi, like the Party, like the dictatorship. But the Church from Below did in fact run *democratically*, even radically democratically.

Under the banner of the Church from Below, Dirk Moldt and the rest of the punks and anarcho-freaks of Open Work felt confident they would now get a building in Berlin. And they were right: a few months later, they signed a contract to take over part of a freestanding parish hall on the grounds of St. Elisabeth Church, a half-destroyed neoclassical gem on Invalidenstrasse in Mitte, originally built in 1835 by the famous Prussian architect Karl Friedrich Schinkel. It took more than a year for all the details to be worked out, but the Church from Below now knew they would have a home base.

Everything had turned out better than in their wildest dreams.

Stasi observers later wrote about the hundreds of punks at the Church Conference from Below—about the way the atmosphere had taken on a par-ticularly "provocative" tone during the hours of "aggressive" punk music. Antitrott, L'Attentat, Kein Talent, Namenlos, and the other bands had people making "wild rhythmic movements." The observers also tried to dismiss the punks as "primitive" and nothing more than a source of irritation at the conference. Reports mentioned their hard drinking and drunkenness, their sneaking of liquor into the event to supplement the beer on hand, and a few of them passing out in the yard. It's true, many punks liked nothing more than to get wasted. But the punks were not a homogenous group, and many among them had played key roles throughout; they were an integral part of the event's success. Government observers also commented on the way punks yelled at Western journalists who tried to take photos of them or interview them. This did not fit with the party dogma that problematic youth cultures like punk were Western-oriented.

What the government observers failed to realize was that the entire joint had been an iteration of punk; punk wasn't music or clothing or novelty haircuts, it was revolution from below, it was creating your own reality, it was action, DIY, it was wresting control of a building and throwing a radically anti-government circus in the middle of the celebration of the city's 750th anniversary, during a carefully choreographed national church conference, in the capital of a dictatorship.

That *was* punk.

Don't die in the waiting room of the future.

52

One common question during the Church Conference from Below had been: *What next?*

The short answer: a hell of a lot.

The next two years would be a flat-out sprint to the finish, with a new structure to help direct punk energy back onto the streets and ultimately down into the foundations of DDR society, shaking it deeply enough to be felt by ordinary citizens, betraying the inherent unsteadiness masked by the outward appearance of stability and strength and power.

But first, there was a reckoning to be had inside the punk scene.

The year 1987 marked the final, definitive break between punks and skinheads. The most dramatic manifestation of that break came on October 17, 1987, during a concert at Zion Church.

Stasi files had discussed skinheads and neo-Nazism in East Berlin as early as 1983, and the authorities had tried to smear DDR punks as harboring fascist tendencies. But once the smear tactics against punks proved ineffective, they seemed to have tried to convince themselves that neo-Nazism was a Western problem. A book published in 1985 by a government-approved journalist, for example, highlighted neo-Nazism's association with Western pop culture: the book described David Bowie calling Adolf Hitler "the first superstar" and reported on Eric Clapton and Rod Stewart's support for xenophobic British politician Enoch Powell, as well as Clapton's racist on-stage tirades against "coons" and "wogs." It was a logical approach. After all, according to official dogma, Nazism was a symptom of capitalism, a product of capitalist society, and as a result could not exist in the communist DDR.

It's true that shaved heads had been part of the punk scene almost from the start. Some committed anarchists also shaved their heads—Stracke, the singer of L'Attentat, had been a skinhead, for instance. In the early years, a shaved head was mostly a mark of someone who liked to fight rather than an expression of a political identity. They were thrill-seekers and button-pushers, but not Nazis. That would change.

Within the Erlöser gang, too, there had always been skinheads, including a group called the Ostkreuz crew, who hung out at a bar near Erlöser Church. As far as the other punks were concerned, some of them were okay. But others had begun to drift to the right, politically—they were, for instance, the only group calling for unification of the two Germanies before the fall of the Wall. The politically attuned punks found these attitudes totally unacceptable.

Several of the leaders of the Ostkreuz skinheads, including Jens Uwe Vogt and Sven Ebert, had grown up with Pankow and were friendly with many other first-generation punks—they had been punks themselves. In fact, almost all of the first-generation skinheads started out in the punk scene. As trouble began to brew, A-Micha was charged with shadowing Sven Ebert and Ebert's brother, Pogo-Bear, whenever the Ostkreuz crew showed up at Erlöser. A-Micha didn't consider either of them racists, it was more that Ebert had a kind of sickness—he just *needed* to fight—and Pogo-Bear always had his back.

One night a young skinhead turned up at the Profikeller in a T-shirt that said FUCK WHITE POWER. Unfortunately, the word *fuck* was hard to read.

A-Micha took a quick glance at the shirt, walked right up to the guy and leveled him with a knockout punch. When the skin woke up, he was pissed off—the shirt said FUCK white power!

"Write it more clearly next time," growled A-Micha.

Skinheads continued to create more and more trouble at Profikeller events. They would profile out-of-town punks, waiting for them to leave the church grounds before viciously attacking them en masse. After one violence-plagued night, the Profikeller punks gathered to decide how to deal with the problem—they wanted to make sure people felt safe coming to concerts, discussion groups, and other events. They decided to make a state-ment at the next concert. They arranged for the drummer of a band playing the show to give a sign, at which point A-Micha, Herne, and others jumped the skinheads they deemed the most problematic, jumped them the same way the skinheads had been jumping isolated out-of-towners.

We will do what we have to do.

The fight at the Profikeller did not take care of the problem for long. Neo-Nazism was spreading and the punks wanted to fight back. Speiche had gone so far as to start an Antifa group at Zion Church. Disagreements over tactics—there was a lot of resistance to violence, whereas Speiche had been fighting on an almost daily basis for years—led to the quick demise of the group. But an Antifa group did take off under the auspices of the new Church from Below. Soon Speiche had a sort of paramilitary troupe—armed only with their fists—that went out hunting for Nazi skinheads to beat the shit out of them.

Still the problem persisted.

In an Interior Ministry memo, the East German government seemed to think the turning point had been in 1986, when skinheads and soccer hooligans had started to openly show fascist tendencies. A report from late 1987 estimated the national skinhead contingent at 800, which represented massive growth in the space of just one year: Berlin alone now had 350 skins, versus 80 the year before and 50 in 1985. An additional 120 skinheads resided in nearby Potsdam, on the outskirts of Berlin.

A-Micha, Pankow, and Speiche began to discuss the neo-Nazi problem with Deacon Lorenz Postler, who was still in essence the sponsor of the punks at Erlöser Church. Postler didn't want to exclude the skinheads—he took the idea of Open Work quite literally and had no desire to nar-row the scope of operations at the church. A-Micha, Pankow, and Speiche vehemently disagreed. And after another series of violent disturbances at the Profikeller, they decided to take things into their own hands in the fall of 1987.

This had to be settled.

Pankow and A-Micha decided to go into the belly of the beast—to go to Hackepeter bar, the homebase of the Ostkreuz skinheads, and try to hash out some kind of understanding with the leaders. After all, these guys were old friends of theirs from the early punk days. But once they sat down and started to talk, Pankow and A-Micha quickly realized the futility of their mission. For one thing, the older skins were surrounded by much younger skinheads—and this new generation of skins had no history with punks. Or rather, no history beyond hatred, beyond seeing them as political enemies, as no better than the disheveled, smelly, useless hippies they also hated. There was no longer any sense of mutual respect, however grudging, and the conversation quickly soured, with the older skinheads making sarcastic comments toward the punks, trying to save face with the younger skins in the room. Sitting face to face with a couple of old punks was now an embarrassment. Punks were the enemy—or at least one of the enemies. In the end, Pankow and A-Micha counted themselves lucky to be able to leave unharmed.

Not long afterward, word came: the Ostkreuz skins had had it, no more talk and no more bullshit. *We are going to beat your ass.*

The Erlöser gang sent back their own message: *Bring it.*

They set a date for a straight-up rumble: Saturday, October 17, 1987.

On the assigned day, the core of the old Erlöser punks assembled ready for battle, waiting at the Profikeller with weapons, including bats and chains, and expecting an all-out war.

But on that same night, Zion Church hosted a huge concert in the main sanctuary. Dirk Moldt and Silvio Meier of the Church from Below had managed to get a popular new wave band from West Berlin, Element of Crime, to headline a show. The pair also grudgingly arranged for the DDR band die Firma to open the show—the band was not well-liked in punk circles, but die Firma had good-quality gear that both bands could use, so Element of Crime could cross the border as normal tourists, with no equipment. The Stasi found out about the show beforehand—both vocalists in die Firma were Stasi snitches—but they did not stop it.

Two thousand people had gathered by seven thirty in the evening, when die Firma started their set. Paul Landers of Feeling B was now playing guitar in die Firma as well; he was a restless musical soul and in addition to Feeling B and die Firma he also played in several side projects—one was an improvisational gypsy-punk kind of thing called Tacheles, and he and Flake had another called Magdalene Keibel Combo, a pun on the addresses of the Stasi headquarters at Magdelenenstrasse and the Keibelstrasse detention center near Alexanderplatz where punks were often taken.

About a mile away, on Greifswalder Strasse, skinheads from all over town—including a few from West Berlin—had gathered at a bar called Sputnik to celebrate the birthday of one of their members. They had spent the afternoon drinking, interrupted briefly for a skirmish with some soccer fans from Leipzig. That's really what most of the skinheads were: soccer hooligans, followers of East Berlin's BFC Dynamo, which was, ironically, the factory team of the Stasi. Despite official denials of the existence of neo-Nazis in the DDR, many high-ranking Stasi apparatchiks—including Stasi chief Erich Mielke himself—had in recent years been directly confronted at BFC matches with skinheads, their fascist and antisemitic chants, and even Nazi salutes.

As the party raged on, Ostkreuz skin leader Sven Ebert wanted to head for Erlöser to settle the score with the punks, as originally planned. But others, including Jens Uwe Vogt and another leader, Ronny Busse, persuaded a group to take a tram to Zion Church, which was nearer anyway, where they could make trouble at the concert instead. So as Pankow and Herne and others waited in the Profikeller for the showdown that never came, a horde of about thirty skinheads headed towards Zion Church. They had no idea of the scale of the concert—they figured if there were two hundred people there, the thirty of them would be plenty to do some damage and keep one another protected.

Element of Crime played their final song around ten. People started to stream out of the church into the dark night. The band's music—melancholic, mid-tempo, almost chanson-like—wasn't the sort of thing that left an audience jacked up. Some groups lingered inside the church, some gathered to chat in front of the church, and others left the church and wandered toward the nearby tram stop.

The skinheads came out of the tram just as the first concert guests reached the stop. A small group of them attacked concertgoers on the street, pouncing on them from the steps of the tram. Most of the skins ran straight for the church. Some engaged people outside while others continued into the sanctuary, where they started punching the first people they encountered while shouting things like "*Sieg Heil*," "*Heil Hitler*," and "*Judenschweine*," which translates as "Jewish pigs."

At first, absolute shock paralyzed the concert crowd.

Screaming, running.

Panic.

But there were still hundreds of concertgoers in the church, including some punks, who started to fight back. Eventually the concertgoers surrounded the skinheads and started chanting "*Nazis raus,*" or "Get out, Nazis," and—led by fist-flinging punks, including members of Antitrott—converged on the skinheads. Eventually the skins were able to retreat back outside, into the dark, where other skinheads were still involved in brawls with other concertgoers.

People outside screamed for help from police. There was no need to call them—a concert like this, with Stasi foreknowledge, attracted a huge police presence. Squad cars were parked all around the church. Uniformed and plainclothes officers stood around, along with conspicuously inconspicuous Stasi operatives. There was even an ambulance nearby, at the ready.

At 10:22 p.m., an emergency call went out to headquarters from police stationed around the church.

The response from headquarters: No intervention necessary. Reinforcements on the way.

None of the police did a thing. None of them reacted. The law enforcement officers of this officially anti-fascist state stood by as skinheads shouted Nazi slogans and pummeled people on the street.

Several truckloads of reinforcements arrived. They, too, did nothing.

Eventually the skinheads made off in a tram.

The East German media reported on the incident but insisted the attack had been engineered by forces from the West. East Berlin skinheads read the articles, met in a bar, and decided to blame the entire thing on a phantom West Berlin skinhead they called "Bomber." In the case of interrogations, everyone agreed to say it was *his* idea, *he* had led the charge. Even if *he* did not exist and the idea was all their own. For its part, the government was happy for Zion Church to come under attack—it turned out, in fact, that at the time of the skinhead attack the Stasi was already planning a tactical operation to bust up the Environmental Library. The government would be all too glad to shift the blame across the Wall and sweep the whole thing under the rug.

But Zion Church activists had other plans. Using connections to Western media—which, unlike the Church from Below, the Environmental Library cultivated—they were able to ensure that West Berlin radio reported on the skinheads and their use of Nazi slogans and on police indifference. A few weeks later, Media Siggi was even able to get video footage of East Berlin skinheads talking about their views—making sure to show Trabants and other signs of the East in the background but never showing the skins' faces—and then smuggle it across for broadcast on a national news show on West German TV.

That there were Nazi-sympathizing skinheads in the DDR was not news to Eastern authorities. They had interrogated skinheads in the wake of the attack on the church. Take this November 20, 1987, interrogation for example:

Stasi officer: What do you know about skinheads?
Skin: I can address that by saying that I myself am a skinhead. I consider myself part of the group known as 'neo-Nazis' . . . The group that I'm part of glorifies fascism the way it reigned during the Third Reich, under Adolf Hitler. I'm against foreigners . . . they should go back to where they came from . . . I'm also for concentration camps. Because I think then we wouldn't have problems like AIDS. I'm also against punks and the skinheads who are in favor of anarchy.

Now, though, the idea that the West had become aware of neo-Nazis in the DDR—complete with video footage—sent shockwaves through the dictatorship. Shame proved an effective motivator. In late November, Ronny Busse, Sven Ebert, and two other skinheads deemed the ringleaders of the attack on Zion were put on trial. Although witnesses used words like *neo-Nazis* and *Faschos*, the political component of the attack was cast aside for the purposes of the court. Sentences ranged from one to two years for simple hooliganism. After protests on both sides of the Wall, as well as the personal involvement of dictator Erich Honecker, Ronny's sentence was doubled to four years.

Still, something was very wrong with this picture. First, representatives of the officially anti-Nazi state had stood by as Nazis drew blood in a church while shouting things like "Heil Hitler." Then they had dragged their feet on charging anyone. Then the political aspects of the case were papered over.

Had the whole thing been a setup? Were the skins working for the Stasi?

The punks' suspicions that the whole thing had been orchestrated by the state were finally confirmed, at least in their eyes, in the early hours of November 25—that's when the Stasi entered Zion Church and raided the Environmental Library.

So that was it, the thinking went, it had been a dress rehearsal, a test run.

The war games were over.

Now came the war.

53

By late 1987 the basement of Zion Church held the printing press used for three separate officially unsanctioned publications: the Environmental Library's *Umweltblätter*, the *mOAning Star*—at least sometimes—and, as of only recently, *Grenzfall*, put out by the Initiative for Peace and Human Rights. Both the *mOANing Star* and *Umweltblätter* were technically legal due to the fig leaf provided by the stamp that designated the newsletters "for internal church use only." *Grenzfall*, however, was illegal: the Initiative for Peace and Human Rights insisted on asserting the right to freedom of expression that was enshrined—at least on paper—in the laws of the DDR.

The dictatorship did not exactly follow the letter of the law when it came to freedom of expression.

In the fall of 1987, the Stasi began to plan *"Aktion Falle,"* an operation aimed at crushing *Grenzfall* and, they hoped, criminalizing the Environmental Library in the process. In order to accomplish these dual goals, the Stasi needed to catch activists red-handed printing the illegal *Grenzfall* in Zion Church. The Stasi had made it obvious to the *Grenzfall* editorial staff that they were being followed and surveilled—which made them nervous about where to print the paper going forward. Then, at the behest of his handlers, a Stasi IM on the *Grenzfall* editorial staff suggested they print the paper at the Environmental Library in Zion Church—that seemed like a safe place, after all, inaccessible to the Stasi and police. The rest of the staff agreed this was a good idea. After the Environmental Library also agreed, *Grenzfall* set up in a storage room in the basement of Zion.

Now the Stasi had everything lined up for their sting.

Through the same snitch, the Stasi was informed that the latest edition of *Grenzfall* would be printed by Environmental Library activists during the night of November 24, 1987.

Perfect.

At precisely midnight—0:00 on November 25—a ten-man commando team stormed Zion Church together with a state's attorney ready to write up charges.

"Hands up!" they shouted.

They ordered the seven activists to line up against the wall and searched them for weapons.

It was the first time uniformed security personnel had forcibly entered a church since the Stalinist era.

At first the Stasi commandos thought they had found what they were looking for: the activists were indeed printing a paper. But it was the wrong paper. They were printing the *Umweltblätter*. It turned out that the duplication of *Grenzfall* had been pushed back a few hours and wouldn't have started until the morning.

Chaos ensued.

The Stasi commando rousted the minister of the church, Hans Simon, from bed. He and his wife had to dress in front of Stasi officers. Upon his arrival at the church, Simon was handed an asset seizure warrant and watched as officers confiscated the copies of the *Umweltblätter* and all of the printing equipment. They also arrested the seven activists, including one who was just fourteen.

By the next morning, the Environmental Library had sprung into action, which as usual included notifying contacts in the West. Meanwhile the Church from Below rallied support for a demonstration, quickly getting its young membership out in force. The first protesters gathered in front of Zion Church at three in the afternoon on November 25. Several were arrested. The crowd, by now several hundred strong, moved inside the church, which was at this point surrounded by police and Stasi officers. The protesters resolved to hold a vigil until three demands were met: the release of the detainees, the return of all the equipment and restoration of the capabilities of the Environmental Library, and an end to state repression of critical voices.

By nine that night, five of the seven detainees had been released—though not before their apartments had been searched. Two remained in custody, having been transported to the main Stasi prison in Hohenschönhausen.

The protests continued.

At 10:30 p.m., police pulled up in military-style transports and carted off the first people who tried once again to take the vigil outside the church. The remaining protesters moved back inside. More people showed up over the course of the night and the next day.

Late in the afternoon on November 26, the people arrested at the vigil the previous night were released. The two original detainees remained in prison.

By then, many known enemies of the state all around the country had been rounded up for detention and interrogation in order to try to hinder sympathy protests outside Berlin. Protests sprang up anyway in cities and towns all over the DDR.

Back in Berlin on the morning of November 27, punks scaled the bell tower at Zion Church and hung a massive banner for all to see. They had smuggled it into the church—through the police lines—the day before. One of them had wrapped it around his body underneath his clothes. Hand-painted across the twelve-foot-wide cloth, it said, in German: *We protest the arrests and confiscations in the Environmental Library.* Western media teams rolled their cameras as a fire truck pulled up to the church and extended a long ladder toward the tower. A man climbed the ladder and carefully made his way across a ledge to pull down the banner.

Official East German media coverage of the incident purposefully conflated *Grenzfall* and the *Umweltblätter*, referring simply to the printing of "hostile" publications. Official media also tried to lump together the environmental activists and the skinheads who had been arrested after attacking the same church the month before—bad apples one and all, enemies of the state. The Church from Below in particular took this as a grave insult, since they had Antifa groups out hunting down Nazis on the street. The bruises on Speiche's knuckles disproved any attempts at equivocation on that front.

But in the end it didn't matter what the East German press said. The final two detainees were released on the morning of November 28, and protests continued for several more days until it appeared the library's equipment would also be returned.

The Stasi had committed a colossal error in judgment. The uproar over the raid and the apparent success of the vigils fanned the flames of the resistance. Seventeen environmental and peace libraries soon opened in churches across the country—*seventeen!*—in big cities like Dresden, Jena, Halle, Karl-Marx-Stadt, and Leipzig, as well as smaller towns in the hinterlands.

Not only had the Stasi failed to eliminate *Grenzfall* and criminalize the Environmental Library, they had actually created a victory for the opposition. They had backtracked in the face of public pressure. That was a dangerous lesson to teach a bunch of aggressive young people whose confidence seemed to be growing every day.

We are the people, we are the power!

54

By late 1987, A-Micha's band Namenlos was in complete disarray.

Jana, the singer, had given birth to their son in 1986 and gradually withdrawn from the band. Kaiser had been chatted up on Alexanderplatz by an Italian woman and ended up falling in love and emigrating. Mita had shifted gears, concentrating more on visual art and other sorts of music; she quit the band.

But A-Micha did not stop, would not stop. Namenlos chugged forward.

Pankow, who had taken up the drums in Fatale, sat in for Mita for some Namenlos gigs in 1987. Fatale had lost steam, too, and Pankow now spent most of his time working with groups outside Erlöser rather than in punk music circles. He still went to shows at Profikeller, but he also worked with Bärbel Bohley and the Initiative for Peace and Human Rights; he worked with Media Siggi and Carlo Jordan at the Environmental Library; he worked with several other groups devoted to causes such as peace activism, liaising with Poland, and objecting to military service and paramilitary training. He could barely contain his contempt for the endless blathering that went on within many of these groups—he and Speiche often sat at meetings and joked bitterly about their all-talk, no-action approach. Yet he still worked with them, still participated in protests, and still gave lectures on topics like how to reject army service.

By that point Pankow was able to get by making and selling clothes. Along with people like Esther Friedemann, he was part of a sort of underground fashion clique. Pankow had even toured with Feeling B: selling clothes at their shows proved good business even if most Erlöser punks considered bands with amateur licenses turncoats. On paper Pankow worked for a writer named Elke Erb, who, as an independent worker, was allowed to hire an assistant. Erb was a member of an official writers union but had frequent conflicts with the government due to her ties to the older generation of peace activists. She had very little money; in fact, in exchange for receiving a legal job slot, Pankow actually helped support her.

Pankow didn't last long in Namenlos—he seemed to be losing his urge to make music. He had never really considered himself a musician anyway; the music had been primarily a way to amplify his rage. Eventually Markus Mathyl from the band Virus X took over on drums and, for a time at least, a woman who went by the nom-de-punk Nina became Namenlos's bassist.

The biggest hole to fill was on vocals. A-Micha had always sung on some songs, but without Jana the band wasn't the same. Jana had been an absolute terror on stage.

In November 1987, Herne and A-Micha's Polish contacts hatched an idea to deepen ties between the two communties: a joint tour of Polish and East German punk bands barnstorming across Poland. Starting earlier that same year, environmental groups in Poland had been permitted to operate openly, and Solidarity was making impressive headway; the Polish dictatorship would back down and make concessions to Solidarity's demands less than a year later, in late 1988. Polish punks were feeling it.

A-Micha combined forces with another band whose lineup was in flux: Kein Talent. Their guitarist had recently left the country, leaving bassist Boris and vocalist Cabi looking for a new opportunity. Together, A-Micha, Cabi, Boris, and drummer Markus hit the road as Namenlos/Kein Talent. They also took along Boris's other band, Wartburgs für Walter, a new entity formed from the ashes of Antitrott—whose biggest gig, at the Church Conference from Below, had also been their last. Antitrott bassist Jörn Schulz formed Wartburgs für Walter with vocalist Ina Pallas—the couple had been living together in various squats since Jörn moved to Berlin—along with Boris, playing his original instrument, guitar.

The bands crossed the border at Görlitz, armed with visas arranged by Herne and A-Micha—the fake Polish cousins system—and were picked up in Zgorzelec, on the Polish side of the border, where Herne had close friends. Everything went as arranged—Polish punks had a tight network. In part this was because the Polish government did not have the option of expatriating their headaches. Whereas the underground was constantly thinned by expatriation in East Germany, in Poland everyone had to stay in the country. Jörn was struck by one solution the Poles had found that was different from the punk squats in the DDR: communes. Everywhere, little communes.

The first night the bands were fed at the home of a Zgorzelec punk, where they also crashed. The next day they went to a club. A proper concert venue. The bands even got a soundcheck. Polish university students also maintained an extremely well organized network, and they could put on punk shows in their clubs with none of the strictures enforced in East German youth clubs. For A-Micha and the others, who had all played only in unlicensed bands, this was truly amazing.

Wow.

Polish audiences rarely saw female vocalists, and Cabi—with Namenlos/Kein Talent—and Ina—with Wartburgs für Walter—blew the crowds away. Then at the end of the night, the club manager gave the bands *money*. It was the first time any of them had been paid to play music. And to top it off, they partied long into the night after the show.

The next morning, their host trundled them onto a train and they headed for the next town, where they were again picked up and taken care of. And paid. To play another club. With a great sound system. The tour took Namenlos/Kein Talent and Wartburgs für Walter to Krakow, Warsaw, and as far east as Bialystock, a city of several hundred thousand near the Soviet border. Each night the East Berlin bands played on a bill with regional Polish punk bands, with the band Trybuna Brudu along for the entire tour. The Berliners met lots of other bands, too. One night they crashed with members of Dezerter, the Polish punk band that had played to crowds as big as 20,000 at Polish festivals.

Clearly Solidarity, glasnost, and perestroika were having major effects in Poland—A-Micha and the other Berliners could feel it. And see it. And hear it. Things were out in the open. Things were changing here. Fast.

After the final tour stop in Szczecin, it was back to the DDR, where earlier that year Communist Party central committee member Kurt Hager had dismissed Gorbachev's reforms as a "change of wallpaper" in an interview with a West German news magazine that was reprinted in official Eastern publications. "And do you really need to change your own wallpaper just because your neighbor has?" he had asked.

It was meant as a rhetorical question, of course, but as A-Micha and Jörn and Ina and Cabi and the other musicians could tell while touring in Poland, the USSR's *other* neighbors were obviously changing *their* wallpaper as well. Soviet leader Mikhail Gorbachev wasn't the exception; East German dictator Erich Honecker was.

A-Micha and the rest left Poland feeling inspired. The bands wanted to plan something back home, something that reflected the boldness and scale of what they had heard and seen in Poland, something big.

55

On January 17, 1988, the East German government staged its annual parade to honor World War I-era communist martyrs Rosa Luxemburg and Karl Liebknecht. Luxemburg in particular had always been a favorite of the *Andersdenkenden*—"dissenters," or, more literally, "those who think differently." The official parade was one that many people otherwise critical of the dictatorship were happy to join, despite the politburo heading the procession.

Following the success of the vigils after the Stasi raid on the Environmental Library, some opposition groups were feeling cocky. Some of them decided to push the envelope: they would try to join the official parade while carrying homemade banners quoting Luxemburg: "Freedom is always the freedom of the *Andersdenkenden*."

The Church from Below opposed this plan for one simple reason: the loudest voices in favor were coming from groups dominated by a newly booming phenomenon, *die Ausreiser*—people who just wanted to flee the country. Would-be emigrants. By 1988, 110,000 DDR citizens had submitted applications to leave. Naturally these people did not share the same goals as the fighters. Many of the *Ausreiser* just wanted to be photographed by the Stasi while taking part in any sort of anti-government activity, in the hope that it would help their chances of being allowed to leave the country. In other words, the would-be emigrants were narrowly self-interested, reckless, and in essence apolitical. And they were starting to create headaches for those who sought to fight the dictatorship rather than run away from it.

A few groups opened up to would-be emigrants. After all, some groups argued, when people submitted an application to leave the country, they sacrificed a lot. They often encountered trouble keeping their jobs, they lost many rights, and then they languished at home waiting to be approved for emigration—which could take years. The *Ausreiser* landed for the most part in human rights groups, despite the fact that they desired just one right: the right to get the fuck out. If *Destroy what's destroying you* was the unofficial punk motto, the motto of the would-be emigrants might as well have been: *See ya, suckers*.

As a practical matter, it proved difficult to absorb *Ausreiser* and still maintain a functional group. When word got around that people tended to be approved for departure after joining some particular group, it made that group even more attractive to other would-be emigrants. The number of such people then ballooned, and the turnover created as people left the country meant there was little familiarity or communication within the group anymore. It was a clusterfuck, and the Church from Below wanted no part of it.

They're not like us.

So when a subgroup of the Initiative for Peace and Human Rights that had been swamped by more than two hundred would-be emigrants started pushing to disrupt the official Rosa Luxemburg parade, the Church from Below urged caution: too many *Ausreiser* were looking to take advantage of the situation, it was the perfect sort of outlet for their selfish notions of how to advance their cause. Their goals put them totally at odds with those—like the Church from Below—who wanted to shape their own future by changing the situation *at home*. By staying and fighting.

A number of groups agreed to participate in the parade anyway. Many of those groups disagreed with the Church from Below on another point: the value of Western media attention. The Church from Below shunned it; many other activist groups courted it. One of the potential upsides of participating in the parade was the chance to make the West German news—this was something both the *Ausreiser* and the Initiative for Peace and Human Rights valued.

But the Stasi, too, had caught wind of the plan to march in the official parade with homemade, unsanctioned banners. And they were in no mood to be embarrassed again, so soon after the Zion Church debacle. On the morning of the parade, police and Stasi detained more than a hundred known activists. It was an attempt to head the problem off before it even got started.

Much of the membership of the Church from Below was at a retreat outside Berlin on the day of the parade—they were holding a national meeting of Open Work chapters. When they heard there had been arrests, they didn't think anything of it: there were always arrests at events like that, but there were rarely serious consequences anymore.

Protests against the mass detentions sprung up in more than forty cities across the country—a repeat, on an even bigger scale, of the reaction to the raid on the Environmental Library two months prior. The protesters had seen this film before, and they knew it had a happy ending.

But then everything went haywire.

Police made a second wave of arrests after the parade, and charges were brought against many of the detainees. Perhaps the government was turning back the clock, asserting control again after the embarrassments of the previous year?

And then the unthinkable happened: faced with charges, many of the detained activists agreed to leave the country for the West—even some of the biggest stars of the older generation, like Bärbel Bohley, Werner Fischer, Vera Wollenberger, Ralf Hirsch, and Wolfgang Templin. To some outsiders, it looked as if that had been the point of the whole exercise—as if the supposed integrity of the reformist activists was nothing but bullshit, and they were really no different than *Ausreiser*.

The nationwide protests collapsed in shock and disbelief. Zion Church became the punch line of a bitter joke: *What's the longest church in East Germany? Zion Church: you enter in the East and exit in the West.*

But it wasn't funny.

The Church from Below cried foul, asserting that church leadership had been complicit in shipping the detainees out of the country in order to defuse the situation. Of course, it was true that an awful lot of the church hierarchy—particularly in Berlin—was in bed with the dictatorship. And the defense lawyer who represented the detainees turned out to work for the Stasi. But what about the activists themselves? Why had they agreed? Since when did anyone believe the Stasi when they threatened draconian jail sentences? After all, the Environmental Library detainees had been released within a few days. These detainees must have known there would be protests on their behalf.

Another thing was clear from the Rosa Luxemburg debacle: Western media attention was no panacea. Apparently it didn't even confer any kind of protection. Many of the activists who had been detained and shipped out of the country were media darlings in the West, having actively sought coverage there. And where were they now? Gone, that's where. Gone.

With the dispiriting reality setting in that so many people from the reformist groups were willing to leave even at a moment when things seemed to be looking so hopeful, punk attitude took on an even more important role. When A-Micha had been offered release from prison to the West, his response was in essence, *Fuck you, I'm staying*.

There was a logic to the punk position: if you wanted to change the world you had to start with your own turf.

We are the people, we are the power!

Plus, the punks were still around and active as other groups atrophied from the huge bloodletting or were overwhelmed by *Ausreiser*. From now on, it seemed to the punks, this fight was going to be theirs and theirs alone.

Punks were the most radical and confrontational group on the spectrum of DDR opposition groups—though that's not quite the right formulation. The groups they dominated, like the Church from Below, were the most radical and confrontational. And since punks formed a significant portion of so many other groups—there were by then more than three hundred independent groups operating nationwide under the umbrella of the Lutheran church, varying in size from five to eighty members—punks were also the most radical and confrontational people within most any group. And even the older generation of punks like Pankow, Speiche, and A-Micha were young by comparison to the aging hippies in many peace and environmental groups. So punks tended to man the frontlines in the increasingly chaotic public protests that would characterize the final year and a half of Communist Party rule in East Germany, with the bulk of the bodies coming from the youngest generation, the kids who had joined the scene after the Stasi crackdown of 1983–84.

Punks were street fighters, willing to endure police batons for those who followed.

They were changing the game.

As a February 16, 1988, report from the Stasi's Department XX explained, since the raid on Zion Church and the Rosa Luxemburg affair, "the Church from Below has strengthened its position as the leading force behind activities." This was unlike the Environmental Library and the Initiative for Peace and Human Rights, both of which were "institutionally weakened" by the same series of events. That was an understatement: the Initiative for Peace and Human Rights was basically dead after the Rosa Luxemburg arrests, done. And there had been a schism inside the Environmental Library in early 1988, too, with a subgroup splitting off and causing in-fighting. The report also stated that "The Church from Below is determined to strongly distance itself from those who just want to leave the country." In addition, the report talked of the Church from Below creating new forms of Open Work, including being able to offer touring versions of their programs, taking music and activism to other groups around the country.

The Church from Below was functioning the way A-Micha had conceived of his own actions since his release from prison—using as a model the Narodniks, the nineteenth-century socialist revolutionaries and forerunners to the Russian revolution. The Narodniks went out to the people and planted political seeds, built revolutionary cells here and there, and then moved on again, counting on the new life to sustain itself and proliferate. Hit-and-run operations designed to create a grassroots movement primed for revolution. Hit-and-run operations designed to allow ordinary people to feel the tremors in society's foundations, the shakiness of government power. Hit-and-run operations designed to leave sparks that could slowly smolder, designed to leave society burning from the inside, with heat and intensity building toward a climactic cleansing by fire.

In early 1988 the Erlöser punks approached Dirk Moldt, who still served as treasurer of the Church from Below. They wanted to put on a massive spring festival to coincide with an annual Free German Youth festival—sort of a music-focused equivalent to the previous year's Church Conference from Below. The event was also inspired by the boldness and scale of what A-Micha, Jörn, and the others had witnessed in Poland.

We will stay and we will fight.

Moldt and the Church from Below agreed to stump up the working capital for the event—much of it the proceeds from the Church Conference from Below.

It was on.

The Erlöser spring festival would be a public spectacle, but one not limited to grabbing attention—especially attention from Western media—the way disrupting an official parade was designed to do.

That was pantomime.

This was punk rock.

56

Herne's alarm went off early on the Saturday morning of the Erlöser festival. His apartment was full of hungover punks from all over the East Bloc. The party had kicked off the night before.

Herne got up and looked out his window.

It was snowing.

Shit.

It was April 23, 1988.

Still, thought Herne, *if this is the worst thing that happens today . . .*

Drama had reigned in the run-up to the festival.

Even the date had been a problem—they had to use fake dates throughout the planning sessions to throw off the Stasi, who always seemed to have ears, even at Erlöser. Hell, getting the minister to consent to the festival at all had even been tough. They had nearly come to blows with him.

Things had only gotten more difficult from there. Herne and his brother Mecki had prepared a fanzine especially for the festival, a one-off newsletter. Originally they had planned to copy it themselves on church copiers, but with the churches more careful since the Zion Church raid, they had been barred from doing it on either of the two machines in town. Someone suggested printing it in Poland and having it transported across. A-Micha didn't think it would be right to ask one of their Polish friends to take the risk of transporting it, though his Polish "cousin" Slipeck could arrange the printing.

"Listen," he told the rest of the festival organizers at the Profikeller, "I have the most experience with this kind of shit."

Namenlos wasn't even going to play the festival, the band was still in flux.

"I've been to prison," he continued. "I've dealt with the cops and the Stasi. And I know the guys in Poland, too. I'll do it. I'll go over and bring the materials back."

His logic was sound.

A few weeks before the festival, A-Micha took a train to Poland, once again using a trusty cousin visa. A-Micha met Slipeck and picked up a thousand copies of the fanzine. His buddies in Poland suggested he sew them into a giant teddy bear, but A-Micha just shoved them into a duffel bag and got onto the train back to the border at Frankfurt Oder.

At the last stop in Poland, his train car emptied. A customs officer appeared at the front of his car. He was the train's lone customs official, and there he was staring at the car's lone passenger.

Shit, must have been compromised by a Stasi informant, he thought.

A-Micha didn't have time to shove his bag under his seat, much less another seat. The officer came straight to him and searched his duffel.

Agententätigkeit!

Activity as a foreign agent.

He could get four to six years, he was told.

A-Micha knew how to handle interrogations. Whenever he was questioned, he would tell a story that was clearly false in order to bait the interrogator into revealing that he knew this or that wasn't true because of this or that reason. It was a ploy to figure out what the Stasi or whoever really *did* know. So when A-Micha was taken to a customs interrogation facility in Frankfurt Oder, he made up a story of having bought the papers at a flea market because they looked interesting. The customs officer took notes. After he had typed up a report, he told A-Micha in a surprisingly friendly way, "The men from Berlin are on their way. I've written down what you said, but you'd better think up something better for them."

Not all functionaries were the same. Some, like this guy, were affable. This guy chuckled along with A-Micha, and his warning wasn't meant as a threat, more like a bit of friendly advice.

The Stasi picked A-Micha up in Frankfurt Oder and drove him back to Berlin. The interrogations started again from scratch.

This time, A-Micha used a story he had pieced together to best take advantage of a legal loophole he'd found out about before setting out on this expedition. If only one person in each country took part in the act, it did not constitute activity as a foreign agent.

He and his "cousin" Slipeck were the only ones involved, A-Micha explained, an East German and a Pole, nobody else. But the Stasi wouldn't relent: they wanted info on the festival.

"You can throw me back in prison before I agree to that," A-Micha insisted.

"Oh no, Herr Horschig, you can forget that. We're not going to do that again. We have other ways to silence you."

They're going to kill me, thought A-Micha.

A-Micha was shaken.

In the end, they struck a deal: the Stasi agreed to release him and he agreed to return the following day and report back on what bands were playing—he would give them info on the festival.

But A-Micha had no plans to honor the deal.

Upon his release from detainment he went to a youth club, ABC, out in Köpenick, where he knew some friends would be hanging out. He was several days late returning, and people were surprised to see him. *You made it!* He had beers with them and explained the situation. A-Micha knew he had been followed by several agents but he and his friends came up with a plan for him to ditch them. All at once, about thirty people inside ABC got up, went outside, and suddenly ran in different directions. There were not enough plainclothes agents to follow them all and A-Micha slipped his tail in the confusion. Then he went to find Deacon Postler and Herne and some others to come up with a plan that could keep him out of jail.

When A-Micha went back to the Stasi office the next day, he took Deacon Postler and another punk with him. That way the Erlöser crowd could be confident A-Micha wasn't a snitch.

Finally, on Thursday, April 21, Herne and company could finally get started on the nuts and bolts—they built the outdoor stage, set up the sound system, set up the portable toilets, assembled the stands for food, beer, and info. Then Friday afternoon, the festival went live with locals Reasors Exzess followed by Aurora, from Hungary, and three bands from Czechoslovakia: O.P.M., Sanov 1, and Do Rady.

Now, Saturday, April 23, the main event, ten straight hours of punk rock. And then the early morning snow that wasn't letting up.

Luckily the sun came out and brought the temperature slightly above freezing by the time the first band started playing, at 12:30 in the afternoon. The snow let up, the stage stayed dry, and when Polish punks Karcer took the stage, things really started to cook. Pogoing and wild dancing started immediately, as S-Bahn trains passed lazily behind the stage, which was draped in a tarp. The crowd kept swelling as the day wore on, and eventually several thousand people watched bands from West Berlin and Italy, as well as plenty of DDR bands.

Re-Aktion, from Potsdam, kicked things off on Saturday afternoon and then closed the night down with their frighteningly aggressive hardcore political punk:

Say goodbye to the Party,
Shout *opposition!*

All told, eighteen bands from six countries had rocked Erlöser. Once again East German punks had managed to spread their message to huge numbers of people, in an event open to the public. Anyone there could feel the tremors shaking society's foundation—and it wasn't just the machine-gun bursts of the double-time drums. Aggression and improvisation; rage and creativity—the spring festival showed once again the power of punk and the shakiness of the regime.

The Stasi had sat by; observing, yes, but not intervening. There were no road blocks or checkpoints around the church grounds, no train stations had been blockaded the way they had been at times in the early 1980s, and the incendiary vocals had boomed out into the open air, not some dank basement.

We will stay and we will fight.

The punks were winning the war.

Members of Polish band Karcer crashed at Pankow's place for the festival weekend. Soon Pankow, too, got into the same sort of trouble that A-Micha had. Pankow and a girl named Sue volunteered to take some printed materials from the DDR across the Polish border for a clandestine meeting with Solidarity. But they were busted by DDR authorities at the border crossing at Frankfurt Oder.

Pankow and Sue were taken off the train and thrown into a detainment facility. The materials themselves never turned up. Pankow had managed to unscrew part of the ceiling in a train car—not the same car they rode in—and hidden the stuff up there for the border crossing. For several days they were interrogated, asked where the stacks of paper were. Pankow was badly beaten in custody. But he held his tongue.

Upon his release and return to Berlin, he felt angry enough to try something quite rash: he decided to sue the Stasi for assault. He went to a doctor, who gave him an exam, documented his various injuries, and photographed his contusions. Then he started looking for a lawyer, but nobody would touch the case. No way. Finally he made an appointment with Gregor Gysi, a prominent pro-Gorbachev member of the East German Communist Party—Gysi's own father was a party hardliner and high-ranking official, but Gregor had defended several dissidents over the course of his career. Gysi agreed to take Pankow's case.

The first obstacle Pankow and Gysi ran up against: it proved impossible to sue the intelligence agency directly. Pankow had to bring a more general complaint for bodily harm at the hands of the state.

Soon after he had started to explore the idea of bringing a suit, Pankow came home one day and happened upon a plainclothes spook trying to break into his apartment. Pankow snapped. He pushed the agent inside the apartment and beat the living shit out of him.

The agent ran out, but no reinforcements came to arrest Pankow. Not that day. Not the next day. Nothing.

Things were really changing.

Pankow's suit—the first of its type—went forward. And he won. But he was never given a written judgment, just an oral affirmation that he had won. He was handed 300 East German marks—about thirty bucks—as compensation.

And that was that.

After Pankow won his suit, Pankow and A-Micha—both of whom were forbidden to travel to Poland after their run-ins at the border—constantly wrote letters petitioning for permission to travel to Poland, just to piss people off. Sometimes they wrote twenty letters a week if they had nothing else going on. Pankow also turned up at the office hours of government commissions and made a public nuisance of himself.

Finally he received a summons to a meeting at the Interior Ministry.

A guy in a drab suit told Pankow in an affectless tone that he would never, *ever* be allowed to leave the country.

57

There was great disparity in the way local authorities addressed problems in East Germany. The provinces were tough. Weimar, for instance, where the punk kids had been sent to Stasi prison in 1983 for spray-painting anarchist slogans on walls around town, was considered a sort of Stasi laboratory—a place where the local Stasi office could try out anything and get draconian on people's asses. The sleepy town was too small and too isolated for any consequences to hamper Stasi brutality there. And they knew it. East Berlin was generally the most relaxed, in part because of the Western media spotlight there. Berliners on both sides of the Wall were the best informed people in all of Germany because of the confluence of media outlets broadcasting views emanating from Washington, D.C. to Moscow and everywhere in between.

Dresden was different. It was tough in Dresden.

Even though it was a large city by East German standards, Dresden sat in the Valley of the Clueless, or *Tal der Ahnungslosen*, limiting the city's exposure to the world at large.

Punks had it tough there, too.

The regional church leadership had managed to deny space to any Open Work or Church from Below type organizations, which also forced the Dresden punks to operate on the mean streets all the time, suffering attacks from citizens and security forces alike. And in 1988 things took a turn for the worse. Punks were totally banned from the central parts of the city. Security forces started to raid known punk apartments. And when a kid named Lars Konrad tried to bring a suit like Pankow's against the police—for bodily harm and an illegal search of his apartment—he was thrown in prison for eighteen months.

In Leipzig, the aborted protests over the arrests of activists before and after the Rosa Luxemburg parade had led to a regular Monday evening peace prayer in Nikolai Church, right in the middle of the historic old town. By May, authorities had started to apply pressure on the church to end the events. One means mirrored a tactic used in Berlin in years past: the church leadership in Leipzig was angling to hold a national conference in 1989, and the state insisted that the church meet its terms, otherwise they could forget convening their pet project. One of those terms was to end the Monday peace prayers, just as in Berlin they had insisted church leadership cancel the Blues Masses.

Up to that point the peace prayers had been organized and run by more or less independent groups working under the roof of the church. The church's initial solution to the Monday peace prayers was to insist on having an actual minister involved in the events. During a summer break in the prayer sessions, the church went one step further: Nikolai Church itself took control of the Monday meetings, wresting control from the semi-autonomous groups. At the first peace prayer after the changeover, on Monday, August 29, 1988, activists initiated a discussion of the organizational changes but were quickly drowned out by the church organist, who started playing at a signal from the minister.

The Leipzig band L'Attentat revised the lyrics of the Wutanfall song *"Leipzig in Trümmern,"* or "Leipzig in Ruins," to reflect the new situation in 1988, post-Rosa Luxemburg debacle:

Das junge Blut hält die Fahne in'n Wind
Die alten Leute im Westen sind
Für Ideale geht keiner in'n Knast . . .

Zum Risiko ist keiner bereit.

The new blood holds the flag in the wind
The old people are in the West
Nobody goes to prison for ideals . . .

Nobody is prepared to take risks

Things were going the opposite direction in Berlin. No thanks to the church, of course, which in Berlin toed the party line even more doggedly than in Leipzig.

On September 29, 1988, about fifty people gathered in front of the Pergamon Museum, the crown jewel of the museums East Berlin had inherited, a museum that housed world-renowned antiquities including the Gates of Babylon and the Pergamon Altar. The crowd milling around outside, organized by the Church from Below, awaited a delegation from the International Monetary Fund—the ultimate imperialist Western institution, the ultimate ideological enemy to a communist government. The problem was the communist government had actually welcomed IMF delegates with open arms: some were staying in a hotel in the East during a conference the IMF was holding in West Berlin—anything for hard currency, apparently— and a delegation was also supposed to visit the museum.

Other church-based groups, like the peace group based in Friedrichsfelde, had planned a week of activities to coincide with the IMF conference, the most ambitious of which was a march between three churches with a stop for a church service in each. But after the government pressured Berlin church leaders, nearly all of those activities had been quashed.

So it was left to the Church from Below to take action.

Church from Below stalwarts like Speiche and Dirk Moldt had already spent the previous night, September 28, calling the hotel to tie up the archaic phone lines. Now, on September 29, it was time for part two of their plan to highlight the hypocrisy of the DDR regime. The well-heeled IMF delegates were easy to pick out as they approached the museum in their fancy Western suits. When they appeared, the demonstrators showered them with small change. It was a punk-style move, bold and funny, Church from Below through and through. Police did not intervene.

Afterward the crowd of protesters started to march toward the U.S. embassy but was stopped; many demonstrators were detained at that point and taken in for questioning. The protesters had one more trick up their sleeves. They had cloves of garlic in their pockets, and while being transported to detention in the back of military-style trucks they ate the raw garlic. By the time they were all herded into holding cells, the entire horde reeked. The garlic wafted across the tables as protesters were interrogated. It filled the detention center.

All were expeditiously released.

They had gotten away with a public demonstration. A very public demonstration, in front of a prime tourist destination. No church, no problem. It was all about the streets now. They had seceded from society and found refuge in churches. Then they had seceded from the church. And now they would take the streets, the streets.

We are the people, we are the power!

There had been one casualty: one of Media Siggi's three precious video cameras was confiscated when he was taken into custody as he walked with protesters toward the U.S. embassy. Luckily the other two were still safely stashed elsewhere.

Especially now that he no longer had a day job, Siggi tried to shoot footage whenever and wherever he could—despite the experience of the Rosa Luxemburg parade and the way the Western media darlings had been shipped out of the country, he still thought it important to give the opposition a voice on Western media. And for whatever reason, the Stasi gave him a long enough leash to do so. They maintained a file on Siggi—code name "Satan"—but it was the same old story: they couldn't conceive of the possibility that Siggi was working independently. It's true that Siggi often worked with a partner in crime, Aram Radomski, but that was the full extent of the operation. Siggi shot footage, handed the tapes to a West German journalist from the news magazine *Der Spiegel*, who as a journalist could pass through the Wall without being searched, and that was that. The Stasi figured TV-quality video production necessitated a huge team. They left Siggi out there so that he might lead them up the chain, to the mastermind of— again—what they assumed was a hierarchical organization. This despite the fact that one of Siggi's closest friends was informing on him and even went so far as to complain to a Stasi handler, "I've collected so much information for you on Schefke—when are you going to throw him in jail?"

Siggi and Aram consistently filmed the physical degradation of the country, whether that was the crumbling city centers where Party planners continued to raze old buildings to make room for more high-rise complexes, or the severe pollution affecting many areas of the country. The urgency of environmental issues became more and more clear even to ordinary citizens as the years wore on. Over the course of 1986 and 1987, for instance, many of the trees that lined East Berlin's streets suddenly died. The likely cause was the leaky hundred-year-old gas pipes still in use throughout the East, but the upshot was that the landscape was withering away right in front of people's eyes. A recent Environmental Library study had concluded that a third of the country's lakes were no longer safe to swim in—they were too toxic. And in late 1988, when East Germany expanded deals it had in place with West Germany to import toxic waste and dispose of it in the DDR—in exchange for hard currency, naturally—groups saw the need for another public action.

On November 11, 1988, protesters headed out to Schöneiche, on the outskirts of East Berlin—the site of a waste incinerator where the poisonous Western materials would be spewed out into the air with no public oversight, in fact with no regard for the public at all. A group from the Environmental Library went by bicycle; a Church from Below group took a train and then walked along an access road used primarily by the trucks that delivered waste to the facility. While walking along carrying banners for the demonstration, the punks and freaks noticed quite a lot of cars coming up the road. This could only be bad. So they stashed first the banners and then themselves in the bushes.

But they got caught.

They were transported to a police station for questioning. They denied any knowledge of a planned demonstration. And again the protesters walked away free, this time with a fine of 300 marks. Okay, that was a small fortune at the time to them, but they could raise the money with a benefit concert or whatever. The important thing was: no extended detention, no trial, no jail time. Following the arrests at the Environmental Library the year before, and surrounding the Rosa Luxemburg parade earlier that year, this was evidence that the possibility of a return to a more hardline approach from the government seemed to have passed. Between the spring punk music festival, the IMF protest, and this attempted demonstration, nobody had gone to jail.

A dangerous signal to give to a bunch of punks and miscreants. With no consequences for their actions, they were bound to get more audacious.

Then, in late 1988, the Polish communist party agreed to enter talks with Solidarity, and head of state General Wojciech Jaruzelski—who had declared martial law back in 1981 in an attempt to clamp down on the union—agreed to resign pending the outcome of those talks. Another dangerous signal. As far as the East German government was concerned, it was glasnost taken too far. The DDR dictatorship seemed genuinely worried about the renewed threat represented by their ostensible allies in the East Bloc, and at the end of 1988 the dictatorship banned the German-language Russian newspaper *Sputnik*.

Once again, people like Speiche could feel the ground shaking beneath the government.

The Honecker government was *scared*.

And in January 1989 the Church from Below finally moved into their permanent home on the grounds of St. Elisabeth Church, just a few hundred yards from Zion Church and the Environmental Library. Bathrooms and a bar had been added to the interior, and a congregation of anarchist non-believers now had virtually an entire building to themselves to use as a cross between a nightclub and an intellectual salon, putting on concerts, readings, lectures, discussion groups, benefits, informational sessions, and, of course, parties—and all of it beyond the reach of the police. Thanks to Speiche and Silvio Meier, it also housed a huge Antifa group that soon created its own newsletter.

We will stay and we will fight.

Speiche volunteered to keep a Friday night bar open on his own, and it quickly became the go-to spot for all-night drinking sessions where opponents of the state could carouse together for hours after regular bars closed. Parties could bring people together and foster new ideas. Parties fueled their own sort of productivity, creativity, and solidarity. And sex. Parties created those connections as well, and in a country where homosexuality was still persecuted, the Church from Below, like the punk scene, offered a safe haven for outcasts of all kind, a place where anything went, where freedom was freedom and all issues were seen as interconnected, and where anyone could end up intertwined with anyone on any given night.

With an actual place to go to get the latest info, open to all, even to those who wore their Mohawks on the inside and felt uncomfortable at Erlöser, the Church from Below now functioned more than ever as an independent national communications hub.

To celebrate the opening of the facility, they put on a concert featuring Leipzig's L'Attentat and Potsdam's Re-Aktion, two stridently political bands:

I'm old enough to go it alone
I don't want to see all this shit anymore
The way you rob me of my future
And ask me to fight for things you no longer believe in yourself

Say good-bye to the Party,
Shout *opposition!*

VI

Disintegration

Punks at the officially licensed Beat Inn, in Berlin-Weissensee, 1988

58

n an East German government report on the "preliminary findings of youth analysis" dated January 12, 1989, punk was identified by authorities as the top problem. Punks had developed a scene independent of DDR officialdom, including, as the report pointed out, the creation of a gray-market economy as well as communications nodes and a national network to facilitate the exchange of information and ideas. "The Church from Below—with its anarchist mode of operation—has become a catchment basin for these punks," and the skinhead attack at Zion Church had strengthened ties between punks in various activist groups, increasing the potential scale of activities going forward.

The report said about a hundred of the core members of the "old classic punks from the years 1983/4" who had been expatriated had ended up involved in anarchist and leftist extremist circles in the West, helping punks still in the East cultivate links to those groups in West Berlin and more broadly in West Germany. In the eyes of the East German government, that was a primary source of trouble: the West.

In some ways the authorities' obsession with the West wasn't surprising. After all, Siegbert Schefke—Media Siggi, with his recording equipment secretly stashed around town—had been smuggling out audio of oppositional musicians and political activities for broadcast on Radio Glasnost and eventually also video footage for mainstream West German news operations; L'Attentat had released an album in the West, and a compilation of

Eastern punk bands had also appeared in the West under the title *Live in Paradise DDR*, further embarrassing the dictatorship; Stracke and Imad of L'Attentat had written for West German fanzines, bringing more attention; West Berlin bands were sneaking into the East to join concert bills at activist churches and even private parties; printing supplies for the illegal publication of the *mOAning Star* and *Umweltblätter* and *Grenzfall* were seeping in from the West; and the West German media was having a field day covering the ongoing existence of East German neo-Nazis.

The dictatorship was so paranoid about former Eastern punks in West Berlin that the Stasi had continued to secretly monitor the group of Weimar punks who'd been jailed in 1983 for spray-painting graffiti—SOLIDARITY, STRIKE BACK, ACTIVE RESISTANCE—even after they were expatriated following their release from prison; this had led to one of the more bizarre incidents in the history of the Berlin Wall. Thomas Onisseit and his older brother, Jürgen—who, unbeknownst to Thomas and his friends, had gotten them sent to the slammer back in 1983 by snitching to the Stasi—along with a small group of former Weimar punks, had decided at the end of 1986 to paint a white stripe along the entire length of the West side of the Berlin Wall. It could take weeks to complete, but they felt compelled to do it. The Weimar punks hated the way the barrier had become a canvas for self-promotion. Celebrity artist Keith Haring, for example, had recently painted a stretch of the Wall. So on November 3, 1986, five former Weimar punks had put on creepy white masks and begun rolling a simple white line at shoulder height along the west side of the Wall, starting in Kreuzberg. On the second day, a little-known aspect of the Wall had come into play. Not only was the entire Wall itself within the sovereign territory of East Germany, the sovereign territory also extended about ten feet *west* of the Wall—this allowed for maintenance, for instance. Few West Berliners realized that if they stood at the base of the Wall, they were actually standing in the DDR, despite being on the west side of the divide. On the second day of the white stripe project, as the painters worked their way through Tiergarten, East German border guards had suddenly popped out of a hatch and, standing in what anyone else would have regarded as *West* Berlin, had pointed machine guns at the painters and shouted, "Hands up or we'll shoot!" Four of them had fled into the bushes of Tiergarten, but one, Wolfram Hasch, froze. He was dragged back through the hatch, put on trial, and sentenced to more than two years in prison. He missed the birth of his son while sitting in a Stasi cell.

But the East German government was missing the real problem. Outside forces weren't fomenting dissent. The DDR was burning from the inside.

Not only were Eastern punks not being steered by the West, they were still largely anti-Western. The Church from Below had chastised Samariter Church minister and Blues Mass organizer Rainer Eppelmann for meeting with West German politicians and grandstanding for personal gain. The Church from Below was still stridently opposed to using Western media to advance its goals. Part of the objection was explicitly anti-capitalist: the punks knew Western news organizations leveraged interest in their articles to sell advertisements, and the punks didn't want their story to become a commodity. But part of it was something else: what they were doing was for themselves, not for international consumption via Western media connections. They also feared—correctly, it turned out—that their motives would be misinterpreted in the West, that they might be seen as anti-communists who wanted German unification, when in fact the only Easterners interested in unification were the neo-Nazis that punks spent a good deal of time and energy combating.

An article in the *mOAning Star* looking back at the Church from Below's 1987 alternative Church Conference from Below dripped with sarcasm when addressing the notion that its organizers were Western puppets. "We have to wake up to the fact that we were perhaps being steered by the West—after all, what Easterners took part in the planning? It's obvious that [West German newspapers] pushed everything along and came up with the flyers . . . It's still completely unclear whether the Church from Below was set up by the USA or by the western media and its shadowy behind-the-scenes figures or by the USSR and Gorbachev-friendly forces."

On the surface, the basic situation in the country seemed unchanged. A few days after the January 12 youth analysis report was issued, Erich Honecker made his famous pronouncement affirming that the Berlin Wall would still be standing in fifty or even a hundred years if the reasons for its existence had not yet been vanquished. And on February 5, 1989, a twenty-year-old East German named Chris Gueffroy was shot in the heart while trying to escape over the Wall in Treptow.

Despite those events, and despite a burst of police activity in February when authorities tried to empty several squatted buildings in Friedrichshain, the Church from Below had its collective gaze fixed on the national elections scheduled for May 7, 1989. The Church from Below had finally gotten its safe haven on the grounds of St. Elisabeth Church, but the pace and scale of protests was actually picking up primarily because protesters were *abandoning* the protective walls of the church and instead taking to the streets. The government might have misplaced the blame but they hadn't missed all the actions, *public* actions.

And even as Honecker's border guards were gunning down Chris Gueffroy—who turned out to be their last victim—the Church from Below was organizing the most audacious and damning public action yet.

59

I t's tempting to think of a dictatorship in simple terms: a government imposed on a populace, one whose rule runs counter to the will of the people. But it's rarely so simple. The communist party of East Germany always touted its landslide electoral victories—*Party garners 99 percent of the vote, again!* While such results may have elicited a collective roll of the eyes in the West, what percentage of the vote did the party really receive?

In May 1989, the political opposition in Berlin decided to find out.

Voting in East Germany was not an actual legal obligation but was considered virtually compulsory because of the consequences for not voting—like losing your job. So voter turnout was usually high, helped along by friendly reminders from security organs for those disinclined to vote. The ballots listed the Communist Party alongside a series of nominally different parties that were in fact sister parties affiliated with the Communist Party in a coalition called the National Front. No opposition parties appeared on the ballot.

There were really just two ways to express disaffection with the ruling coalition: one was not to vote. The punks at Erlöser held parties on every election day—revelers were admitted only with an unused voter card, and the parties ended in a bonfire of those cards. The other way to express disaffection was to fill out the ballot in a way that wasn't an affirmation of the listed parties—like crossing them out. In theory, this could create a gap between the number of voters and the number of votes in favor of the Communist

Party and its National Front coalition partners. And still, after every election the Party announced another victory with 99 percent of the vote.

Not surprisingly, elections in East Germany were assumed to be fraudulent above and beyond the system designed to create high voter turnout while offering no choice. But citizens had the right—at least on paper—to monitor the election officials who counted the votes. Activists from a peace group in Samariter Church had made a small-scale attempt to monitor the vote a few years prior. They had stationed their people at eight voting locations near the church and had witnessed in those few locations as many ballots intended as "no" votes as were officially acknowledged in the entire precinct, which included dozens more voting locations. The stories from that limited sample were legendary. One ballot had a big, fat anarchist A scrawled on it. "It could stand for *all*," offered a vote counter. Chalk one up for the Party. On another ballot, someone had written, "You're more idiotic than the *Nationalelf*," or the National Eleven—the country's notoriously unsuccessful national soccer team. "Well, at the very least that's not a no," said a vote counter. Chalk up another vote for the Party.

Now, in 1989, the Church from Below and other groups planned not only to monitor the vote-counting at a large number of polling stations but also to educate voters on how to properly cast a no vote with none of the ambiguity of an anarchist A. Already in the lead-up to the election, the Stasi had catalogued more than one hundred incidents of criticism of the vote, mostly attempts to distribute flyers or hang posters. In the run-up to the May elections, the Church from Below held meetings every Wednesday night to clarify how to cast a no vote and explain the legal basis for monitoring the vote and how exactly to exercise it. Loads of young people turned up, many of whom had heard about the effort at concerts either at St. Elisabeth Church or Erlöser.

More and more people seemed interested in *doing* things, taking action. *Don't die in the waiting room of the future.*

On the day of the election, Sunday, May 7, 1989, hundreds of volunteers headed to the schools, gyms, and municipal buildings that made up the polling locations. Teams of monitors blanketed the stations in three East Berlin districts: Prenzlauer Berg, Friedrichshain, and Weissensee, and more limited monitoring took place in Leipzig, Dresden, Erfurt, Rostock, Potsdam, Halle, Magdeburg, Weimar, Karl-Marx-Stadt, Jena, and other cities. In Berlin's Weissensee, monitors attended 66 of 67 polling stations; in Friedrichshain, 82 of 89; in Prenzlauer Berg, 41 stations, which represented a third of the total.

Once polling stations closed at six on that sunny spring evening, election officials dumped the ballots out on big tables, organized them, examined them, and counted them. There was no attempt to shut out the monitors—in every location, monitors managed to sit by and watch as the votes were counted.

By nine that night, nearly all the monitors in Berlin had taken their results to the Church from Below at St. Elisabeth Church, where hundreds gathered for an election party. According to numbers tallied by the monitors, the Communist Party and its affiliated sister parties had received 85 to 90 percent of the vote at various stations. Of course, the Party and its election commissioner, Egon Krenz—Honecker's number two and long assumed to be next in line to take over the dictatorship—announced another landslide victory: 98.85 percent of voters had cast their ballots in favor of the ruling party slate. Even if it was only a 10 to 15 percent discrepancy versus the official numbers, the Church from Below now had hard evidence of election fraud.

The repercussions began immediately.

On the night of the elections, the Church from Below's party evolved into a minor demonstration. Some West German reporters had caught wind of the monitoring effort and attended the party at St. Elisabeth Church; the fraudulent results quickly made their way across town to West German news organizations and made the late news, where it was heard by East Germans tuned to Western stations. Between that and the more limited monitoring in other cities across the DDR, similar demonstrations sprung up all over the country. In Leipzig, a thousand people took to the street. A hundred were arrested and detained overnight.

As West German media reported, East German security forces made "free use of their batons" against protesters in Berlin and other cities, including Leipzig.

The following day, May 8, was the weekly Monday peace prayer at Nikolai Church in Leipzig. Since the dispute over control of the prayer sessions, activists had started gathering *outside* the church. The shift mirrored Berlin and the Church from Below: the formerly church-based groups had in essence seceded from the church and taken to the streets. Once again Party pressure had backfired, as a prayer session previously cloistered away in the church became a public spectacle, even if it was still small in scale.

On May 8, police ringed demonstrators in front of Nikolai Church in Leipzig, just as they had surrounded about a hundred protesters the week before as they tried to stage an alternative Mayday march on the important labor holiday.

On May 10, the details of the election commission's counts were published in official Eastern media. Obviously the specific numbers didn't jibe with the monitors' figures any more than the initial numbers had. In Prenzlauer Berg, for instance, monitors in just one third of the total polling stations counted 2,659 votes against the ruling party slate; the official tally for the entire district acknowledged just 1,998 against. Fraud. In Friedrichshain, monitors had counted more than three times the number of no votes as officially acknowledged. Fraud. And voter participation numbers appeared cooked, too: in Weissensee, where monitors attended all but one polling station, the government claimed 15,000 more total voters than the 27,680 ballots counted by monitors. Fraud.

Was a dictatorship simply a government imposed on a populace, one whose rule ran counter to the will of the people? Not exactly. Most people actually went along. The vast majority of people, in fact. But the dictatorship had falsified the vote anyway.

The opposition now held proof that elections were a sham.

The regime was going to pay.

60

On May 26, 1989, die Anderen and Feeling B played a concert in West Berlin's Ecstasy club, in the Schöneberg district. It's difficult to know for sure why authorities green-lit the gig. Perhaps they hoped the bands wouldn't come back, that sending them over for a concert was even easier than expatriating them. Perhaps the ministry of culture thought Eastern bands might be able to develop a following in the West and create another source of hard currency for the DDR. Whatever the reason, the ministry had approved one-day visas for the members of Feeling B and die Anderen.

On the day of the show, the bands had traveled together in an official bus, together with a minder from the ministry of culture.

The bus pulled to a stop at the checkpoint at Invalidenstrasse—it was still morning and the bands would have all day in West Berlin.

Toster, the frontman of die Anderen, had never been through a border checkpoint before. He was practically pissing himself with anticipation.

An East German soldier climbed into the bus.

"You got anyone hidden in here?" he asked.

"No, no," everyone assured the guard. They had all the right paperwork and even a ride-along minder.

The bus continued on, across the death strip and toward the second wall, the one facing the West. With the exception of Aljoscha, none of the members of Feeling B or die Anderen had ever witnessed the scale of the security curtain the East had erected—normally you weren't permitted to get close to the checkpoints.

Toster experienced an otherworldly feeling—how strange it was to be crossing the border on a bus chartered by the cultural authorities of the DDR rather than fleeing, as so many others had tried to do.

I can't believe how easy this is, he thought.

A few yards past the second wall Toster felt overwhelmed.

This was only a few *yards* from where he had spent his life, and yet here he was in the middle of a totally different world. He thought of all his friends who had left the country in various waves over the past years.

After pulling beyond the checkpoint, the bus drove past the Reichstag—the former capital building next to the Brandenburg Gate. The members of Feeling B and die Anderen stared in amazement at the field in front of the building. A pair of ultra-light aircraft were sitting there, parked on the lawn, surrounded by Allied military police vehicles. It turned out the miniplanes had landed there at 4:30 that morning, just as the early summer sky was beginning to lighten, after two Western brothers had flown into East Berlin's Treptower Park to extract a third sibling still living behind the Wall. The three brothers—two in one aircraft, one in the other—had then flown back over the floodlit death strip at an altitude of only about five hundred feet and aimed for a landmark where they would be sure they were touching down on the correct side of the serpentine Wall. Reunited and ready to celebrate, they abandoned the planes right in front of the Reichstag.

The bus drove on to the venue and the bands did a quick sound check. Most of the guys were meeting friends they knew in West Berlin.

Feeling B guitarist Paul and keyboardist Flake had decided in advance not to get stressed out by trying to see everything on this, their first trip to the West. They went for a late breakfast at the apartment of Christian Jäger, a friend of theirs who had played in the band Happy Straps before his departure from the DDR.

Before they headed back to Ecstasy, they stopped for their first-ever döner kebabs. When they went to sit down and eat them, the owner of the kebab stand shooed them away.

Huh?

They had cans of Coke they'd bought somewhere else.

"You can't sit here with those drinks! Get out!"

Toster of die Anderen had something specific he wanted to do on his first trip to West Berlin. He wanted to ride one of the subway trains that passed beneath East Berlin territory, rolling through stations that had been sealed off by the DDR. Toster had felt those trains pass beneath him, trains from another world, another country, just beneath his feet in the East. It was like something out of science fiction, he always thought, and he wanted to ride on one of those ghostly trains just once.

Unfortunately, the friend he planned to meet and ride the trains with was late. So the manager of Ecstasy—who had himself never been to *East* Berlin—asked Toster if there was something he might want to do. The club manager had an old Italian sports car, so Toster suggested they go see the highway that entered West Berlin from the southwest.

"I want to see the part beyond the sign I always see—last exit in the DDR."

He and the club manager trundled into the Lancia and drove down to the checkpoint between Wannsee and Potsdam, then came back.

That afternoon Toster spent his share of the band's earnings. First he bought guitar picks—up to then he'd always played with homemade picks he cut out of the tops of jelly jars. Then he invested the rest of the money in cans of Becks beer. It had to be *cans*. Neither he nor any of his friends had ever had beer out of a can before, and he wanted to take them back for all the friends he knew would be waiting at their local hangout in East Berlin upon their return.

Back at Ecstasy, the guys couldn't believe all the things they experienced for the first time. There was a billiard table in the bar—*just like in the movies!*—and Flake tried to play pool. He and Paul ordered Campari and orange juice with their free-drink tickets but found themselves struggling to pronounce the exotic name of the bitter Italian liqueur. And there was a backstage area at Ecstasy. In the East they sat at the bar with the audience before a show.

A lot of people they'd known in the East turned up for the show, people who had fled or applied to leave only to find themselves unemployed in West Berlin, struggling to get by. Despite their presence, the concert wasn't very well attended. But it didn't matter. The bands were so excited that they sped through their songs.

When they all boarded the bus after the show, the minder from the cultural ministry addressed them.

"If you don't want to go back, just get off here," the minder said. "I don't care."

The band members stayed put.

The minder shrugged his shoulders and off they went. The bus pulled through the checkpoint and returned to a different country—a country without bright streetlights and kebab stands and sunset-colored glasses of Campari and orange juice.

Toster didn't care.

He was looking forward to passing out cans of beer to his friends.

61

The first of what became monthly protests over the election fraud was called for June 7, 1989, one month after the vote.

Everything about the protest plan was bold.

First of all, activists distributed hundreds of flyers announcing a demonstration, depositing them by hand in mailboxes around town. Then there was the plan for the demonstration itself, which involved burying a crematorium urn marked "Here lies democracy."

They planned to meet in front of a centrally located church administration building and from there go to Alexanderplatz. Police caught wind of the plan, though, and mustered a massive presence all around the area. Fewer than a hundred people managed to reach the planned location.

It was a bust.

But there was a backup plan: activists met at Sophien Church that same evening at seven. Sophien was a pretty eighteenth-century baroque church nestled among the tight little streets of an old quarter near Hackescher Markt. This time, about five hundred people made it. Herne, who still booked bands at Erlöser, was pissed off at the turnout. Since 1983 he had held a day job at a concrete factory and as a result he knew a lot of normal working people; he knew that they, too, had started to grumble openly about the bullshit they saw, and about the sham elections specifically. Herne could tell the mood was changing—some of the workers he knew had decided not to vote at all, or to cross out the candidates on their ballots—and yet those people, *normal* people, weren't here at the protest, at least not in big numbers. Where were they? Were they still afraid to protest, even in the face of actual fraud? There must have been thousands of ordinary citizens, maybe tens of thousands, who knew they'd had their votes stolen. And here were just five hundred souls.

The plan at Sophien Church remained the same: to bury the urn to mark the death of democratic elections and to march through the streets. At least, that's what people like A-Micha and Dirk Moldt thought. After some speeches and discussions, those two guys and a handful of others got up and headed to the doors of the church with the urn in hand.

The church doors opened onto a fenced yard. Beyond the church grounds: swarms of police and rows of military-style troop transporters in which to carry off detainees.

As he walked out, A-Micha turned to look back at the church doors, expecting to see hundreds of people streaming out behind him.

Nobody was following.

The church pews were full.

A-Micha and Dirk and the rest went back inside. A-Micha went to the front of the church and began to speak at the top of his lungs. He thought he could get the more timid people to their feet, get them out of the church, get them to face the police, to stand with him and Dirk, to stand together for all those whose votes had been disappeared, for all those whose futures had been usurped.

"You can't let a handful of people go out there on their own and get taken away by the Stasi," he yelled. "If we *all* go out, nobody will go to prison."

Again he went to the doors with Dirk and the urn, and again he started across the churchyard. Again he turned to look behind him.

Again they were alone.

God damn it!

Again he went in and exhorted the crowd.

"Together is the only way!"

A-Micha stalked out a third time.

This time, a few people got up. This time, a few people followed him. And then a few more, and a few more. Soon hundreds of people flowed out into the yard toward the street.

By the time the majority of the group had exited the churchyard and spilled onto Grosse Hamburger Strasse, the assembled police and Stasi came running at them with batons.

"Everyone sit down," yelled A-Micha.

He figured the security forces hoped the crowd would try to push through their lines. That would justify any violence—which was just what the government forces wanted. The police started to beat protesters, knock them with batons, and drag them away by their hair.

"Do not fight back," A-Micha implored.

Most people did as he urged. They sat down. And they were hauled away one by one and transported to the central Stasi facility at Magdalenenstrasse.

As he waited to be processed, A-Micha watched others have their information recorded by Stasi officers. A chill went down his spine, an icy dagger of fear, something he rarely felt, even in situations like this: he recognized some of the Stasi officers' faces. The team processing the demonstrators included some of the very same officers who had processed him when he'd been arrested with the rest of Namenlos back in 1983, the day they rounded up the whole band, the day they executed Jana's dog, Wotan.

This is not good, he thought.

But the officers did not seem to recognize A-Micha, and he never let on that he recognized them.

After a few hours, everyone was released.

They had done it again. They had taken their rage into the open, aired it in public, off church grounds. They had made it onto the streets, if only briefly, and they were back out and ready to fight. Battered, yes, some bloodied, yes, but all ready to fight on.

A-Micha, who had been counting down since 1979, sure the battle would take just ten years, was beginning to believe.

Ten, nine, eight, seven, six, five, four, three, two, one . . .

62

Even the gray-area acts with *Einstufungen*, the government-sanctioned amateur licenses, were getting salty by 1989.

Die Art, a Leipzig band with an *Einstufung*, scored a major underground hit with the song "Wide Wide World." The band was already selling hundreds of its homemade tapes, and their 1989 cassette, *Dry*, set what is thought to be a DDR record for private tape album sales with nearly two thousand copies—which doesn't come close to accounting for all the copies of copies that circulated. "Wide Wide World" could never have been recorded through official channels because of the lyrics:

> Gray in gray is our city,
> I want to see the colors of the world

But with their amateur license die Art could still play the song at official events, such as the Free German Youth's spring festival, where they sang it for 15,000 people from a big open-air stage. The Erlöser and Church from Below crowd may have hated this kind of footsie-playing, but those yearning lyrics were easy to decipher.

Criticism hardened in the wake of the official East German reaction to China's violent suppression of student protesters on Tiananmen Square on June 4, 1989—which also happened to be the same day Solidarity managed to capture every parliamentary seat it was permitted to contest in the first semifree elections in Poland. Chinese students had occupied Tiananmen Square for weeks—public action against the dictatorship. China had criticized the protests as "counterrevolutionary" and then declared martial law. Finally, Chinese troops supported by tanks and armored vehicles cleared the square, leaving hundreds or perhaps thousands dead.

News of the violence led to demonstrations in front of the Chinese embassy in East Berlin on June 6, followed on June 7 by the protests on the one-month anniversary of the East German election. On June 8, the East German People's Congress passed a resolution supporting China's use of force against the demonstrators on Tiananmen Square, and Egon Krenz—Honecker's anointed successor—reiterated the government's support in comments to Western media; Krenz would later hint at the implementation of a "Chinese solution" to the increasing unrest in the DDR.

It was all too much. At least for some musicians.

The night of June 10, 1989, the Berlin band Herbst in Peking took the stage at another Free German Youth open-air festival, in Brandenburg, north of Berlin.

The singer, Rex Joswig, had moved to Berlin a few years before, working as a roadie for licensed jazz musicians and getting to know Aljoscha, Paul, and Flake from Feeling B, as well as Toster from die Anderen and many others. With his long blond hair and his enthusiasm for classic rock, he wasn't a traditional punk, but the Sex Pistols had been transformative for him, too, and the Pistols' kiss-my-ass attitude he'd adopted had gotten him kicked out of school in the dipshit town well north of Berlin where he'd grown up. He'd put Herbst in Peking—the name taken from a book, *Autumn in Peking,* by French poet Boris Vian—together in 1987 after a few false starts, and despite his fundamental desire to be confrontational, he had decided to do that within the context of the amateur licensing system—like most of his friends. After getting their *Einstufung,* the band developed a good following, and played eight to ten gigs a month.

That June night, as the last streaks of high summer light seeped from the sky, Rex addressed the crowd of several thousand: "We'd like to start with a moment of silence for the victims of the massacre at Tiananmen Square," he said.

Some boos echoed out in the crowd.

What the fuck, thought Rex. *People get run over by tanks and these assholes don't have a problem with it?*

A voice spoke to him through his vocal monitor, a voice from the sound booth.

"Don't say shit like that on our sound system."

The guys running the sound were afraid the omnipresent Stasi agents would think they were in on Rex's tirade. They were shitting themselves.

But Rex felt a visceral hatred for the DDR authorities in the wake of their reaction to the massacre, outraged by their support for China's murderous actions and the veiled threat the East German government's support represented to DDR citizens. *We will roll right over you, too,* they seemed to say.

Later in the show, Rex was at it again.

"This next song is for our bassist, who on Wednesday spent twenty-four hours in detainment because he didn't agree with the vote on May 7, because he wants secret ballots and doubts the accuracy of the vote count."

Whoa.

At the end of the band's set, a few people made a point of telling Rex how cool they thought it was for him to bring up Tiananmen Square, but the festival organizers just wanted to get the band the hell out of there. The other bands at the festival wanted them gone, too—speaking out made the other bands look like cowards for not saying anything. The local police seemed more intent on washing their hands of the problem than anything else. They immediately escorted the band's vehicle away from the festival grounds and out of their jurisdiction.

As the band drove off, the keyboard player said to Rex, "Today is the end of the road, today we break up the band."

I don't think so, thought Rex.

Two days after the performance, Rex and the band received a summons to the culture ministry in Berlin. Rex knew there was going to be trouble. And he had a statement in mind.

Fuck it, he thought as he stopped by a seafood shop on Stargarder Strasse to get the right prop for his statement.

"You have anything that's gone off?" Rex asked the fishmonger.

The guy retrieved a stinking, spoiled carp and wrapped it in a newspaper for Rex.

When Rex and the other members of the band sat down in front of the commission at the culture ministry, the officials started to rattle off all the evidence. They had Stasi reports with every word Rex had said. At the end of the presentation they announced the verdict: the band's amateur performance license had been yanked indefinitely. They could no longer legally play gigs. Venues across the country would be notified of the revocation of Herbst in Peking's *Einstufung*. They were poison.

"Do you have anything to say," the band was asked.

Rex did.

"Yes, I'd like to say something. First, we brought you something, a gift from the band," he said, putting his parcel on the table in front of the commission. "It's a fish that stinks from the head. If you know anything about the history of the Italian mafia, you know what that means. And one more thing: time is on our side."

Rather than break up, Rex rallied the band to record a song that would become the hit of the fall of 1989, played in heavy rotation on West Berlin radio after a friend of Rex's smuggled the master tape out. The song was called "Bakschischrepublik," and the chorus, bristling with Rex's rage, went:

Schwarz-Rot-Gold ist das System
morgen wird es untergehen

Black-red-gold is the system
Tomorrow it will fall

63

Another demonstration against election fraud was planned for Alexanderplatz on July 7. Only about sixty people made it there, but it took a thousand security personnel to thwart the demonstration. Government forces closed nearby subway stations and shut down access roads. They also beat and arrested innocent bystanders—collateral damage. It was another mistake, as ordinary people were rarely confronted with ugly state-sanctioned violence. *Not my problem, they're not coming for me* . . . except now some ordinary citizens had bruises and bloody noses, and many other ordinary citizens had seen bruises inflicted and noses bloodied.

The Erlöser punks and Church from Below had already taken advantage of the collective repulsion that many ordinary citizens—even committed party members—felt at the East German government's reaction to Tiananmen Square. At the end of June they had organized a week of twenty-four hour drumming as a protest. Church leadership at St. Elisabeth Church, which housed the Church from Below, complained that the round-the-clock drumming was a disturbance of the peace. Of course, that was the point, and despite threats the Church from Below did not get evicted.

In September, the monthly electoral fraud demonstration once again tried to take Alexanderplatz, with protesters blowing whistles and lining up in T-shirts that spelled out ELECTION FRAUD and then splitting up again. Police dragged protesters away by their hands and feet to police vans, battered and beaten, one with a broken arm. Nearly a hundred were arrested and held overnight. Three days later in Potsdam, just outside Berlin, Antifa activists attempted to join an officially sanctioned rally in remembrance of the victims of fascism. The kids carried signs that translated "Warning! Neo-Nazis in the DDR!" and "Against Nazis" and "War never again—fight it from the start." Police brutally beat them.

Meanwhile the crisis over would-be emigrants had taken on a dynamic all its own. Thousands of *Ausreiser* had fled to Poland, Czechoslovakia, and especially Hungary, where the government led by Miklos Nemeth had taken perestroika and glasnost so far as to dismantle the wire fence dividing Hungary from Austria—the first break in the Iron Curtain—with the cryptic blessing of Soviet premier Mikhail Gorbachev, who told Nemeth that border security was Nemeth's own problem, not his. On August 19, 1989, Hungarian activists had staged a "Pan-European Picnic" near Sopron, directly on the Austrian border, during which hundreds of East Germans were allowed to push through a border gate and enter Austria. So began a flood of humanity. By September 10, Hungary had officially opened its border to the West and refused to stop East Germans from exiting, despite bitter complaints from the Honecker regime. People left East Germany in droves—tens of thousands fled during the next few weeks of September. Immediately after the border opened, the tenor of demonstrations back in East Germany changed—especially in Leipzig.

Ever since the attempt by church leaders to hijack the Monday meetings at Nikolai Church, people had taken to gathering outside the church on Monday evenings. This continued even after the church had relented and allowed activists once again to lead the Monday peace prayer themselves. By summer of 1989 the outdoor public gatherings had built from a few dozen to a few hundred strong, packed with members of the punk scene in Leipzig and nearby Halle. One of them was Connie, now twenty-three, who had been jailed at age seventeen for spray-painting FREEDOM FOR JANA, MITA AND A-MICHA after the arrest of the members of the band Namenlos in 1983. Connie and others from the Mockauer Keller gang went to the Monday gatherings week in and week out, though they couldn't stand the *Ausreiser*, who, they felt, selfishly pursued their short-sighted personal goals at the expense of those fighting for change at home. When the would-be emigrants chanted *"Wir wollen raus,"* or "We want out," Connie and other Leipzig punks even mockingly chanted back: *"Wir bleiben hier,"* sneered the punks, "We're staying here."

After the opening of the Hungarian border, would-be emigrants no longer made up such a large portion of protesters outside the church on Mondays, but the crowds continued to swell anyway.

On September 11, 1989, about six hundred people gathered in front of Nikolai Church and were attacked by police after refusing to disperse; a hundred were detained. On September 18 about a thousand gathered, and so brutal was the police response that several protesters had to be hospitalized; about a hundred and fifty were detained. Over these weeks, the *Ausreiser* chant of *"Wir wollen raus,"* or "We want out," was increasingly drowned out and replaced by a strong, defiant, *affirmative* version of the punks' chant: *"Wir bleiben hier,"* or "We're staying here."

Instead of mocking those who wanted to leave, this was now a threat: *We're staying here . . . for a reason.*

Now the people on the streets planned to stay, they refused to throw in the towel, they refused to flee the problem but instead vowed to fix it, to *destroy* it. This was perhaps a scarier prospect for the government than just a few weeks prior, when so many had just wanted to get the fuck out.

We are the people, we are the power.

The number of participants skyrocketed to five or six thousand on Monday, September 25—despite police brutality and mass arrests the previous week. Or perhaps because of the brutality and mass arrests. Because ordinary citizens cringed at the violence being inflicted on peaceful demonstrators in the town center. The boomerang effect.

Also on September 25, demonstrators tried for the first time to leave the area around Nikolai Church to march along the broad ring road that encircled the old town center. Nothing had been planned, and Connie looked around at all the Stasi cameras and police and wondered what was going to happen. She knew many people had been arrested in previous weeks just for loitering near the church, and now thousands of people were trying to stage an actual march. Still, she wasn't afraid. On the contrary.

Finally, finally! I've been waiting for this moment!

Again police used batons and dogs and made mass arrests, and managed to halt the marchers' progress along the ring road in front of the main train station. Again average citizens—who increasingly hung around to watch the events—seemed repulsed by the violence. The marginal youths who made up the foot soldiers of the protests were accustomed to being beaten; they weren't used to being viewed sympathetically by the populace. Things were changing fast.

On October 2, over ten thousand joined the Monday march in Leipzig. Typical of the explosion in the crowd was another young punk with a similar name, Conny, famous around town for her bright red Mohawk. She was a regular in Open Work and had promoted concerts in the Mockauer Keller. Conny and others from the circle around the band L'Attentat had attended the Monday gatherings from the start, back when only two or three dozen people stood outside Nikolai Church. But now Conny's mother joined her, appalled at the regime's violence to such a degree that she did something she had never before contemplated: she protested.

We are the people.

That same Monday, October 2, solidarity vigils began in East Berlin, too, to protest the detainment of demonstrators in Leipzig in previous weeks; similar protests sprung up elsewhere around the country. From October 2 on, thousands of Berliners attended candlelit vigils held nightly in front of Gethsemane Church, in Prenzlauer Berg.

A-Micha was still living in his squatted apartment on Schliemannstrasse, just around the corner from Gethsemane Church. In the chaos around him, and in the reports he heard from Leipzig and elsewhere, he recognized this as a do or die moment: either the dictatorship was going to fall now, right now, or he and all the rest would be crushed and the momentum would be lost—perhaps forever. Rumors had spread in opposition circles of Stasi prison camps being hastily built on the outskirts of Berlin, and despite the increasing number of demonstrators it still seemed to A-Micha as if things could go either way. A-Micha felt compelled to do something—anything—to ensure the outcome went the right way. He began to print flyers and distribute them to people around Gethsemane Church, whether they were there to protest or just to gawk.

A-Micha's flyer began: *Wir dürfen jetzt nicht einschlafen!*

We cannot let up now!
We cannot abandon the political prisoners to their fate!

... We cannot leave our fate and that of our country to the politicians
(here or over there)—after all WE are the ones who want to, and must,
live here!
We are the power—we can and must make demands!

The flyer called for people to join the marches from the Schönhauser
Allee S-Bahn station to Alexanderplatz every Monday.

You can help us determine the way forward!
Together with Leipzig, Dresden, and other cities we will enforce our
will!

Then in all caps:

KEEP THE PRESSURE ON! INTO THE STREETS!

On October 7, East Berlin was to serve as the backdrop for celebrations
of the fortieth anniversary of the founding of the DDR. That morning, in a
move often made prior to major public events, police arrived at the doors
of many Erlöser punks and detained them to ensure they didn't cause difficulties during the celebrations. Protests took place anyway, and police
brutally suppressed demonstrators during and after the official celebrations;
one demonstrator died and about five hundred were detained as protestors
roved the streets of Prenzlauer Berg. Similar clashes took place all over the
country. Again ordinary citizens were confronted with state-sanctioned
violence inflicted on peaceful protesters, in Berlin, in Leipzig, and in many
other places big and small. By the next day, three thousand protesters were
in detainment around the country—in Leipzig, many of them held in horse
stalls outside of town.

Yao Yilin, a Chinese Politburo member and hardliner who had advocated the crackdown on Tiananmen Square protesters earlier that year, attended the DDR anniversary celebrations to great fanfare. Egon Krenz had also just returned from China, where he had celebrated the fortieth anniversary of the People's Republic and said, "In the struggles of our time, the DDR and China stand side by side." The East German regime seemed to be hinting once again at a Tiananmen solution to the building chaos.

Soviet premier Mikhail Gorbachev had also reluctantly flown in from Moscow for the anniversary celebrations—behind closed doors he referred to Honecker as an "asshole" and said that he hadn't been anxious to take part in Honecker's self-congratulatory fête.

Along the parade route on October 7, East Germans had chanted Gorbachev's name, some even calling out, "Gorbi, help us!"

While in the East German capital, Gorbachev told seventy-seven-year-old dictator Erich Honecker, *"Wer zu spät kommt, den bestraft das Leben."*

Translation: He who is too late is punished by life.

64

t takes a magical, spontaneous, mass uprising for a revolution to take place.

No one group can ever bring it about.

First there is a feeling of shakiness underfoot, a faint tremor, discernable only by those doing the shaking and stomping—in this case, in East Germany, the punks, the freaks, the young people who realized that the authorities were scared, that the dictatorship was wobbly. Then, if the stars align, other people, normal people, those who would otherwise just go about their lives, happy to get by in the system as it exists, *not my problem*, no reason to make waves . . . if the stars align just right, then those people might eventually feel it, too. The tremors. The shakiness. And maybe, just maybe, they come out of their apartments and their houses to see what's happening, to see what is causing the tremors. And maybe, just maybe, they even join in, *I'm not sure exactly what I'm doing out here, what brought me outside, but I don't like the way those people are being treated . . . and . . . well . . . I don't like this regime either; I'm staying out here in the street*. Maybe these people, the normal people, the ones not inclined to step out of line, maybe they help to rock the joint, too, maybe they help to shake and stomp. And perhaps, if the magic holds just right, and everyone feels it and everyone joins in, *we are the people*, the tremor becomes an earthquake and the foundation crumbles. It all comes apart.

Revolution.

And that is what happened in the fall of 1989 in East Germany.

By early October, the groundwork laid by punks and other activists influenced by the punk mentality was becoming a magical, spontaneous, mass uprising, being joined by people from all walks of life, all now chanting Otze's line: *We are the people.*

Both participants and Party officials expected the number of people at Leipzig's weekly Monday demonstration to swell on October 9, 1989. So, too, would the number and type of security forces present. For the first time, the Party called in troops from the National Volks Army, armed with live ammunition; Stasi chief Mielke issued orders for all Stasi operatives to carry their guns; regional hospitals were put on alert. For weeks, every Monday protest had been bigger than the previous; for weeks, the violence of the official response had also intensified. Which side was winning? And what would happen next?

Siegbert Schefke—Media Siggi from the Environmental Library—snuck out of his Berlin apartment in the pre-dawn hours of October 9, ditching the group of Stasi tails waiting for him outside his place by creeping across the roofs of adjoining buildings before dropping down and driving to Leipzig with Aram Radomski and one of their cameras, switching cars several times to make sure they weren't followed. All around them they saw convoys of military-style vehicles also chugging toward Leipzig. When they reached town, the pair hid in a church tower that faced the ring road in central Leipzig. From that vantage point they filmed the biggest demonstration yet as it slowly snaked around the ring road.

This time, for the first time, security forces did not attack demonstrators despite the military-style build-up prior to the event. With close to 100,000 peaceful protesters working their way around Leipzig's historic city center, police, Stasi, National Volks Army troops, and paramilitary groups all hung back.

Siggi and Aram smuggled the footage out via their West German correspondent contact, and it was broadcast the next night for everyone in East Germany to see via Western TV. The snowball effect, the magical spontaneous uprising of a broad spectrum of society—of normal people, working people, those who usually just went along—had reached critical mass for all to see. No longer just punks and freaks dared to take to the streets, but grandmothers and shift workers, the bedrock of society, all across the country . . . the tremors becoming ever more frequent, ever more powerful, the foundations shuddering underfoot, shaking, shaking, shaking.

Even core members of the Party could now feel the tremors reverberating beneath them.

The following Tuesday, October 17, at the weekly meeting of the Politburo, Erich Honecker was deposed. The Politburo installed Egon Krenz in his place, who, despite having spoken openly of a "Chinese solution" to the country's unrest, despite having overseen the election commission that was proven to have falsified the vote back in May, now began to speak of change.

People on the streets were not buying it.

The tremors did not let up.

We are the people, we are the power.

On November 4, 1989, three Stasi officers knocked at A-Micha's door at seven in the morning. "These are the colleagues who will look after you today," the ranking officer said, gesturing to the other two. "We don't *have* to arrest you, but we *can* arrest you."

Then one officer took up a position in front of the building, and one behind. Wherever A-Micha went, they went. And if he were to go in the direction of Alexanderplatz, where a demonstration was scheduled, he knew what would happen.

It didn't matter that A-Micha and other known agitators couldn't go.

November 4 was a Saturday, making the demonstration that day the first not scheduled on a workday. Half a million people gathered on East Berlin's Alexanderplatz to demand real change, fundamental change, not Egon fucking Krenz change. The tremors had become shockwaves. The tremors had fatally cracked the foundation. Revolution was at hand.

We are the people.

Back in August, Erich Honecker had quoted an August Bebel rhyme during a promotional visit to a microprocessor factory in Erfurt: *"Den Sozialismus in seinem Lauf hält weder Ochs noch Esel auf,"* which means "Neither ox nor donkey can halt the progress of socialism." Honecker had repeated the phrase on October 6, with Gorbachev in attendance on the eve of the celebrations of the DDR's fortieth birthday.

The final sentence of the fall issue of the *mOAning Star* newspaper read: *Die Anarchie in ihrem Lauf hält weder Mielke noch Erich schon gar nicht mehr auf.*

Translation: Neither Stasi chief Erich Mielke nor dictator Erich Honecker can halt the progress of anarchy any longer.

Truth.

65

I t was cold on November 9, 1989. As the sun sank early that evening, it got colder.

Feeling B and die Anderen were on their way to another gig in West Berlin that night at a venue called Pike Club, in a back courtyard on Glogauer Strasse, in Kreuzberg. The club was fairly close to two border checkpoints, one at Heinrich-Heine-Strasse and the other at the Oberbaumbrücke, a bridge from Warschauer Strasse in the East to Schlesisches Tor in the West.

The bands' previous gig together in the West—back in May—had taken place barely a week before the Chinese government crushed the student uprising on Tiananmen Square. That had been an *oh-shit* moment for some members of the bands.

Should I have stayed in the West?

But Feeling B had soon after been granted another set of travel visas, lengthy ones that allowed them to go on tour in West Germany during the summer of 1989. Visiting the other side of Berlin was one thing; traversing West Germany was another. The state concert agency assigned the band a driver, a cushy Russian Lada sedan, and a trailer to haul their gear.

In the case of die Anderen, the reward for their return after the May show came that fall of 1989, when authorities granted them permission to play the show at Pike Club. This time die Anderen received visas that allowed unlimited exit and entry for a month, from late October to late November, as well as the right to use any checkpoint.

The members of die Anderen had already crossed to Kreuzberg and back earlier the same day as the Pike Club gig to buy a few cans of beer and a newspaper.

They'd been drinking all day.

Dafty was playing guitar in die Anderen at this point. Toster had gotten him back into the music scene upon Dafty's return from the army, having him work as a roadie for die Anderen before Dafty started his own group, which eventually imploded. Dafty—with his serious punk background, his run-ins with the cops, his detainments, his friendships with the Erlöser punks and Church from Below crowd—simply couldn't believe he had this visa in his hand.

But he did; they all did.

And when they turned up for the gig that cold November night, they were already drunk. They kept drinking as the other bands played, with Feeling B playing their set just before die Anderen went on.

Unlike back in May, this time the venue was full, and as die Anderen played the crowd seemed to swell further.

The band spotted a lot of familiar faces in the audience, but that wasn't unusual. They always ran into a lot of people they knew in West Berlin—people who had fled recently through Hungary or people who had left or been expatriated over the years. But as die Anderen ripped through their set, people started holding up East German ID papers and waving them in the air.

Strange.

Still, drunk themselves, the band members figured the people in the crowd were probably drunk, too—shit, maybe they were making fun of the band or something.

They continued to play.

More familiar faces. The British musician PJ Harvey was at the show—along with her mom. Harvey was still practically a teenager, but the band she was in at the time, Automatic Dlamini, had played in East Berlin over the summer and she'd gotten to know die Anderen.

So many familiar faces.

And the ID papers waving in the air.

More and more East German ID papers held aloft.

What the fuck was going on?

Finally, as die Anderen were playing their final song of the night, Dafty spotted another familiar face. And this wasn't someone who had fled the country. He had seen this person earlier *that day*, back in East Berlin.

It began to dawn on him . . . *but wait, that's impossible!*

He just couldn't wrap his hazy head around what was happening. If these people were here . . . in *West* Berlin . . .

I must be really drunk.

Of course everyone already had a sense that something big was on the verge of happening. Things had already taken place in the last few weeks and months they thought they'd never see. Honecker had stepped down. Tens of thousands had taken to the streets in Leipzig and Berlin, half a million had filled Alexanderplatz just a few days ago. But still. This . . . this would mean . . .

When the band came offstage, they were mobbed by friends from East Berlin, all talking at once, and it was true, it was true: the checkpoints were open.

The Berlin Wall had fallen.

As news spread inside the club, the bar passed out free beer.

Unbeknownst to the people at the concert in Pike Club, East German government spokesman and Politburo member Günter Schabowski had announced an immediate end to travel restrictions at a press conference earlier that evening. Though Schabowski had told the mayor of West Berlin ten days prior that travel restrictions would be liberalized, and West Berlin had prepared its public transport system for that eventuality, it seemed as if East Berlin had not prepared for the policy change. After the press conference ran live on Eastern TV and the news was broadcast and re-broadcast on West Berlin TV and radio, East Berliners had gathered at some checkpoints, demanding to be let through. Guards at the checkpoints had received no specific orders, however, and struggled to reach superiors at night; as the crowds began to build, the guards just had to wing it and decide on an individual basis how best to deal with the situation. A little-known checkpoint between Waltersdorfer Chausee in the East and Rudow in the West opened first, at around 8:30 p.m. Then, faced with a huge crowd of perhaps tens of thousands, having themselves seen the news conference, and unwilling to open fire to maintain control, the guards at Bornholmer Strasse checkpoint opened their gates at around 11:30 p.m. Word spread, and other checkpoints, including Checkpoint Charlie, soon followed suit.

A carload of the bands' friends had driven through the Invalidenstrasse checkpoint in their old Volga and then found their way to Kreuzberg and Pike Club, where they knew Feeling B and die Anderen were playing.

Despite the excitement, the members of Feeling B just wanted to go home. But the scene at the checkpoints was so crazy, they couldn't get back across. In the end one of their friends bought a bottle of whisky and they, too, joined the party.

The members of die Anderen walked over to the checkpoint at Heinrich-Heine-Strasse and stood there watching their countrymen flood through. They rapped on the tops of Trabants, Easterners greeting other Easterners as they entered the West.

People chanted and sang. It was a huge street festival in the middle of the night.

The Berlin Wall had fallen.

Toster and Dafty and the rest of the band wandered the streets of West Berlin all night with friends, smoking dope and drinking what seemed like a hundred beers.

The band also made a decision right there and then: die Anderen broke up.

The Wall was done and so was the band.

For the punks of East Berlin it was simple: mission accomplished.

Or was it?

The battle of Mainzer Strasse, 1990

VII

Lust for Life

66

It's easy to look at the images of Easterners and Westerners dancing arm in arm atop the Wall and think that was it; everything changed in an instant.

But it didn't.

When Otze of Schleim-Keim went home on November 10 after a night of partying, his brother met him at the door.

"The Stasi were just here," he told Otze. "They're looking for you."

The day after the fall of the Wall, Stasi officers went to work. The police went to work. Border guards still stood at attention with machine guns at their sides. The East German Communist Party's annual three-day conference even continued with little mention of the opening of the border.

In the immediate aftermath of the fall of the Wall, it wasn't clear how much had changed, and it wasn't clear what was going to happen. Groups like the Church from Below and the Erlöser punks had never spent much time thinking about what might come *after* the fall of the Wall.

In hindsight, it's seen as inevitable that the two Germanys would reunite. But none of the people who had laid the groundwork for the fall—those who had started the tremors and endured the security forces' brutality—envisioned a unified Germany. Those people had sacrificed their places in society for the chance to form a *new* one, something *different* and distinct, an independent East Germany built from scratch. They hadn't looked to the West for inspiration before, and none of them looked to the West for salvation now that the border was open.

336 BURNING DOWN THE HAUS

The political situation quickly spiraled out of control—specifically, out of the control of all of those people who had fought so hard to bring down the dictatorship. Not even the new political organizations that had mushroomed during the final days before the fall of the Wall—some of which, like *Neues Forum*, or New Forum, ostensibly had tens of thousands of members—seemed to have any influence. As demonstrations continued after the opening of the border, the chants on the street transformed with frightening speed from "We are the people" to "We are *one* people."

That was the sort of nationalist sentiment that sent shivers down the spines of anti-Nazi Antifa groups. A unified Germany was just about the worst outcome they could imagine. But their nightmares were about to be realized—in more than one way. Skinheads joined the continuing demonstrations, skinheads attacked those voicing anti-unification sentiments, skinheads operated openly in the streets.

Antifa groups began to mobilize.

Among those moved to action was Grit Ferber, the woman who'd been among the teenagers imprisoned for spray-painting anarchist graffiti in Weimar in 1983. She was living in West Berlin in 1989, having left East Germany not long after her release from prison.

In December 1989 Grit went back to her home town, alarmed at what was happening on the streets of East Germany. Grit and a group of friends joined a big Antifa demonstration in Weimar. Afterward they secured speakers to the top of Grit's VW Beetle to serve as a makeshift PA, and drove around the streets shouting things like *"Deutschland muss sterben,"* or "Germany must die."

After her release from prison back in 1984, Grit had become increasingly paranoid about the Stasi—about being surveilled and about them trying to set her up in order to throw her back in prison. She and her friends had refused to go straight to the West from prison, but once on the outside she changed her mind. She had landed in Kassel, a mid-sized city in the middle of West Germany. After about six months there, she had moved to West Berlin and started a band with two other exiled women from Weimar and two women from Kassel. And now she was driving around her old haunts shouting into a microphone that Germany must die.

One day in early 1990, Grit and the drummer in her band ran into some friends.

"We squatted a building in the East," they said.

"Squatted a building?" said Grit. "I want to do that!"

She had two small children now and had always dreamed of bringing them up in a communal setting. The squats in West Berlin never suited her— the people all wore black and shat on the idea of being in a relationship or having kids.

She began to talk to her bandmates about the idea of squatting a place in East Berlin together. One of the women originally from Weimar immediately rejected the idea. She had been together with Wolfram Hasch when Hasch had been arrested at gunpoint in 1986 while painting the white line on the West Berlin side of the Wall; she had given birth to their child while he was stuck in Stasi prison; she said she would never, ever set foot in the East again.

Grit decided to explore the idea anyway. She heard about a squatters council that had been set up and went to one of their weekly meetings in January 1990. The more she listened, the more interested she became.

By early 1990 about fifteen buildings had been squatted in Mitte, Prenzlauer Berg, Friedrichshain, and Lichtenberg, including Köpenicker Strasse 137 and Kastanienallee 85/86, which still exist in largely the same form today, as residential collectives. On the facade of Köpenicker Strasse 137, residents painted a slogan: *Die Grenze verläuft nicht zwischen der Völkern, sondern zwischen oben und unten*. Loosely translated: Borders don't run between nations but between those at the top and those at the bottom. Emancipation—true freedom—was predicated on an equitable economic system, and unification would not bring that.

Aljoscha, the singer of Feeling B, put down roots in Schönhauser Allee 5. Because of the travel privileges he'd enjoyed with his Swiss passport, Aljoscha knew he didn't like the West. He also knew that if they were going to make anything out of the East, they would have to get an independent infrastructure up and running—and fast, since he expected Western investors to swoop in and take advantage of the situation. The only way to block Western real estate speculators was to scoop up the real estate before them.

With more than thirty apartments in its original configuration and a courtyard in the middle, Schönhauser Allee 5 was ideal: Aljoscha wanted to establish something big. Schönhauser 5 offered plenty of space to create the arts center he envisioned, with concert venues, band rehearsal spaces, music and art studios, video editing facilities—within months he would even erect broadcasting facilities for a pirate FM radio station, called Radio P.

But first things first: the pub, with a bar made of stacked beer crates, opened almost immediately.

67

Squatted in the gathering dusk of December 29, 1989, Schreinerstrasse 47, in Friedrichshain, was arguably the first of all the buildings squatted after the fall of the Wall.

Core members of the Church from Below, including Dirk Moldt and Silvio Meier, squatted this imposing nineteenth-century apartment building; A-Micha joined them a short time afterward. For them, it was a logical extension of how they had always done things: if the political process was going off the rails, they would create their own world, their own reality. DIY. Punk.

What they felt they needed were building blocks that could be scaled up to a societal level, cells that could form a whole organism. They had carved space out within the dictatorship—negative space, outside society; now there was nothing but negative space, a political vacuum, and they would create islands—positive space, a living model for a new society. The possibilities seemed endless: on top of all the derelict old buildings, many of which were still scheduled for demolition, there were tens of thousands of apartments left empty by those who decamped for the West once the border opened.

Dirk and Silvio withdrew from the Church from Below and devoted themselves to the new project full-time. In addition to making the space livable, they had to fortify the building to fend off potential police attempts to oust them as well as to protect against increasingly bold and frequent attacks by skinheads.

A statement they issued upon squatting the building began by talking about how the overthrown rulers of the DDR had betrayed the country, warning that international capital now had free rein to plunder the country. It continued:

> We hereby declare that we have squatted Schreinerstrasse 47 in Berlin Friedrichshain in order to give our hope for socialism, understanding, and solidarity at least a tiny chance of survival . . .

> We didn't stay in the noncapitalist world through the long, bitter years of the dictatorship just to sit by passively and watch the breaking up and selling off of our country. Our moral values—solidarity, nonviolence, education, participation, our shameless lust for life, and rage—allowed us to survive the era of Stalinism. And we will make a stand against the far worse dictatorship of global capitalism by using the exact same means . . .

> We urge everyone to follow this example and to take buildings, workshops, educational institutions, bars, cafés, etc., under your own control. It's the only way we see to deny the inhumane "free market" a base in the DDR . . .

> In a spirit of hopeful desperation, we cry: don't let us waste this last chance for free self-determination!

The plan for Schreinerstrasse 47 included a meeting space where communal issues could be addressed and projects—like creating a playground on an adjacent empty lot—could be managed. Drawing on past experience that had taught them the importance of independent media sources, they also installed a printing press, allowing them to produce informational flyers as well as a newsletter devoted to the squatting movement they hoped to catalyze. The renovations also included a café, because, of course—it was right there in their manifesto, after all—*lust for life.*

Another one of the very first buildings squatted after the fall of the Wall went one better: at Rosenthaler Strasse 68, in Mitte, living space was totally secondary to the goal of creating a revolutionary party venue. Or as the squatters themselves described it, an "independent art, culture, and communications center."

The gang who squatted it on January 17, 1990—mostly people loosely associated with the bands Ich-Funktion, Freygang, and die Firma, including Paul Landers of Feeling B—dubbed the building *Eimer*, which meant bucket. The name came from the hundreds of buckets of rubble the squatters had to remove from the damp, dark, derelict building when they took it over. The ground floor of the old building was already collapsing, so the squatters ripped it down and created a cavernous basement concert space. Upstairs was soon to be another bar, with a smaller stage and dance floor.

Even as they worked on the building, the Eimer crew immediately began to put on concerts, performances, and parties, open to all. They assembled the best sound system ever heard in the East, built a recording studio and rehearsal spaces, and installed guest quarters where musicians and artists could crash after events. The Eimer squatters also stuck to their ideological guns, establishing a simple, equal distribution of pay: whatever income was left after costs was split evenly between all who worked and lived there, no exceptions.

Speiche joined Eimer about two weeks after it was squatted and became a key figure within the collective. He booked bands and DJs, and helped get the word out for events. He also handled security—which would prove quite a job, as the leftist squats quickly came under attack from right-wing skinheads. At times, Speiche also served as Eimer's punk conscience. When, a few years down the road, someone tried to install a cigarette machine and coin-operated slot machines, he knew how to take care of the problem: he threw that shit right out the window.

Not commerce.

Culture.

Eimer functioned not only as the home of the first burst of experimental post-Wall culture, but also as the jumping-off point for the most important squat in the evolution of the city. Eimer eventually became crowded enough that a group split off and started to look for another building. Eimer had appealed to its occupants in part because it was scheduled for demolition as part of government plans—plans still being executed despite the opening of the border; in essence, Rosenthaler 68, which became Eimer, no longer existed in official records. Many places in the old streets around Hackescher Markt were designated for demolition, including a sprawling complex on Oranienburger Strasse that the breakaway group from Eimer was eyeing.

The complex dated from 1909 and had been built as an elegant shopping center. The structure was among the first in Berlin to employ steel, so even though it had been damaged during World War II, and even though Eastern authorities had started years before to demolish the rear walls of the building, it was still surprisingly sound—especially given how skeletal it looked, particularly in the back, where the exterior walls had been blasted off and the space was completely open to the weather. The building took up about half a block and the view from the open rooms at the back looked out over a vast vacant lot—altogether, the property covered almost six acres.

On February 13, 1990, the team from Eimer—led by a musician named Leo Kondeyne—struck.

Borrowing a surplus fire truck owned by Tatjana of die Firma, a group of fewer than ten people climbed into a second floor window of the five-story complex, went downstairs, opened the boarded-up ground floor, and then got to work securing the place—like the other squats, it had to be heavily fortified.

This building is hereby squatted.

It was a huge job.

Leo's gang had to secure the structures and the yard, get water and electricity running, clear the chimneys to allow them to heat. Demolition of the complex had been so imminent that the group had to pull explosives out of holes demolition experts had already drilled. And then they started to craft the place to fit their goal: to provide more space for people who had the urge to create art and music, to create *culture*—a new culture that could form the basis of a new society, one being created from scratch, one they hoped to conjure up as a living model. Depending on how the political situation shook out, it might serve only as a basis of an antisociety, but they were used to playing that role; and even if their vision didn't become a living model for something larger, they themselves would still be living in a world of their own creation, by their own ideals.

Speiche took a sleeping bag and did not leave the complex for five days straight as the group worked around the clock. They had brought a generator and got music and lights on by day two; over the next few days they tapped into electrical lines they located in the building.

Leo Kondeyne, the ringleader of the group, wasn't a traditional punk. He was a bit older, slight and soft-spoken, really more in tune with the hippie generation; he had worked as a soundman for the Eastern heavy blues outfit Freygang. But in the mid 1980s he had met Alexander Kriening, the drummer in the initial lineup of Feeling B. Kriening did Leo a great favor in urging him just to make music—winning him over to the punk DIY ethos. It didn't matter what you played or how well, just start making a racket. And when Leo and Kriening started doing just that, Leo loved the results.

Soon an ever-shifting array of guest musicians from the punk scene came and went within Leo's anarchic group, a strictly improvisational affair without a set lineup or repertoire. The shapeshifting combo was dubbed Tacheles, taken from a German idiom derived from Yiddish: *Tacheles reden*, which means to speak frankly. Feeling B guitarist Paul Landers was a frequent member, but because of the nature of the project, Paul played clarinet in Leo's band. Of course. Clarinet. Paul—as well as his Feeling B compatriot Flake—went on to become technicians in the newly squatted complex, helping to build the first sound system out of old parts, fashioning stages in various bars and performance spaces inside, working behind the scenes on theater productions, even pulling out the asbestos lining in part of the building.

Leo saw the squatted building complex as a logical extension of the band. He wanted to bring to life—to concrete reality—the spontaneity and creativity of the band, the ever-expanding sense of solidarity nurtured by the interchangeable lineup, and, just as important, the *chaos*. And it worked.

Partly because of the scale of it, Leo's complex on Oranienburger Strasse—more than any other place established in the rush to stake out physical and philosophical space for a new society—came the closest to being a fully fledged alternative world. It was a magical realm where anything seemed possible—where *everything* seemed possible. And it quickly became the hub for the entire scene that sprang up in East Berlin after the fall of the Wall.

Early on, someone hung a banner on the pockmarked facade of the new squat, the grand, five-story former department store, bombed-out, soot-caked, grotesquely disfigured, now with music and the clink of beer bottles echoing through the damp, cavernous space.

It read: *Die Ideale sind ruiniert, retten wir die Ruine.*

Translation: The ideals are ruined, we're saving the ruins.

They named these ruins Tacheles.

Ruins like Tacheles—places where time had stood still since the end of World War II—became the means of transport into the future: you opened the door to these crumbling monuments of the past and entered a new world, a colorful vision of a new way of life created amidst the grim rubble of history.

In coming years, Tacheles came to encompass bars, theaters, a cinema, a printmaking studio, video editing facilities, and a sprawling sculpture garden that doubled as a biergarten—all in addition to the art studios and living quarters.

The main bar, Café Zapata, on the ground floor, became a popular destination. And a subterranean space beneath the bar became the first new club in East Berlin—a club representative of a different world, the world Tacheles residents wished to make real, a physical manifestation of their collective ideals. Radical democracy reigned inside the club, just the way they wanted it to outside the club. There was no door policy. The restrooms were not divided by gender. Photographs were forbidden—a policy continued in many other Berlin clubs through the years—adding to the atmosphere of spontaneity, participation, and total lack of self-consciousness. A mix of sweat and dirt dripped from the low ceiling as unnamed DJs—there were no stars in this environment—dropped tunes and a wild mix of people danced.

It was a free space, where everyone took part, everyone played a role, and thus everyone experienced the collective euphoria of the party.

Tacheles also became a sort of musical petri dish—the place where a musical mutation first took place, where punk philosophy extricated itself from the stifling constrictions of traditional rock instrumentation. Otze of Schleim-Keim, who lived under a staircase in Tacheles for a year or so, began to experiment with electronic production while there. It all made sense to an old punk like Otze: producing on a computer demanded even less technical know-how than playing punk-rock guitar, it had even more of a leveling effect, it broke down the barriers between listener and musician even further. And DJs did not demand attention like a band. DJs empowered people to have fun on their own terms. DJs stood at ground level—at least at a place like Tacheles—and partied along with everyone else. Techno was punk as fuck.

Eastern bands died off quickly after the fall of the Wall. It wasn't just that people now could hear music from all over the world, it was also that previously existing forms of music seemed mired in the past, the soundtrack to a bygone era. For Eastern punks, the original enemy had been vanquished. And even if Western colonization and the sudden rise in neo-Nazi violence presented new challenges, the music—and the message—needed to change.

After all, the occupants of Eimer and Tacheles and other squats were trying to build now rather than destroy.

For that, they needed a form of music as new as the idealized society they were inventing, a sound forged in the present and pointing to the future.

68

Bohemianism is typically formed in opposition to some status quo, set in relief against an existing society. But East Berlin in 1990 was a totally blank slate: the system of government, the material culture, even the names of the streets in many cases—everything was gone. Everything. An entire society had been wiped from the earth, and here were the physical remains, waiting to be redeveloped into something else, something new, something formed not in reaction to a status quo but conjured out of thin air, built from scratch by those willing to create a new world, a new reality, DIY.

What was suddenly happening in East Berlin wasn't bohemianism, it was pure magic: the imposition of something completely new on this blank slate of a city, a collective imagination being brought to life. And for that reason alone, the crumbling wasteland of central East Berlin became the most beautiful place on earth just then, an entire city of limitless possibility.

East Berlin was basically a complete nineteenth-century city standing empty. But instead of being in the middle of nowhere, abandoned like some ghost mining town, it was fused to a bustling, modern city—West Berlin—and was served by an enviable and still functional infrastructure: subways and trains and buses and trams, a great water supply flowing from every tap, reliable electricity. Everything was in place beneath this half-empty paradise of elegant ruins, this dilapidated gray metropolis just waiting to be imbued with the color and life of a brand new society.

The call to action issued by Schreinerstrasse 47 had not fallen on deaf ears. An informational pamphlet produced by the squatters council in the spring of 1990 showcased eighteen buildings, plus two blocks of buildings: Kreutzigerstrasse 18-23, and Mainzer Strasse 2-11, both in Friedrichshain.

The dream of scaling up a society based on socialist anarchist cells seemed to be working. East Berlin had become an autonomous zone on par with the Paris Commune of 1871, and unlike nineteenth-century Paris, Berlin had no central government to fight, no national troops threatening to invade—there was in essence no central authority at all in the aftermath of the collapse of the communist regime.

"Our growing movement," read the introduction to the pamphlet, "is composed for the most part of young people who wish to put into practice their own ideas about collective living," to build a "self-determined neighborhood culture," and to keep usable buildings from sitting empty and further deteriorating.

Over the years, punk activism helped save hundreds if not thousands of historic buildings throughout the DDR. For an indication of the scale of East German "redevelopment" plans, 10,900 residential buildings in the city of Dresden were planned for demolition by 1990 as part of a program that would have ripped down 30,000 by the year 2000; for comparison, during World War II, when Dresden was repeatedly firebombed, 25,000 residential buildings were destroyed, with an additional 18,000 heavily damaged. There were similar plans for mass demolition in Berlin's historic districts. One would have razed two-thirds of the buildings in some sections of Prenzlauer Berg. In Friedrichshain, all six of the buildings squatted on Kreuzigerstrasse were slated for demolition in early 1990. If not for the rethinking caused by the takeover of spaces like Tacheles, many of the planned demolitions throughout East Berlin might have still taken place before unification, gutting the city of much of its historic housing stock.

A squat was not first and foremost about living rent-free on an urban island of egalitarian hedonism. If you wanted to create a new society, your goals couldn't end at the front door. Many of the buildings built playgrounds or opened day cares. The squatted blocks on Mainzer and Kreutziger offered communal meals for elderly neighborhood residents. This new way of life had to work from birth to retirement. There were food cooperatives, bicycle repair facilities, carpentry workshops. And nearly every building housed a bar or "info-café." Bars and cafés in the squats brought in money, of course, though not much, and the profits were set aside to pay for meals and supplies. More important, the bars and cafés were places to socialize and party together with the wider community.

A squat drew the rest of the world in through its bar or café. And the rest of the world just might take away the seed of an idea from that interaction; if that seed took root elsewhere, it just might grow into another outpost working toward the formation of a new society. If all these outposts continued to expand and stayed at least loosely tied together, they might actually form the basis of a new way of life. It was in any event the only hope for a new society once the election of March 18, 1990, determined that the territory of the DDR would be split into its constituent states and absorbed by West Germany; from the point of view of those who had fought and marched and chanted "We're staying here," the speedy annexation of East Germany represented straight-up colonization.

The pamphlet's introduction ended with another call to action: "Don't isolate yourselves. Build your own projects in your neighborhood!"

By the time that pamphlet was published, Grit Ferber, the Weimar punk, had squatted in one of buildings in Kreutzigerstrasse, too. The building had been listed in a log of empty spaces maintained by the squatters council. Others who had already moved into the street were anxious to get more of the empty buildings around them filled because they kept getting attacked by gangs of skinheads. One obvious solution to the problem seemed to be strength in numbers.

The buildings on Kreutzigerstrasse were in terrible shape. The building Grit ended up in had windows in the front, but the back was open to the weather, and many of the floors had collapsed. The coal ovens were not in working order. The first two things Grit and her friends did were secure the ground floor with heavy doors and install a communal kitchen in one of the intact floors at the top of the building.

Grit and her compatriots scoured other empty buildings for supplies, salvaging water pipes, wiring, fixtures, lamps, anything. One afternoon as they were loading her VW with supplies rummaged from an empty structure on Mainzer Strasse, two East German cops approached them and said, "You can't take that stuff, you're going to have to take it all back into the building."

What can they do? thought Grit.

She had West German license plates on her Beetle, and she had never been one to cower in fear of authority—if you could even call the *Volkspolizei* an authority now, after the election.

"Go home," Grit said to the cops. "You can't tell us what to do anymore." The cops did not respond.

Grit finished loading her VW and then drove back to Kreutzigerstrasse.

The move back to the East had cost Grit her band. But she ended up meeting two other women on her first day in Kreutzigerstrasse and together they formed a new band and quickly started playing the bars and clubs in other squats all over the central parts of the East, including Eimer. When she wasn't playing with her band or working on the building, she took her turn working at the bar, dubbed Pilatus, where everyone in the house had a shift.

Even with more houses in the area squatted, the attacks from skinheads did not subside. If anything, they were increasing: neo-Nazis had realized they, too, could take advantage of the political vacuum.

Tacheles was attacked with Molotov cocktails one night, and one of the squatters defending the place went screaming through the café with his clothes on fire.

The squatters council eventually appealed for help, reaching out to personal contacts and leftist organizations in West Berlin and urging them to come occupy more buildings in the East. By August 1990 there were a hundred and twenty buildings squatted in East Berlin.

These increasingly numerous outposts, bursting with color and energy, were beginning to set the tone. Even if, after the March elections, everyone knew these cells would not be part of the political structure of a new country, they were beginning to define the culture of a new city.

69

The political limbo—the de facto anarchy—during which the initial burst of creativity in East Berlin took place, ended in a legal sense with the official annexation of the East by West Germany, on Oct 3, 1990. After unification, the West German regime quickly asserted its authority.

And the West Germans did not fuck around.

In November 1990, police were tasked with emptying a city block in Friedrichshain that was almost completely squatted. Thus began the battle of Mainzer Strasse, in essence a small-scale civil war. Residents of the squatted block erected barricades, lit cars on fire, and threw Molotov cocktails at the police, who eventually rolled in with armored vehicles and violently removed the squatters.

It would be easy to say everything changed after that first year, after unification, after Mainzer Strasse was cleared in a military-style operation, but that wouldn't be accurate. The sense of anarchy, the feeling of limitless possibilities, lasted for years. Some squatted buildings, like Eimer, held on in nearly the same form for another twenty years; others, like Schreinerstrasse 47, managed to legalize their status while retaining their soul. Grit Ferber still lives on Kreutzigerstrasse in a building with a communal kitchen. Herne, who had set up the concerts at Erlöser Church in the 1980s, still books shows at Köpenicker Strasse 137.

Tacheles, the grandest and most audacious of all the squats, was fatally weakened by an internal rift, but the death spiral lasted two decades. Not long after it was squatted in 1990, the original occupants of Tacheles had invited a group of West Germans to move in—they'd been kicked out of an abandoned hotel near Anhalter Bahnhof, in West Berlin, where they had set up an artist collective. At first, the Westerners seemed to share the same goals as the Eastern artists already living in Tacheles, and things worked well. The newcomers brought fresh energy and skills, and a lot got done. But slowly the relationship soured. Spearheaded by Ludwig Eben, the Westerners wrested control of the money-generating parts of Tacheles and milked them for personal gain—creating profits at the bar became the overriding priority, and creating culture took a back seat to this new priority among the group from West Berlin. Ludwig Eben became a millionaire while Leo Kondeyne, the original mastermind of Tacheles, was eventually forced out of the building altogether.

It was a terrible blow to the fundamental vision behind the project, which had been built as a collective dream rather than a personal one: the bars were supposed to provide modest funding for art, music, and culture.

Gone was the anarchist ideal of democratic control of the workplace.

After years of wrangling, the bank that by then held the deed to the property insisted on emptying Tacheles in September 2012.

"This is the theft of a work of art, supported by the police," said a Tacheles spokesman as the building was finally cleared.

But by then, there were over a hundred lawsuits pending between various parties within Tacheles, most related to the ongoing battle between two factions—on one side, the artists; on the other, the group that ran the bars and clubs. Any semblance of solidarity within Tacheles had evaporated. Not only did the battle for the building complex not rise to the level of Mainzer Strasse, the police encountered no resistance at all.

The world inside had long since capitulated to the world outside.

It's tempting to grumble about the death of the grand experiment of the post-Wall years, tempting to look back at the early 1990s with a nostalgia that suggests the city is no longer *that way*, to say that the creative anarchy of the year with basically no government was just a freakish anomaly, a moment in time, unsustainable and unrealistic, a product of a once-in-a-lifetime circumstance, magical but inevitably short-lived. And it's true that the city isn't the same as it was then, and that the transient nightlife scene of the 1990s has largely been replaced by a more formalized scene, with leases, fire exits, and professionalization.

And yet, artists and musicians still flock to Berlin, activists and whistleblowers seek haven here, and tens of thousands of people come to the city every weekend to party.

What draws people to Berlin today is not nostalgia for some bygone era. What draws people to Berlin today is the fact that it is still unique. And while the continued existence of Köpenicker 137 and Schreiner 47 and old squatted cultural centers like Acud, Zosch, and Schokoladen is heartwarming, what makes Berlin unique today isn't the few lingering bastions of the 1990s. What's important isn't the locations that survived but the *spirit* that survived, a spirit that has continued to evolve in its particulars and to breathe life into new institutions, a hyper-political spirit that continues to imbue the city with the ethos of East Berlin punk.

These days, club life is not only Berlin's most famous attraction; it is also a window on the city's soul. The contemporary club About Blank offers a glimpse of that soul. It sits unmarked on a street lined with scrub trees and corrugated metal fences, an apparent wasteland sandwiched between rail yards, construction sites, car lots, and a cut-rate grocery store. All that's visible from the outside are two graffiti-covered doors in a concrete block. Inside, you pay a modest cover and walk down a bare entrance hall. There is no velvet rope, no VIP area, no dress code, no branding, no *bullshit*. Here, cool is not for sale. A few feet beyond the hall, you are totally immersed in another world—the darkness and smoke are so thick and disorienting that you feel as if you're suspended in air, and any sense of time or space fades. There is just the austere *boom-tick-boom-tick* of the city's signature sound, minimal techno, and the thump of the bass compressing your chest, practically lifting you off your feet. Sexual politics are a non-issue in here, and people—gay, straight, bi, women, men, transgendered—writhe as one, slip-sliding up against each other awash in sweat, smoke, and jubilation.

The club was founded by a twelve-person collective, almost all of whom have connections to squats in the former East, particularly to Köpenickerstrasse 137. The About Blank collective, consisting mostly of feminist punk women, set out a political framework for the project even before they discovered a location. The complex where they ended up had originally been a kindergarten for the children of East German railway employees, and then had sat empty for about fifteen years. By 2009 the property belonged to the city, which agreed to rent it out until it is eventually razed to make way for a highway. There was nothing left in the building—no heat, no plumbing, no electricity, no windows. But rather than take out bank loans to improve the place, the members of the collective set to work themselves, calling in friends to perform tasks they couldn't manage alone; any extra money they needed they borrowed from leftist groups connected to various squats.

There's also a lot more to About Blank than techno parties: one building on the property holds workshops for artisans and rehearsal spaces and studios for musicians. Another building holds a gender and queer studies center that puts on concerts, readings, and other events. About Blank also hosts benefits for feminist, anti-racist, and anti-fascist groups, and is part of a network that helps rally people for political demonstrations. Another point insisted on by the collective from the beginning: anyone who works here— not just the original twelve, but over a hundred people at this point—makes the same wage per hour, whether they are booking DJs, slinging beers, or cleaning the toilets.

Nowhere inside the club does it say THIS IS A RADICAL LEFTIST VENUE, but it *is* one, and the hope is that the atmosphere—how people work together and treat each other, the sense of mutual respect and inclusion, the experimentalism, the unfettered freedom—rubs off on partyers. There can be a political element to partying, after all. At its best, partying can make people question normality—the normality they encounter beyond the doors of a place like About Blank, perhaps the normality they know in another city or another country altogether.

70

By far the most famous club in Berlin today is Berghain.

Opinions of the place vary—to some, it's been irrevocably sullied by coverage in American media outlets, or it's lost its edge because of all the tourists who flock there to party. But Berghain was the largest and most easily identifiable institution at the moment when the world decided Berlin was the coolest city on earth, and it is still the gravitational center of the scene, allowing lots of other places to operate in the relative anonymity of its outer orbits.

The building that now houses Berghain was originally part of the physical plant for a grand Stalinist residential development that runs east from Alexanderplatz out to Frankfurter Tor. The centerpiece of the 1950s development was a series of impressive apartment buildings lining Stalinallee, now Karl-Marx-Allee—still the most impressive avenue in town. What's most striking about Karl-Marx-Allee is its scale: at ninety meters wide and two kilometers long, the avenue is comparable to the National Mall in Washington, D.C. Tucked out of sight in what at the time was open land near the main East Berlin rail yards, the building that became Berghain originally provided steam to heat these showpiece housing blocks.

The steam plant was abandoned in the 1980s.

When Berghain opened, in December 2004, the space was left largely as the club owners found it, in keeping with Berlin's makeshift style. The main dance floor is in the old turbine room, where concrete columns support a sixty-foot-high ceiling. The rest of the venue remains mostly undecorated, a disorienting industrial maze that provides secret spaces where anything goes, a dark tangle of social, sexual, and musical pleasures.

In a club where photography is strictly forbidden and the staff consciously avoid the media, the most familiar aspect of Berghain isn't the dark, industrial interior or even the Socialist-Bauhaus exterior of the old power plant; it is the bulldog-like glower of Sven Marquardt. Sven is Berghain's *Türsteher*, which could be translated as "bouncer," but in a scene where there is virtually no violence it really means something else. Sven is the public face of the club—a bearded face with tattoos of barbed wire and thorns snaking around his left eye and steel rings bristling from his lips and nose.

Sven Marquardt is also an old East German punk, a man who represents the past, the present, and the future of the city: a physical connection between East Berlin punk and twenty-first-century Berlin.

Yes, all the bands died. Yes, the idea of an independent, idealistic country died. Yes, Tacheles died.

But the spirit of East Berlin punk rock lives.

Silvio Meier, a member of the Church from Below's inner circle who helped squat Schreinerstrasse 47, died—murdered by neo-Nazi skinheads in a subway station in 1992. Aljoscha of Feeling B died—gasping for breath during an asthma attack in 2000, seven years after bandmates Paul Landers and Flake left to form a band called Rammstein. Otze of Schleim-Keim, whose song "Prügelknabe" included the line *We are the people*, died—while in a high-security mental institution in 2005 after splitting open his father's head with an axe.

But the spirit of East Berlin punk rock lives.

The ethos of East Berlin punk infused the city with a radical egalitarianism and a DIY approach to maintaining independence—to conjuring up the world you want to live in regardless of the situation or surroundings. Berliners today still fight for the right of self-determination with a seriousness not seen in other Western cities.

A straight line connects Major and Esther to the anti-gentrification movement that has left smoke billowing from the charred remains of hundreds of luxury cars in Berlin in recent years.

Say it, speak it, shout it out loud.

A straight line connects Planlos and Namenlos to Eimer and Tacheles, to Berghain and About Blank, and on to all the other clubs that will inevitably follow.

Were you really born to be subordinate to it all?

A straight line connects the Church from Below and the Schreinerstrasse squatters' manifesto to the unique sense of freedom that defines Berlin to this day.

We are the people, we are the power.

And sometimes, if you stand at the edge of the dark river as rosy-fingered dawn clutches at the Eastern horizon and the music thumps behind you in Kater Blau, Salon zur Wilden Renate, or Griessmühle, you can almost hear the city whispering: *Don't die in the waiting room of the future.*

Create your own world, your own reality.

DIY.

Revolution.

Acknowledgments

I WOULD LIKE to thank first of all Micha Kobs, who first exposed me to the East German punk scene twenty-five years ago. If there was one person in particular who set this book in motion, it was Kobs. I met him early in my Berlin years and figured out he had played guitar in one of the earliest punk bands in East Berlin—though it wasn't until many years later that I realized just how significant his band, Planlos, had been. He worked at the bar in one of the venues where I deejayed, and I always looked forward to our end-of-the-night chats over a closing-time whisky or two. Eventually Kobs showed me scrapbooks of materials from the early 1980s that he had carefully hidden during the years of the dictatorship, and looking through those photos and papers in his apartment, something clicked inside me. Years later, when I eventually started working on a book that would tell this story, Kobs introduced me to his former bandmate Michael "Pankow" Boehlke, who proved the single most important person in making the book a reality. Pankow generously put me in contact with dozens of his punk compatriots, opened the archive he had assembled for a museum show and book and DVD of his own on DDR punk, and patiently helped me for years as I went about researching the book. In short, this book would never have been conceived without Kobs, and would never have been completed without Pankow.

When I began my research, I assumed Stasi files would provide the most significant information. But as I went through files, I was surprised at the mundane nature of what the famed spy agency collected. The Stasi rarely had detailed, reliable information that might form the basis for cinematic storytelling. Instead, the interviews I conducted became the key to writing the story. Many of the people I interviewed spent several hours with me, sometimes over the course of multiple days; many allowed me to follow up in order to straighten things out as I learned more over the course of my years of research.

Among my interview partners I would particularly like to thank: Grit Angermann, Jan Bayer, Major Bergmann, Tatjana Besson, Abouto Blanko, Michael Boehlke, Chaos, Belinda Cooper, Alec Empire, Esther Friedemann, Gilbert Furian, Henryk Gericke, Arne Grahm, Torsten Hahnel, Herne, Michael Horschig, Norbert Jackschenties, Rex Joswig, Daniel Kaiser, Micha Kobs, Leo Kondeyne, Olaf Kretschmar, Paul Landers, Ronald Lippok, Frank Masch, Irina Meyer, Dirk Moldt, Siegfried Neher, Thomas Onisseit, Key Pankonin, Karsten "Dafty" Richter, Mita Schamal, Siegbert Schefke, Jana Schlosser, Stefan Schüler, Jörn Schulz, Sven Schwiegelshohn, Speiche, Curt Stauss, Johnny Temple, Olaf Tost, Frank "Trötsch" Tröger, and Mirko Whitfield.

Many others contributed to the insights and the richness of detail in this book, and I thank them as well. I'd like to add a special thanks to the many individuals who gave me access to their personal Stasi files and to those who shared with me their diaries or other writings from the time. And a note about the transcripts of Stasi interrogations used in the book: the Stasi would summarize the contents of hours of conversations into relatively short documents written in an oddly formal, bureaucratic style of German, which is why the responses don't sound like the typical language you would expect of a teenage punk.

I realized early on that accurately transcribing these lengthy interviews was going to be a challenge for a nonnative speaker, and for help I turned to three close friends: Klaus Stimeder, Steve Winkler, and Julia Wilton. All three provided not only terrific transcriptions but also encouragement, help, and ideas, and, in the case of Stimeder, a valuable first read of the draft manuscript, as well—thank you.

Two important figures in this book had already died before I started my research, so for material on Dieter "Otze" Ehrlich, I am particularly indebted to the book *Satan, kannst du mir noch mal verzeihen*, by Anne Hahn and Frank Willmann, and for material on Aljoscha Rompe to Ronald Galenza and Heinz Havemeister for their extensive oral history *Feeling B—mix mir einen Drink*. There were also a number of existing books featuring interviews with, and first-person accounts by, Eastern punks, which proved invaluable resources, and from which I cribbed liberally throughout my own book. Among them are *Too Much Future*, *Wir wollen alle artig sein*, *Auch im Osten trägt man Westen*, *Macht aus dem Staat Gurkensalat*, *Haare auf Krawall*, and *Zonen Punk Provinz*—see bibliography for complete details on these terrific books.

Despite my reliance on interviews to bring this story to life, I was also able to gain important information through archival work. Thanks once again to Michael Boehlke for allowing me total access to the Substitut Archiv; to Sylvia Griwan, Günter Nepp, and Dr. Ulrich Mählert at the Bundesstiftung zur Aufarbeitung der SED-Diktatur; to Christoph Ochs, Frank Ebert and Tom Sello at the Robert-Havemann-Gesellschaft; and to the Lichtenberger Museum and the New York Public Library.

I also wish to acknowledge those who went before me in writing about this period, and who were willing to offer support as well as expertise, especially Dirk Moldt, Henryk Gericke, Frank Willmann, Anne Hahn, Gilbert Furian, Alexander Pehlemann, Ronald Galenza, and Heinz Havemeister.

Thanks to Maik "Ratte" Reichenbach for letting me spend a day at his apartment going through his photo archives; thanks to Karoline Bofinger, Micha Kobs, Paul Landers, Stefan Mai, Lutz Schramm, Jörn Schulz, and Dirk Teschner for opening up their personal photo collections.

Thanks also to: Holly Austin, Joseph Braude, Jason Buhrmester, Jamie Byng, Joao Manuel Bouza Da Costa, Community Bookstore (Brooklyn), Cookie, Frank Dabrock, Katy Derbyshire, Erin Edmison, Birgit Fordyce, Danny Francis, Harriet Fricke, Leopold Froehlich, Steffen Fuchs, David Gedge, Pia Goetz, Brezel Göring, Brittany Hazelwood, Heike Highlife, Thomas Hoeffgen, Markus Hoffman, Andrej Hüsener, Hilary Kavanagh, Trip Khalaf, Wieland Krämer, Birgitta Kröll, Alexander Kühne, Frank Kuenster, Seth Kugel, Andreas Kump, Kevin Lane, Jacob Levenson, Markus

Linnenbrink, Bob Love, Ian MacKaye, Dan Mandel, Steve Martin at Nasty Little Man, Edna McCown, Duff McKagan, Andrew Miller, Stephanie Mohr, Tom Mohr, Jason Murtagh, Markus Nägele and the team at Heyne Verlag, Joel Najar, Christopher Napolitano, Johnny Perez, Martin Petersdorf, Natalie Reed, Brian Reyes, Michael Reynolds, Germo Robra, Daniel Ryser, Katie Salisbury, Ben Schafer, Mathias Schwarz, Damion Searls, Paul Stanley, Ken Steen, Riky Stock, Gerhard Stöger, Falko Teichmann, Spencer Theile, Jürgen Teipel, Anita Thompson, Virginie Varlet, and Lucas Wittmann. Special thanks also to Steffi de Velasco, whose writing inspired me to push against stylistic limitations in order to make the storytelling worthy of the story, and to Anna Stein, whose unbridled enthusiasm renewed my confidence in the manuscript.

I am also very grateful to Betsy Gleick and the team at Algonquin for taking a chance on me and believing in the power, importance, and timeliness of this story.

And finally a heartfelt thank you to Erin, Greta, and August for your collective love, patience, and understanding during the long years of research and writing, and to my parents, Elizabeth and James, who instilled in me the curiosity and openness that allowed me to learn so much during the Berlin years and beyond.

Bibliography

Boehlke, Michael, and Gericke, Henryk. *Too Much Future: Punk in der DDR* (Verbrecher Verlag, Berlin, 2007)

Denk, Felix, and von Thülen, Sven. *Der Klang der Familie* (Suhrkamp Verlag, Berlin, 2012)

Furian, Gilbert, and Becker, Nikolaus. *Auch Im Osten Trägt Man Westen: Punks in der DDR und was aus ihnen geworden ist* (Archiv der Jugendkulturen e.V., Berlin, 2008)

Galenza, Ronald, and Havemeister, Heinz. *Feeling B: mix mir einen Drink* (Schwarzkopf & Schwarzkopf Verlag, Berlin, 2010)

Galenza, Ronald, and Havemeister, Heinz. *Wir wollen immer artig sein: Punk, New Wave, Hip-Hop, Independent-Szene in der DDR 1980–1990* (Schwarzkopf & Schwarzkopf Verlag, Berlin, 1999)

Gieseke, Jens. *Der Mielke-Konzern: die Geschichte der Stasi 1945–1990* (Deutsche Verlags-Anstalt, Munich, 2001)

Gutmair, Ulrich. *Die Ersten Tage von Berlin: der Sound der Wende* (Tropen Verlag, Stuttgart, 2013)

Hahn, Anne, and Willman, Frank. *Satan, kannst du mir noch mal verzeihen: Otze Ehrlich, Schleimkeim und der ganze Rest* (Ventil Verlag, Mainz, 2008)

Hahn, Anne, and Willman, Frank. *Der Weisse Strich: Vorgeschichte und*

Folgen einer Kunstaktion an der Berliner Mauer (Ch. Links Verlag, Berlin, 2011)

Hentschel, Christian and Matzke, Peter. *Als ich fortging . . . Das grosse DDR-Rock Buch* (Verlag Neues Leben, Berlin, 2007)

Jadke, Ulrich; Holm, Kirsten; Luther, Jörn; Onisseit, Thomas; Haufe, Rüdiger (Hg). *Macht aus dem Staat Gurkensalat!* (WJS Verlag, Berlin, 2011)

Kirche von Unten (Hg). *Wunder gibt es immer weider—Fragmente zur Geschichte der Offenen Arbeit Berlin und der Kirche von Unten* (Kirche von Unten Eigenverlag, Berlin, 1997)

Knabe, Hubertus. *Gefangen in Hohenschönhausen: Stasi-Häftlinge berichten* (Ullstein Verlag, Berlin, 2007)

Kowalczyk, Angela "China." *Negativ und Dekadent: Ostberliner Punk-Erinnerungen* (CPL Verlag, Berlin, 2003)

Kowalczyk, Angela "China." *Punk in Pankow: Stasi-"Sieg": 16-jährige Pazifistin verhaftet!* (Anita Tykve Verlag, Berlin, 1996)

Kowalczyk, Angela "China." *Wir haben gelebt!* (CPL Verlag, Berlin, 2006)

Lange, Sascha. *DJ Westradio: meine glückliche DDR-Jugend* (Aufbau Verlag, Berlin, 2007)

Mählert, Ulrich. *Kleine Geschichte der DDR* (Verlag C.H. Beck, Munich, 5th edition, revised 2007)

Mareth, Connie, and Schneider, Ray. *Haare auf Krawall: Jugendsubkultur in Leipzig 1980–1991* (Connewitzer Verlagsbuchhandlung, Leipzig, 2010)

Marquardt, Sven, with Strittmatter, Judka. *Die Nacht ist Leben* (Ullstein, Berlin, 2014)

Moldt, Dirk (Hg). *mOAning star: eine Ostberliner Untergrundpublikation* (Robert-Havemann-Gesellschaft, Berlin, 2005)

Moldt, Dirk. *Nein, das mache ich nicht!: selbstbestimmte Arbeitsbiografien in der DDR* (Ch. Links Verlag, Berlin, 2010)

Neubert, Ehrhart. *Geschichte der Opposition in der DDR 1949–1989* (Ch. Links Verlag, Berlin, 1998)

Pehlemann, Alexander, and Galenza, Ronald. *Magnetbanduntergrund DDR 1979–1990* (Verbrecher Verlag, Berlin, 2006)

Rapp, Tobias. *Lost and Sound: Berlin, Techno und der Easyjetset* (Suhrkamp, Frankfurt, 2009)

Rauhut, Michael. *Rock in der DDR* (Bundeszentrale für politische Bildung, Bonn, 2002)

Rüddenklau, Wolfgang. *Störenfried:DDR-Opposition 1986–1989* (BasisDruck Verlag, Berlin, 1992)

Sarotte, Mary Elizabeth. *The Collapse: The accidental opening of the Berlin Wall* (Basic Books, New York, 2014)

Stephan, Gerd-Rüdiger (Hg). *"Vorwärts immer, rückwärts nimmer!": Interne Dokumente zum Zerfall von SED und DDR 1988/89* (Dietz Verlag, Berlin, 1994)

Von Hallberg, Robert, translated by Northcott, Kenneth. *Literary Intellectuals and the Dissolution of the State: professionalism and conformity in the GDR* (University of Chicago Press, Chicago, 1996)

Westhusen, Mark. *Zonen Punk Provinz: Punk in Halle (Saale) in den 80er Jahren* (Verein Zeit-Geschichte, Halle, 2005)

Willmann, Frank. *Leck mich am Leben: Punk im Osten* (Verlag Neues Leben, Berlin, 2012)